COCKTAILS

KNACK®

COCKTAILS

More than 300 classic and contemporary cocktails for any occasion

CHERYL CHARMING

PHOTOGRAPHS BY Susan Bourgoin

Guilford, Connecticut
An imprint of The Globe Pequot Press

Editor-in-Chief: Maureen Graney
Editor: Katie Benoit
Text Design: Paul Beatrice
Layout: Kevin Mak
Cover photos by Susan Bourgoin
Interior photos by Susan Bourgoin

CIP DATA: A catalogue record for this book is available from the British Library.

ISBN 978-0-7627-5929-3

Globe Pequot Press International
Footprint Handbooks
6 Riverside Court
Lower Bristol Road
Bath
BA2 3DZ
UK
T+44 (0)1225 469141
F+44 (0)1225 469461

Printed in India by Replika Press Pvt Ltd

About the author

Cheryl Channing has the knack! Known as the "Martha Stewart" of modern cocktail culture, she is the author of nine books on the subject. She has tended bar in the United States and beyond for more than three decades. She lives in Orlando, Florida. Visit the author at www.misscharming.com.

CONTENTS

INTRODUCTION
Behind the Wood

Behind the wood: the shiny, jewelled bottles filled with potable potions, the liquid gold that flows from a tap, the thirst-quenching concoctions served in ice-frosted glassware, the intriguing tools and techniques, the enticing smells, sights and sounds, the warm smile housed in a well-groomed body.

For centuries, being the body behind the wooden barrier (eventually abbreviated to 'bar') has held a fascination for many. The flexible beauty of bartending is that its skills can be showcased on a small-scale, novice level at a party at home, where just a few recipes can dazzle friends, or on a high, professional level in a famous bar that calls for an in-depth knowledge of mixology. So there's a level for all, including you.

In 1976, I dipped my first toe into the water of the hospitality biz by landing a job as a pizza waitress at Ken's Pizza in Benton, Arkansas in the USA. Soon I left the small town of Benton and jumped into the big pond feet first, as a server at my favourite theme restaurant in Little Rock, John Barleycorn's Vision. One night, the manager said that he needed a cocktail waitress for the upstairs bar and that I was to report to the bartender. My feelings were ambivalent; I was scared of the dimly lit room with tinkling glassware and echoes of laughter but extremely curious at the same time. After a couple of weeks working the bar, I applied for a job as a cocktail waitress at a new nightclub called Cabaret, but my goal was to make it behind the copper-topped bar. I morphed into a bar sponge and sopped up everything bar related: recipes, trivia, bar tricks, techniques and so on, and I was quickly promoted to bartender and then to head bartender.

Learning to make new drinks was fun (and that's probably one of the reasons why you purchased or were given this book), but my fascination was with twisting recipes, flavours and presentations. I quickly realized that I was a small-town girl with big-city talent. I took a bartender position on a cruise ship in the Caribbean, travelled the

country, and then made my way to bartending at Walt Disney World. Never during this time did I stop scribbling on cocktail napkins all things bar- and cocktail-related that I came across. The end product is this, the book that you hold in your hands right now – 33 years of what I've learned as a bartender condensed into these pages, and I'm very grateful and honoured to pass it on to you.

To develop the knack of how to tend a bar – and the knack of how to make cocktails (because they are two different knacks) – it's always best to start with simple, classic recipes, so that you create a firm foundation of cocktail knowledge on which to build your skyscraper of cocktails. Almost every chapter in this book shows you the basics, and with each turn of the page you'll begin to see how a simple cocktail combined with imagination can be twisted into unlimited possibilities, as long as you develop a knack for knowing what flavours mix well together.

An important part of building a firm cocktail foundation is learning the history of the spirit, ingredient or recipe used. I did not make this history connection until about 20 years into my bartending career. As an author, I was forced to look back and connect the cocktail culture dots of what I had experienced. It was then that it hit me why specific cocktails were developed, why cocktails had certain names, and why some recipes worked and others did not. As you flip through this book and read the tidbits of trivia and history that accompany the recipes, you'll discover that a cocktail time travel trail will start to link in your mind. For example, why aren't there any recipes from cocktail books of the mid-1800s that call for Coca-Cola? Answer: because Coca-Cola wasn't available until the 1890s. Why was the number one cocktail across America rum and Coke in 1945? Answer: a popular singing trio, the Andrews Sisters, came out with a hit calypso song

entitled 'Rum and Coca-Cola'. This is a perfect example of how the introduction of products and the influence of the media shape the cocktail culture timeline.

According to cocktail historian and author David Wondrich, the word 'cocktail' first appeared in print in a newspaper called *The Farmer's Cabinet* on 28 April 1803. An excerpt from the paper, referring to the cocktail as a morning drink, reads: 'Drank a glass of cocktail – excellent for the head . . . Call'd at the Doct's. [F]ound Burnham – he looked very wise – drank another glass of cocktail.'

Over the past 200-plus years the artform of the cocktail has risen and fallen, but recently there has been a rebirth of the cocktail. Modern mixologists and liquid chefs are behind the bar, studying and respecting the historic cocktail, then twisting it with modern ingredients. A liquid culinary marriage using fresh ingredients is taking place, and it's catching on thanks to those souls dedicated to spreading the cocktail gospel. Even extinct and previously banned ingredients from cocktail books of the 19th century are being raised from the dead.

There are several types of bars and several types of bartenders behind them. The one you choose to be is up to you. Today, the bartender spectrum extends from extreme-flair, bottle-flipping bartenders to purest-of-the-pure mixologists. More than likely you, like me, will fall somewhere between these two, but understand that something can be gained from both these extremes. Take what interests you and make it your own.

So let's recap. The first step in learning to mix cocktails is to start crafting the classics. Next, study some cocktail history. After that, your hands will be itching to get some hands-on experience. To begin, pick out a few cocktails from this book that you'd like to make. For example, if you like Margaritas, then turn to the Margarita chapter and begin with the first three. Look in the directions for the ingredients needed to make these cocktails. Of course, you'll need to buy the booze, but there are other garnishes, mixers, tools and gadgets involved as well. But to begin, simply start with baby steps.

Practise your bartender mechanics by combining your bar tools with some bottles filled with water. Stand at the bar (or the kitchen worktop) at home and practise your pouring techniques. Practise shaking, stirring, measuring, muddling, layering and more. As you develop these techniques, strive for safety, cleanliness and precision. The skills will come with repetition and a passion for being a good bartender.

Learn to make one cocktail really well, and then move on to a new one. You'll soon get the knack of making a good drink. Next, you need to incorporate the knack of bartending. Yes, this includes making cocktails but that is only a piece of the cocktail pie. Bartending also includes personality, good grooming, a great smile, good memory, average maths skills (if money is involved), efficiency, knowledge of alcohol and physical strength – to carry heavy bottles and to haul out the empties.

So, have you decided what kind of bartender you want to be behind the wood? Maybe you're just interested in having friends over to try a new concoction, and that's great! Maybe you want to make a living from it. Fantastic! Whatever your interest may be, my only hope is that the information I've gathered from my experiences and the rich images in this book jumpstart your desire. Please visit my website (misscharming.com) for more information. My best to you. Cheers!

POURERS & OPENERS

Learn basic tools and techniques all bartenders should know

One of the best tools you can invest in is a bottle pourer. Twisting off spirit bottle caps and 'glug-glugging' spirits work well for a neat drink ('neat' means a drink poured straight from the bottle into a glass without ice), but for precise and smooth control a pourer is the best choice. Simply unscrew a bottle cap and then push the pourer into the bottle. If your bottle has a wide mouth you'll have to buy a wide pourer. If you're using pourers for a party, just keep your bottle caps until you are finished, then screw them back on. Once you are comfortable with pouring, bump it up a notch and try a long pour. Simply raise the bottle higher, creating a longer stream of spirit. Then you can graduate to reverse pouring, which is grabbing the neck of the bottle in reverse and pouring.

Using exact measures in a cocktail is crucial, and that's why jiggers and measuring devices are helpful. There are many sizes to choose from, especially in two-ended jiggers. I prefer

Pourers and Pouring

- Pourers add a professional touch when making cocktails. Use them in bottles that are used most often.
- Pourers come with options such as colour, size and material (plastic or metal).
- When pouring, flip up the bottle quickly and vertically. Practise with a bottle of water.
- Cut (the downward movement when you finish pouring) quickly down in a smooth motion.

Jiggers and Measures

- The most professional bartenders use jiggers and measuring glasses for accuracy.
- Invest in a couple of jiggers of different sizes.
- For control, rest the edge of the jigger on or near the lip of the glass while pouring from the bottle, so that you create one fluid movement of pouring and dumping in the glass.
- Try to rinse out jiggers as you go, especially when using creamy liqueurs.

the jiggers and measuring glasses marked with measured lines. These have a wider range of use.

Openers are tools that can open beer bottles, wine bottles and cans. The cool, flat, hip beer bottle openers called 'speed openers' are designed to operate at the speed that is needed behind a high-volume bar. They are produced with many ways to store them on your body, from magnetic clips to retractable reels. For medium- to low-volume use, my favourite is a chrome bottle opener ring, because you can pop off the cap and aim for the rubbish bin all in one motion. There are many kinds of corkscrew on the market, from the rabbit to winged corkscrews, but you need to learn to use the waiter's corkscrew.

Openers

- Crown cap bottle openers are available in plenty of styles – hip, practical and novelty.
- Buy the kind of bottle opener that works best for your needs.
- Professionals will use nothing less than a waiter's corkscrew for wine bottles.
- Can openers punch open a can. They usually have a bottle opener on the other end as well.

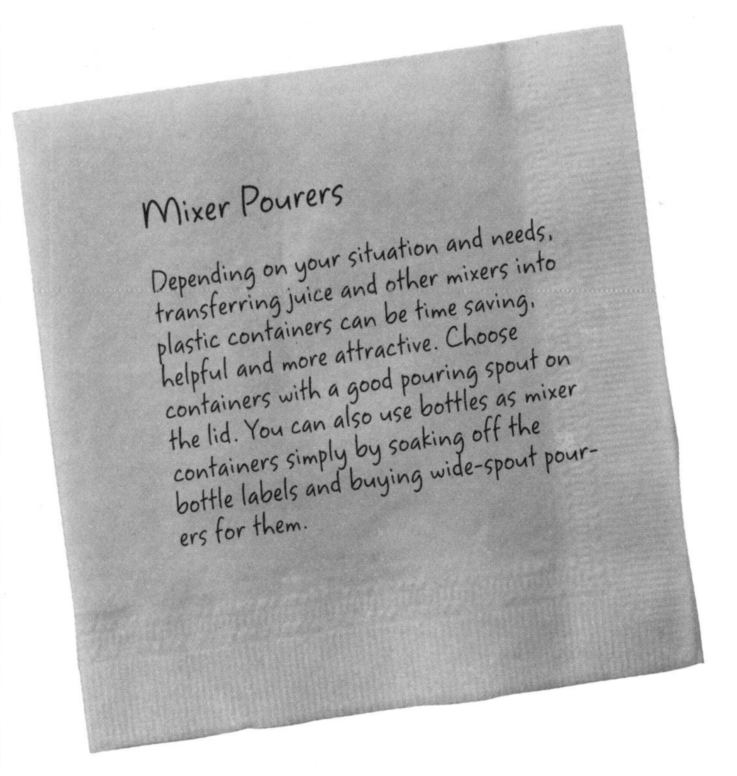

SHAKERS & STRAINERS

Learn techniques that will have you stirring and shaking

Mixing glasses can be used for stirring a cocktail, muddling and for the other half of a Boston shaker.

Bar spoons have long, twisted handles. They can be found with a variety of ends, such as the traditional red knob, disc, and even a fork. The forked end is used to get olives out of a jar. I find that using the disc-ended spoon works best when it comes to stirring.

The julep strainer is used with mixing glasses so that you can strain the cocktail without the ice falling into the glass. It has a concave shape that fits into the glass.

There are two types of shaker: Boston and cobbler. The cobbler is a three-piece shaker – you shake it, take off the little lid, then strain through the built-in strainer. These shakers became popular in America during Prohibition in the 1920s, when they were produced in many novelty shapes, such as boots, bullets or lighthouses. Stephen Visakay owns the

Mixing Glass and Bar Spoon

- A mixing glass is a tempered 50-cl glass. A thick, untempered pint glass can be substituted.
- Use a mixing glass when a recipe calls for stirring instead of shaking.
- Stirring chills a cocktail without adding air bubbles to the drink, as shaking does.
- Bar spoons are long so they can reach the bottom of tall glasses.

Julep Strainer

- The julep strainer is believed to have originated as a tea strainer and crossed over to the bar in the late 19th century.
- The top two drinks that use a julep strainer are the Classic Martini and the Manhattan.
- Practise with a glass of iced water to develop the feel for this strainer.
- Vintage julep strainers can sometimes be found in online auctions.

largest collection of shakers in existence – over 1000 – and displayed them in his book, *Vintage Bar Ware* (1997). Jimbo Walker of Denton, Texas, owns the world's second largest collection, at almost 600 shakers.

The Boston is the shaker that serious and professional bartenders use. It consists of a mixing glass that fits into a shaker tin. Just tap firmly on top of the glass to ensure a tight fit, then shake, glass side up, not in front of you or by your side, but professionally over your shoulder, for a minimum of ten seconds. To release, hold vertically tin side down, then firmly tap on the top of the tin on the side that is not touching the glass.

Ice is an important factor when making a cocktail. Ideally, cocktail ice should be large. Preferably use 25-mm cubes. Larger ice cubes create less water dilution and keep cocktails cold longer.

Boston Shaker

- A basic Boston shaker consists of a 50-cl mixing glass fitted inside a 85-cl steel shaker tin.
- Other sizes of shaker tins are available, from small (cheater tins) to large (Mako tins) to accommodate all needs.
- Powder- and rubber-coated tins are available in a rainbow of colours, such as hot pink, neon green, black sparkle, white and tie dye.

Hawthorne Strainer

- The Hawthorne strainer has a coiled ring that fits inside a shaker tin.
- This strainer requires a firm but light touch.
- When straining, press firmly inwards towards the inside of the tin, not down, or you will stop the flow, and instead liquid will seep out around the sides of the strainer.
- Hawthorne strainers can be found in a variety of colours, styles and coatings.

MUDDLING & LAYERING

Muddle and layer your way up to the next level of bartender techniques

Every bartender should know a few ways to strain a drink. You should understand that straining is all about keeping ice and other solid ingredients out of the cocktail. If you don't happen to have a julep or Hawthorne strainer, you can split strain. This means that you are slightly pulling the mixing glass and shaker tin apart, creating a small opening for the liquid to stream from while keeping the ice in the shaker. Another way to strain is to insert the clean bottom end of a mixing glass into the tin to hold back the ice. Double or fine straining is when you strain with the shaker in one hand while the other holds a mesh strainer over the drink to catch small herb particles, pulp, seeds and so forth.

Split Strain

- Begin by positioning yourself with feet slightly apart for proper grounding.
- Split straining takes a little practice, so start with a Boston shaker of ice and water until you master this technique.
- It helps to use a vinyl- or rubber-coated shaker tin so your hands can tolerate the cold.
- Bar supply stores sell modern tins with built-in strainers.

Muddling

- Never use a muddler that has been stained or varnished. This poison will flake off during use and end up in the drink.
- The wide flat end is the business end of a muddler.
- Invest in a taller-than-normal muddler in case you find yourself muddling in a shaker tin.
- The most popular drink that requires a muddler is the Mojito.

A muddler in its basic form is like a pestle that mashes and grinds ingredients in a mortar. A muddler is a long stick used to crush ingredients for drinks. This crushing releases the oils and flavours from ingredients such as herbs. There is a variety of muddlers on the market, from vintage to modern.

GREEN LIGHT

Gently rub a mint leaf with your fingers to release the oil. Now smell it. Amazing aroma! You just mini-muddled that leaf. Now take a piece of citrus rind (lemon, lime or orange), hold it up in front of you and squeeze. The oil will spray out. Smell it. These are the flavours and oils that are released by muddling.

Remember that practice makes perfect for this skill.

Layering

- Practise layering at home with ingredients from your kitchen such as oils, vinegars, water and juice.
- Layering requires a steady hand.
- You can break the fall of the liquid with practically anything. Most bars use a spoon or a cherry.
- When layering several spirits and liqueurs, or several drinks, have all your bottles in a row and ready to go.

Stylized Layering

Layering takes a bit of practice, but once you get it you've got it. An advanced and stylized way to layer is to use a disc-ended bar spoon. The disc end goes into the glass, and you pour the spirit or liqueur on the spiral handle. It spirals as it travels down into the glass.

SPECIAL TOUCHES

Chill out then warm up to the idea of some special touch techniques

There's nothing worse than preparing a nicely chilled cocktail, then pouring it into a warm, room-temperature glass. The temperature of your cocktail immediately begins to rise. Always chill the glass before pouring a strained drink. Also, with the recent Martini craze, glasses have become very important. Look for smaller cocktail glasses, no larger than 200 ml, to keep your cocktail chilly to the bitter end.

Making a hot drink in a room-temperature glass works the opposite way. Instantly the glass lowers the temperature. To avoid this, start with a preheated glass. Also some people like to have their cognac or brandy warmed. One way to accomplish this is to pour 60 ml of hot (but not boiling)

Chill and Warm a Glass

- To chill a glass, fill it with ice and water (or carbonated water) and leave it to sit while you make the drink.
- Chill glasses that will be used for cold strained cocktails.
- Another way to chill glasses is to keep them in the freezer.
- To preheat a glass or mug, simply fill it with hot water, then leave it to sit for about a minute.

Rim a Glass

- Rimming a glass requires two things: something wet or sticky and your chosen edible ingredient.
- Saucers and plates work well for holding your ingredients.
- Lemon juice mixes well with sugar-based rims, and lime juice mixes well with salted rims.
- Rimming ideas are limited only by your imagination.

water into a brandy balloon and allow the glass to warm for about a minute. Pour the water out, then pour in the brandy. To take it another step you can serve it with the balloon bowl resting in a glass filled with a little hot water so the steam warms the brandy.

GREEN LIGHT

Strive to rim the outside edge of the glass only. Salt falling into a Margarita will change the taste of the drink. And the same goes for sugar falling into a Lemon Drop. The flavoured rim and the flavour of the cocktail are meant to complement each other when they combine to enhance the taste as it reaches your lips.

Rimmers with ingredient compartments can be purchased at bar supply stores.

Coloured and Flavoured Rims

- Use plastic bags and food colouring to colour salt and sugar.
- Visit cake decorating and sugarcraft suppliers for a larger assortment of colourings and other edible items.
- Crush biscuits and sweets in plastic bags.

Sticking Power

The easiest way to wet the rim of a glass is to take a slice of citrus and rub it around the rim. But sometimes this does not give enough sticking power to hold biscuit and sweet crumbs. You may have to use simple syrup, honey or even golden syrup. If you have the time, apply it with a paintbrush.

GARNISHES

Cut, zest and flame your way down the cocktail-making technique trail

You must always take precautions when cutting fruit and garnishes. You may even consider wearing rubber gloves to avoid the sting of citrus juice on your hands. Always use a knife that is longer than the length or width of whatever you are cutting. Make sure you wash, rinse and dry the fruit and vegetables, and don't forget to wash your hands.

Non-organic citrus fruits are usually sprayed with wax after picking to preserve the skin, but if your ingredients are unwaxed or organic, you won't need to scrub them as much. You can wash citrus fruits in a solution of 750 ml water, 750 ml white vinegar and 25 ml bicarbonate of soda, then rinse and dry them.

Cutting

- Always use a sharp knife when cutting and always pay close attention to what you are doing.
- You can use serrated or regular knives to cut fruit. It's up to you.
- For fruits, don't use cutting boards that have previously been used for cutting animal products or concentrated flavours like garlic.
- Place a wet towel under the cutting board for traction.

Zesting

- 1. When making a zest spiral, first cut off one end of the lemon, then hold both the fruit and the zester firmly in your hands.
- 2. Press and pull the zester around the fruit while turning it with your other hand.
- With practice you'll be able to zest the entire lemon in a continuous strip.
- Use the multiholed part of the zester to make tiny scrapings of zest.

Zest is prepared in three different ways. Each looks different and serves a different purpose. The long, spiral strip that is made with a zester (also called a canelle knife) is twisted to release the oils, then rubbed on a glass rim or twisted over the top of the cocktail. Fine scrapings of zest are used for infusing spirits, making liqueurs, adding extra flavour to a shaken-then-strained cocktail, or mixing with ingredients for rimming. Zesters to make these two types can be combined in an all-in-one tool, or they can be purchased separately. At a pinch you can use a vegetable peeler as a makeshift zester, but it's better to buy the right tool for the job. The third kind of zest is a 25-mm oval slice cut from the rind of a navel orange or thick-skinned lemon. You use it to flame the oil for a cocktail, so when you hear the bar term 'flamed zest', this is what it means.

Flaming a Zest

- 1. To flame zest, hold an oval piece of citrus zest about 25 mm from the top of the cocktail.
- 2. Then hold a flame above the edge of the glass.
- 3. In one motion, squeeze the zest so that the flame ignites the citrus oil spray.
- 4. The burnt oil freefalls on to the cocktail, creating a caramelized layer gently floating on the surface.

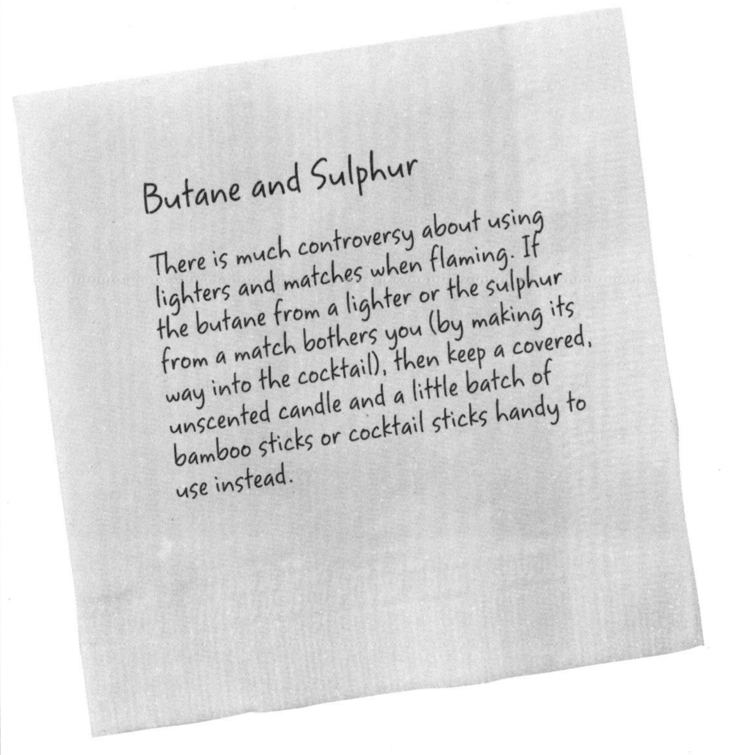

BARTENDING TOOLS

Try your hand at some heavy-duty techniques to really juice things up

Blenders can range in price from £20 to £1,000. For one that will last a lifetime on your kitchen worktop, go for a commercial model costing around £150–200. When blending, add your liquid ingredients first, then slowly add ice.

Manual juice extractors are available, but if you're serious about buying one, then you'll want an electric juicer that can extract the juice from dense ingredients such as carrots, rhubarb, ginger, wheatgrass, pineapple, pears and apples. It will cost around £150–200 as well. Electric citrus juicers are used for oranges, grapefruit, lemons and limes because you can't juice the peels through the juicer. Well, you can, but you don't want to because of their bitterness. You can juice citrus

Blending

- Cracked or small ice works best when making drinks in a blender.
- Start with less ice than you think you need because you can always add more.
- Strive for a pourable consistency, but if you go a notch over the thickness, simply use a bar spoon to help the mixture into the glass.
- You can use a blender to purée as well.

Electric Juicing

- Juice extractors are used for all vegetables and fruits except citrus.
- Make only what you need for 12 hours, because juice will begin to spoil after that unless you freeze it.
- Electric citrus juicers are good for high-volume use.
- Valencia oranges are best for juicing, and navel oranges for garnishes.

flesh through a juicer, but it foams. Besides, electric citrus juicers are economical. You can buy one for about £20, or get a citrus press attachment for a juicer or food processor.

Manual citrus juicers come with a variety of options. The most modern and popular to use for cocktails is the two-handled squeezer, with which juice can be squeezed straight into the drink, mixing glass or shaker tin.

Ice crushers are available in electric and manual versions as well. The one to choose is the one that best fits your needs.

MAKE IT EASY

It's worth the investment to purchase a good blender. Cheap blenders have low-powered motors that will burn out fast and leave you frustrated. Look for professional quality American models, available from catering suppliers, which have plenty of power to grind ice and other ingredients. They're also the best for making perfect smoothies.

Manual Juicing

- Manual juicers are good for low-volume use.
- Using room-temperature fruits will yield more juice.
- To avoid pulp and seeds, double-strain through a mesh strainer. An easy mesh strainer to use is the type designed to steep loose tea leaves in a cup. It will sit perfectly in the glass as you squeeze into it.
- Store lemon and lime juice in squeezy plastic bottles for easy use.

Crushing Ice

- 'Crushed ice' in bar terms doesn't necessarily mean ice crushed to snow consistency. However, you can use this form of ice if you find a recipe described as a frappé or mist, and also for a mint julep.
- Cracked ice can be made by placing ice cubes in a canvas bag, then hitting it with a large heavy object such as a muddler or a rolling pin.

THE SMALLEST GLASSWARE

Learn the small differences between these pocket-sized glasses used behind the bar

Shot glasses come in a plethora of styles and can be made of almost anything. Some people even have a collection of shot glasses, because wherever you travel you find these glasses in souvenir shops. Novelty shot and shooter glasses are endless. You can buy necklace shot glasses, shot glass rings, test tube shots, glasses that light up, and glasses that are split in two so you can pour one spirit on one side of the divider and something else on the other. They can also be found in practically any shape imaginable, such as boots, bullets, body parts, animals and cacti. You can get edible shot glasses, and glasses made of chocolate, candy, fruit gums, ice or any liquid that will freeze can be found. You can even find chess

Shot and Shooter Glasses

- A shot glass will measure 30–60 ml.
- Shot glasses are available in a wide variety of shapes and sizes.
- A shooter glass will measure 60–150 ml.
- Shooter glasses can be found in many shapes and sizes, too.

Pony and Cordial Glasses

- In bar terms, a 'pony' is a unit of measurement of 1 US ounce, or 30 ml, so pony glasses will always measure 30 ml.
- Pony glasses are always stemmed.
- Cordial glasses can range in size from 30–90 ml.
- A serving of cordial or liqueur would be served in a cordial glass.

and draughts sets that use shot and shooter glasses as the playing pieces.

Sometimes pony and cordial glasses are used as shot and shooter glasses, though bars don't seem to carry them any more because they get stolen. They're used domestically for dinner parties. A pony glass is a cordial glass, but not all cordial glasses can be called 'pony glasses' because of their size. All liqueurs and cordials such as crèmes, creams and schnapps can be poured into cordial glasses.

ZOOM

'On the rocks' is a familiar bar term that means to pour the spirit over ice. That's how the rocks glass gets its name. A drink on the rocks will have spirit only. You can have anything on the rocks that you desire, but the most popular choices are whiskey, Scotch, amaretto and Irish cream.

Rocks Glasses

- Rocks glasses should measure 150–200 ml.
- Rocks glasses are meant to hold a portion of spirit without mixer over ice.
- Rocks glasses come in a variety of shapes and sizes.
- Shooters are often strained into rocks glasses.

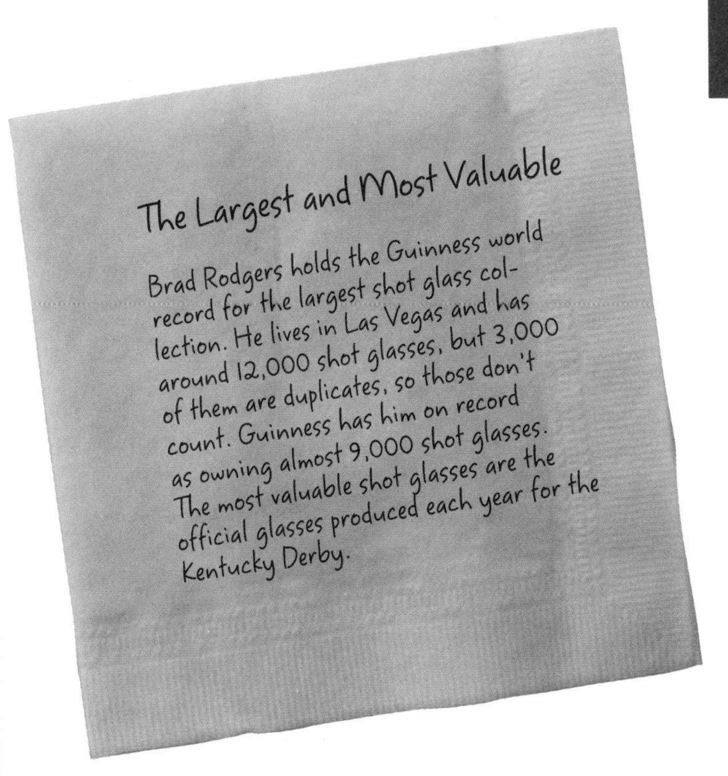

The Largest and Most Valuable

Brad Rodgers holds the Guinness world record for the largest shot glass collection. He lives in Las Vegas and has around 12,000 shot glasses, but 3,000 of them are duplicates, so those don't count. Guinness has him on record as owning almost 9,000 shot glasses. The most valuable shot glasses are the official glasses produced each year for the Kentucky Derby.

THE STURDIEST GLASSWARE

Strong and steady glassware can be handled firmly

A lot of bar glassware requires a delicate touch or else a stem will snap or the lip will chip. You still have to care for the glassware discussed on this page, but most can be handled quite roughly with little wear and tear.

Basically, these glasses are just slightly different from each other in size and measurement. The highball is a mixed drink that has been around since the 19th century. Its name more than likely came from standing tall at medium height. There are a couple of stòries about its origin. One is that a highball is a drink taken before dinner when the sun is a big ball in the sky. Another is that it came from the American railroad practice of raising a ball on a pole to indicate a clear line ahead. The most popular highballs are Scotch and Soda, Gin and Tonic, Bourbon and Coke and Seven and Seven.

Bars often stock old-fashioned glasses and call them their 'highball glasses'. What they mean is that they make their

Highball Glasses

- Highball glasses should measure 200–300 ml.
- A highball consists of one spirit and one mixer.
- Originally a highball was a drink made of rye whiskey and ginger ale over ice.
- Today the traditional medium-tall highball glass is not often used in bars. Instead bars use an old-fashioned glass, so the names of the glasses get interchanged all the time.

Old-fashioned Glasses

- Old-fashioned glasses should measure 200–350 ml.
- These glasses are shorter and squatter than traditional highball glasses.
- They are sometimes referred to as 'lowball glasses' because the height of the glass is less but it can also be used for a highball cocktail.
- These glasses get their name from the cocktail that was originally made in them, an Old Fashioned.

highballs in old-fashioned glasses, but most people don't know the difference. The double old-fashioned glass is excellent for when you want a double.

A collins glass is named after the drink Tom Collins. Traditional collins glasses are frosted with a clear lip.

ZOOM

The 1938 film *Jezebel*, starring Bette Davis, is set in New Orleans in 1852. The first scene shows a man pulling up in his carriage next to the Louis-House to 'have a ball', as he says. It's assumed that he means a highball because the next scene shows him and other gentlemen standing and drinking at an elegant lobby bar.

These glasses hold more than the old-fashioned glasses

Double Old-fashioned Glasses

- These glasses are larger than old-fashioned glasses.
- A double old-fashioned glass can measure 350–450 ml.
- Most men prefer to have their drinks in a short, sturdy glass instead of a tall one, so this glass works well for this purpose.
- This glass is called a 'bucket' in some parts of America.

Tall and Collins Glasses

- The collins glass is a tall, straight-sided glass that can measure 300–350 ml.
- A collins glass is also called a 'chimney glass' because of its shape.
- A tall glass in the cocktail world can measure 300–600 ml.
- Tall glasses are available in a variety of colours and shapes.

STEMMED GLASSWARE

Learn the different uses for this tall and elegant stemware

The cocktail glass symbolizes the cocktail culture. The cocktail glass was fairly small, usually 120–200 ml, until around the millennium. It was around that time that the Martini craze took over. Froufrou fruity Martinis required more mixers, so the glass had no choice but to become larger. These millennium Martinis can be made in a tall glass with ice, but when strained into elegant and sexy glasses they seem more appealing and fun. The downside is that that much liquid without ice warms up pretty fast, especially when you are touching it with your hands.

The classic Margarita glass (shown in the photo below with salt, ice, and lime) is supposed to resemble a sombrero. If you want your Margarita to be truly authentic it should be drunk from Mexican bubble glass.

When you see a hurricane glass, you should think of Pat O'Brien's Bar and New Orleans in the 1940s, because that's

Cocktail Glasses

- Cocktail glasses can measure 120–350 ml.
- These glasses are the icons of the cocktail world.
- All Martini glasses are cocktail glasses, but not all cocktail glasses are Martini glasses.
- The cocktail determines the size of the glass to be used.

Margarita Glasses

- Margarita glasses can measure 240–480 ml.
- Because Margaritas can be served straight up, on the rocks or frozen, there is a variety of glassware to choose from.
- Some bars use an all-purpose glass, such as a pint glass, for 90 per cent of their drinks, and a Margarita will be served in that.

where it originated. Today in New Orleans hurricane glasses are everywhere and are available in every colour imaginable, but the most prized is the souvenir glass from Pat O'Brien's itself, imprinted with the Pat O'Brien's logo. It will hold exactly $10 in pennies.

ZOOM

The Bombay Sapphire gin company holds an annual competition to design a Martini glass. The glasses that are created by design students from around the world will leave you breathless. One winner from each country competes in a final competition. The showcase of glasses can be viewed each year at the Bombay Sapphire Blue Room exhibition, which tours the world.

Hurricane Glasses

- Hurricane glasses can measure 360–780 ml.
- Some bars will invest in hurricane glasses and use them to serve their frozen and tropical drinks.
- The shape of the glass was derived from the shape of a hurricane lamp.
- It was originally used to serve Pat O'Brien's Hurricane, a fruity rum cocktail.

Poco Grande Glasses

- Poco grande glasses can measure 300–400 ml.
- Stems on a poco grande can vary in shape, but the curvy shape of the bowl will stay the same.
- This glass is sometimes called a 'tulip glass'.
- This is another glass that some bars will dedicate to their frozen and tropical drinks if they make the investment.

SPECIALITY GLASSWARE

Historic speciality glassware is still used today

In France during the 19th century, absinthe was served in a glass standing on a saucer. Most establishments had their logo imprinted on the saucers, and patrons would stack them neatly on the table. When they were finished, their bar tab was calculated by how many saucers were in the stack.

Ceramic tiki mugs were a feature of Polynesian-style tiki culture, which exploded and flourished in the USA between 1933 and 1973. There were tiki bars, lounges and rooms with a wide assortment of exotic tropical drinks on their menus. A tiki drink was usually accompanied by extravagant garnishes and decorations, such as paper umbrellas, Chinese back scratchers, tropical flowers, sugarcane sticks, dry ice to create mist, fruit and more fruit. Tiki mugs are in a category all of their own, and many people collect them. It's possible to find tiki skulls, Easter Island heads, fruit-shaped mugs, volcano mugs, barrels, figures and more.

Absinthe Glasses

- Absinthe glasses can measure 200–300 ml.
- Some absinthe glasses have built-in reservoirs so you can pour the exact amount of liqueur into the bottom of the glass without measuring it.
- The glasses come in a variety of shapes and sizes, but they almost always have an ornate quality.
- A pierced spoon is used to hold a sugar cube, over which water is poured to dilute the drink.

Irish Coffee Glasses

- Irish coffee glasses should measure 180-300 ml. Any more, and the alcohol portion will need to be adjusted.
- These glasses are available in a variety of colours, but clear glass is the most often used.
- There are two basic styles: the footed glass mug with a handle and the stemmed bowl.
- You can serve an Irish coffee in this glass, but all other hot and warm bar drinks are served in this glass as well.

The world's most expensive mint juleps sell for $1,000 each at the Kentucky Derby. Each year Woodford Reserve bourbon sells 'millionaire mint juleps' for charity. Sometimes the ingredients are local, and sometimes Brown-Forman (the company that owns Woodford Reserve) travels the globe to collect mint from Aspen or Ireland, sugar from Australia or South America, and ice from icebergs or the Bavarian Alps. The juleps are served in gold-plated cups with silver straws.

ZOOM

Absinthe had a bohemian following. Many artists and other creative figures drank absinthe, and there's even an unproven story that Van Gogh cut off his ear after drinking it. Many paintings by the masters feature absinthe, including Van Gogh's 1887 *Still Life with Absinthe*, Picasso's 1901 *The Absinthe Drinker*, and Degas's 1876 *L'Absinthe*.

GLASSWARE

Tiki Mugs

- Tiki mugs can measure 200–600 ml.
- Over 30 varieties of tiki mugs are available in many shapes and sizes.
- The word *tiki* refers to a carved statue of a Polynesian god.
- Tiki mugs are usually ceramic and made by slip casting in a plaster mould, then dried, glazed and fired in a kiln.

Mint Julep Cups

- Mint julep cups can measure 180–360 ml.
- You can serve a mint julep in a variety of glasses, but a silver cup is the traditional way to serve it.
- Using silver or pewter means the cup becomes nicely coated with frost.
- Mint julep cups and glasses abound in Louisville for the Kentucky Derby at the beginning of May.

MIXERS 1

Learn the basics of the most common mixers

In July 2008, New Orleans became the first city in America to be granted an official cocktail by the Louisiana legislature. The cocktail granted was the Sazerac. The Sazerac was invented in the early 19th century, and the recipe calls for Peychaud's (pronounced pay-SHOWDS) bitters.

About 90 per cent of professional bartenders reading these words know of only one brand of bitters that sits behind their bar: Angostura. And they probably pick it up only to jerk a few dashes into soda water to drink for a stomach ache. Occasionally they may use it to make a Manhattan or Old Fashioned, or to soak some sugar cubes for some Champagne cocktails. Well, I'm here to tell you that bitters have made a comeback and are a staple among modern mixologists worldwide. Some are making their own bitters! Bitters that have been dead for over a hundred years and are found in historic cocktail books are being revived.

Bitters

- The first known definition of the word 'cocktail' lists bitters as one of the ingredients in the recipe. It dates from 1806.
- Bitters are concentrated witches' brews of herbs, roots, seeds, alcohol and other ingredients.
- Bitters do not make a drink taste bitter. They add a punch of flavour to cocktails.
- The most popular bitters brand, which has lasted the test of time, is Angostura.

Juice Mixers

- Juice provides four elements in a cocktail: sweetness, colour, texture and flavour.
- Juices used for cocktails should be as fresh and pure as possible.
- Juice can derive from fruit or vegetables.
- The most common juices found behind most bars are orange, grapefruit, cranberry and pineapple. Since the millennium you will also find lemon, lime, pomegranate and white cranberry juice.

Regan's Orange Bitters No 6 is a great example of the revived orange bitters that so many recipe books call for. It was invented by cocktail and spirits expert Gary Regan. Fee Brothers of Rochester, New York, a four-generation-old manufacturer of quality cocktail mixes, now produces seven bitters: lemon, orange, mint, peach, whiskey barrel aged, grapefruit and old fashioned. So, get bitter!

GREEN LIGHT

More and more bars are pushing for fresh juice to be used for their cocktails. Freshly squeezed juice is more expensive but makes a huge difference in taste. Mid-sized electric juicers are popping up on the front and back counters of many bars. To remove the pulp, simply strain the fresh juice through a mesh strainer.

Sweet Mixers

- Sweetness can play a very important role in cocktails.
- Simple syrup (sugar and water) is the most common sweetener used in a cocktail.
- A sweetener like grenadine can add colour as well as sweetness.
- Other cocktail sweeteners include maraschino and hibiscus syrup, coconut cream, flavoured syrups, liqueurs and cordials, maple syrup, honey, gomme, orgeat, purées and lime cordial (such as Rose's).

Dairy Mixers

- Single cream can be used for cocktails (most American bars use half-and-half, a blend of milk and cream that is slightly lighter than single cream with about 12.5 per cent fat).
- Soy milk can be substituted as an eco-milk or cream.
- High-end bars make their own fresh whipped cream rather than using canned aerosol products.
- Other dairy mixers include ice cream, yogurt, unsalted butter and eggs.

MIXERS 2

A second round of mixers can be added to your cocktail repertoire

The most overlooked cocktail ingredient is ice. Ice is not just for chilling a cocktail. The dilution melts into a cocktail and changes the taste, especially if the ice machine you are using does not have a filter! If the ice machine makes ice from a city water supply, you are diluting chlorine and other contaminants into your cocktail.

Cocktail ice should be made with filtered water and the ice cubes should be large for minimal dilution. Machines that make 25-mm cubes are ideal. How many times have you ordered a cocktail at a bar, and within one minute the wafer-thin kitchen ice was already melted halfway up the glass? Bars and restaurants that respect cocktails install a dedicated ice machine that makes big, beautiful cocktail ice.

Bloody Marys are adaptable enough to withstand a myriad of mixers being added to them. One extra ingredient I've been using for years, in addition to Worcestershire sauce, is

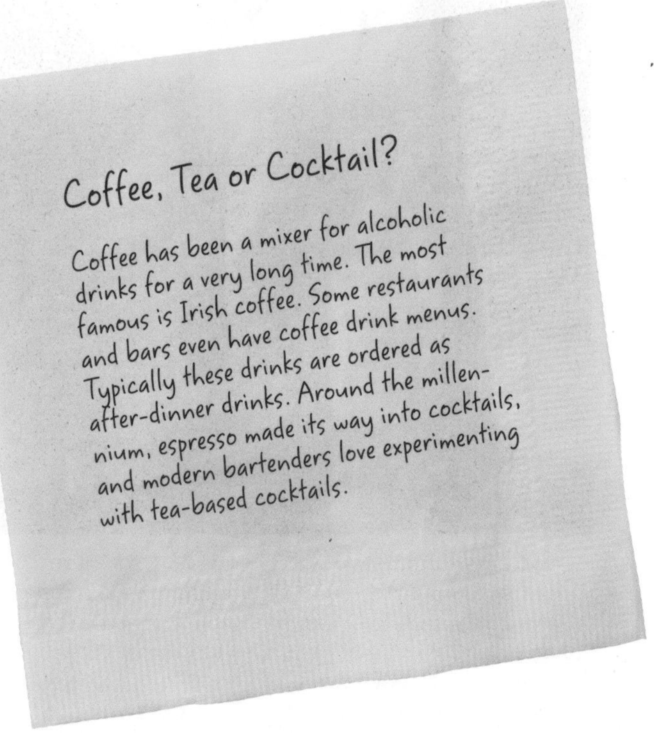

Water-based Mixers

- The most important water-based mixer for a cocktail is water itself.
- Ice plays an extremely important role in a cocktail.
- When you shake, stir or serve a cocktail with ice, the melting ice is considered an essential part of the cocktail.
- Other water-based mixers include coffee, espresso, tea and dry mixers blended with water such as powdered cider or chocolate.

a little bit of brown sauce. Most people don't know that I've mixed a little into their drink, but many comment on how good the Bloody Mary tastes.

A small grater works well for grating nutmeg. It's essential to grate it freshly, as its flavour deteriorates very quickly.

ZOOM

John Lea and William Perrins, two Worcester chemists, made the original Worcestershire sauce in the early 19th century. A fermented relish based on ingredients encountered by the British in India, it is still made in Worcester and is exported all over the world. The sauce is aged in wooden casks for 18 months before bottling. The company is now owned by H.J. Heinz.

Savoury Mixers

- The most common savoury mixers are hot sauces, Worcestershire sauce, beef bouillon, brown sauce, tomato juice, clam juice and tomato-clam cocktail.
- These ingredients can be mixed before or stirred in after as seasonings.
- Popular cocktails made with savoury ingredients include the Bloody Mary, Bloody Bull, Bloody Caesar, Bloody Maria, Red Eye and Prairie Fire.

Dry Mixers

- Dry mixers used for cocktails include salt, celery salt, chilli pepper, cayenne pepper, white pepper, cocoa powder, cloves, cinnamon, spicy seasonings, powdered hot chocolate and powdered apple cider.
- Dry mixers can be added at anytime in the cocktail-making process.
- Often dry mixers are sprinkled on top of a cocktail.
- Always try to use the freshest ingredients possible.

CUTTING WEDGES & WHEELS

Grab some citrus and a sharp knife and learn to cut your first garnish

A sharp knife is crucial. A dull knife is dangerous because it can slip off the food you're cutting and cut your fingers instead. Serrated knives have little teeth that grab hold of citrus fruit, which can be better for beginners, and they don't need sharpening. You can keep other knives sharpened by using a steel or other types of knife sharpener.

Always make sure your hands, the knife and whatever you are cutting are all dry before you start cutting. When you come to a stage of cutting when the blade is getting too close to your fingers, simply curl them under while still applying firm pressure.

Wheels for drink garnishes are very decorative. However, they are not practical to squeeze into a drink because of the mess doing so will make on your hands. Wedges are designed to be easily lifted off the edge of a drink and then squeezed to add flavour in one smooth motion. Some people cut off

Wheels: Step 1

- Wheels can be cut from any fruit or vegetable with a circular shape. The most common is citrus.
- For this demonstration, a lemon is used.
- 1. Begin with a secure, clean surface. Cut off the ends of the lemon.
- 2. Make a lengthwise cut to the centre of the lemon if you want the wheels to rest on the rim of the glasses.

Wheels: Step 2

- 1. Hold the lemon firmly down with one hand.
- 2. Carefully slice the lemon widthwise into wheels about 4 mm thick.
- If you need to make several wheels or desire very thin wheels, use a kitchen slicer or mandolin.

the ends of a piece of fruit and then cut wedges, but I don't like that amputated dogtail dock look, because you lose the beautiful curve of the fruit. And when you squeeze it, your fingers touch the flesh of the fruit instead of being protected by the peel.

YELLOW LIGHT

For hygiene and courtesy to the guest, it's usually best for bartenders to set a wedge of lemon or lime on the rim of the glass and allow the guest to taste the drink first, then decide if he or she wants an extra burst of flavour. Even though bartenders often wash their hands, they are constantly touching things.

Wedges: Step 1

- Wedges can be cut from any fruit or vegetable with a circular shape. The most common is citrus.
- For this demonstration, we are using a lime.
- 1. Begin with a secure, clean surface, then slice the lime in half lengthwise.
- 2. If the wedges are going to be set on the rims of glasses, make a slice into the flesh of the lime widthwise, without cutting through the peel.

Wedges: Step 2

- 1. Turn the lime half over and hold it down firmly with one hand.
- 2. Carefully slice along the length of the lime at an angle.
- Each half lime should yield three or four wedges.

MAKING TWISTS

Take a spoon and a knife in your hand and do the twist!

The bar term 'twist' refers to a thin strip of lemon rind that is twisted over a cocktail to release its oils, then gently rubbed around the rim of the glass so that the pungent citrus oil can be tasted when taking a drink. A twist is the thicker and sturdier brother of a lemon zest, and often the two words are used interchangeably.

One twist that is often confusing to bartenders and guests is the lime wedge twist. I believe that the practice of calling a wedge of lime a 'twist' came about because TV and film writers did not know the difference. Typically, people will order soda water 'with a twist'. What they really want is soda water with a *wedge* of lime.

The most popular drinks that a lemon twist *can be* used for are classic Martinis (think James Bond), whisky neat or on the rocks, and a cup of espresso. The recent resurrection of the Sazerac calls for a lemon twist, but the twist is not dropped

Twists: Step 1

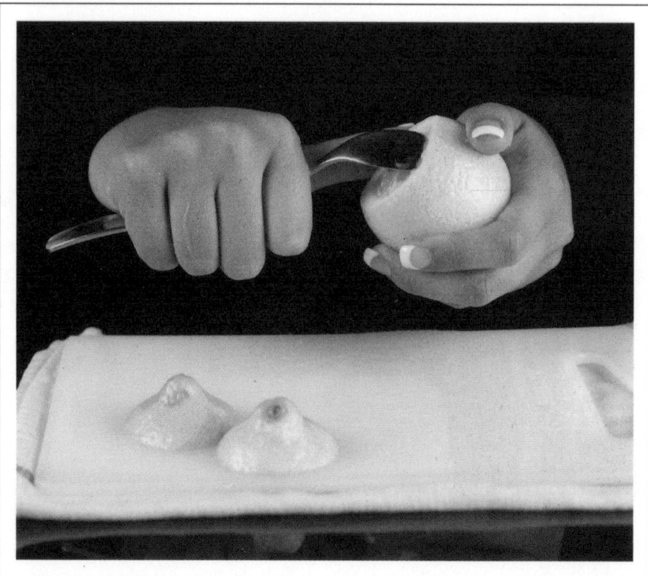

- 1. Cut the ends off a lemon.
- 2. Slip a spoon between the rind and the flesh, then run it around the lemon at both ends.
- The goal is to separate the flesh from the rind.
- Another way is to make a lengthwise cut in the rind, then separate the rind from the flesh with your fingertips or a spoon.

Twists: Step 2

- 1. Vertically slice the whole rind once. Or, if you prefer, you can lay the rind on its side and make one slice.
- This slice is the lengthwise slice you'd be making in the other way using your fingertips or spoon.
- Be sure to save the lemon flesh for juicing.

into the cocktail. The reason why I say that a lemon twist *can be* used is because it's something that a guest will request. It's not part of the recipe, as it is in the Sazerac.

And that brings me to talk a little about cocktail garnishes. Garnishes are meant to enhance a cocktail either by taste or appearance. A garnish should tell you something about the ingredients in the drink. For example, a drink with pineapple juice could be garnished with a pineapple slice. If candied ginger is part of a garnish, then I would assume that there's something 'ginger' in the cocktail. Guests can choose not to eat the garnish and set it aside on a cocktail napkin or push it into the drink.

Be extra careful when working with slippery rinds.

Twists: Step 3

- 1. Tightly roll up the lemon rind.
- 2. Secure the rolled rind with a bamboo or cocktail stick by pushing it all the way through the rind.
- Securing the rind makes the next step of slicing easier.
- Some people don't secure the rind and just hold it tightly with their fingers. It can be done but be warned of its slip factor.

Twists: Step 4

- 1. Slice the secured rolled rind to make twists.
- An average lemon can yield up to eight twists.
- Fatter lemons make for longer twists.
- Another way to make twists is to cut lengthwise strips around a lemon, then cut off one end. You can then pull off a twist as you need one. However, these will be shorter.

CUTTING A PINEAPPLE

Learn how to cut this exotic fruit to slip a new trick up your sleeve

Of all the garnishes I show people how to cut into slices, the pineapple is always their favourite. It seems that they feel they just learned a cool new trick, like making a balloon animal or whistling by placing two fingers into their mouth. You will need a larger space than normal when cutting a pineapple. And a larger knife.

You can also save the top end of the pineapple (with the fronds). It can be used as decoration in a display, or you could stick bamboo-skewered fruit kebabs into it. The fronds can also be torn off and used as a garnish. You'll have to trim the bottoms of them a little for the sake of appearance. You can also spear fronds on a pineapple slice. A fancy way to attach

Cutting a Pineapple: Step 1

- 1. Begin with a secure, clean surface.
- 2. Slice off the ends of the pineapple.
- 3. Carefully cut the pineapple in half lengthwise.
- 4. Discard the ends.

Cutting a Pineapple: Step 2

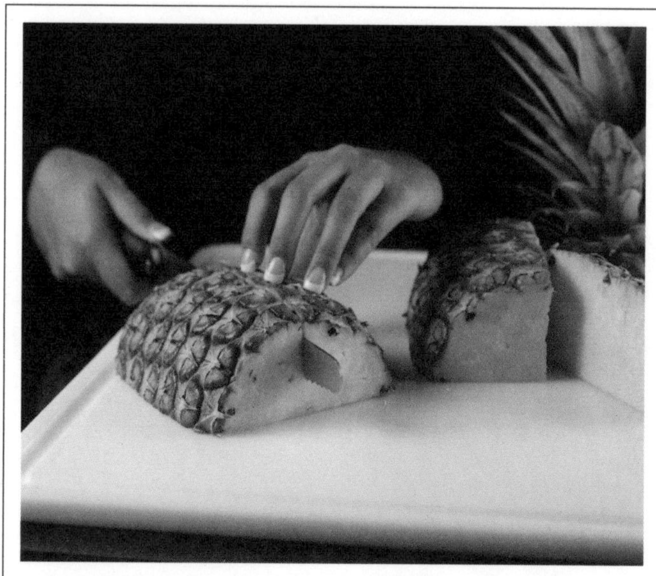

- 1. Lay the pineapple halves flat for cutting stability.
- 2. Slice both pineapple halves lengthwise.
- The result will be four lengthwise pineapple quarters.
- After some practice, you may discover that you prefer to cut the quarters in half to make eighths. This will yield more slices.

the fronds to a pineapple slice is to make an incision in the edge of the slice, then insert a couple of fronds down into the incision, point side up. For punches made with pineapple juice, just throw a handful of fronds in for fun.

Drinks that could get a pineapple slice garnish are Piña Colada, Bay Breeze, Planter's Punch, Singapore Sling or any tropical drink made with pineapple juice.

ZOOM

The pineapple is native to southern Brazil. It got its English name because European explorers thought it looked like a pine cone, and it was successfully cultivated under glass in Europe from 1720. The Spanish introduced it to Hawaii, where the first commercial plantations were planted in the late 19th century. Over 14,000 million tons of pineapple are now grown around the world.

Cutting a Pineapple: Step 3

- 1. Firmly hold down a pineapple quarter (because the outside curve of the pineapple is unstable). Make a careful 12-mm lengthwise cut into the pineapple flesh.
- 2. This will allow the slices to rest on the rim of a glass.
- 3. Repeat with the other three pineapple quarters.
- 4. The result will be four lengthwise pineapple quarters with rim slices.

Cutting a Pineapple: Step 4

- 1. Turn the pineapple quarter on its flat, stable side, then hold firmly.
- 2. Make many slices widthwise.
- 3. Repeat with the other three pineapple quarters.
- 4. The result should be 30–40 pineapple slices that will rest on the rim of a glass.

ADDITIONAL GARNISHES

Discover the ever-growing world of cocktail garnishes

The top four garnishes every bar will have are lemons, limes, olives and maraschino cherries. From that foundation a tower of garnishes can be built. Next in line would be oranges, pineapples, strawberries and mint.

There's really no limit when it comes to garnishes. Some bars carry non-typical garnishes because of their signature cocktail menu. These can include peaches, grapes, mango, wild hibiscus flowers, orchids, rose petals, berries, pears, apples, kiwi, watermelon, cantaloupe, bananas, basil, rosemary, sugared ginger and sugarcane sticks. Unusual garnishes in this book include chocolate-covered strawberries, chocolate-dipped fortune cookies, lychees, edible gold, crushed biscuits and sweets, coconut flakes, celery salt, a frosted doughnut, red candy lips, gummy worms, flowers and liquorice bootlaces.

Non-edible additions to a drink are called 'decorations' and 'tools'. Sometimes a decoration can also serve as a tool, such

Making Flags

- Originally a flag was an orange slice speared with a cherry.
- Today a flag is anything that has been speared with a cherry.
- You can cut and spear the fruit any way your heart desires.
- Look for fun and interesting cocktail sticks to make flags.

Stuffing Olives

- 1. To make stuffed olives, first buy some large, green pitted olives, preferably unstuffed. If you can find only pimento-stuffed olives, simply remove the pimentos.
- 2. Now stuff with your chosen ingredients.
- Olives can be stuffed with practically anything you like.
- Some popular stuffing choices are blue cheese (or any cheese), whole almonds, garlic, pearl onions and jalapeños.

as a paper parasol speared with a cherry. There are unlimited choices when it comes to straws, sticks and stirrers.

Some drinks automatically get a characteristic garnish. Limes are used for Margaritas, tonics (Gin and Tonic and so forth), Cape Codders and Cuba Libres. Lemons are used for teas (Long Island, Long Beach and so forth), and orange flags are used for sours (such as Tom Collins and Whiskey Sour).

MAKE IT EASY

Get creative with your Bloody Marys! For example, why not make a pizza Bloody Mary? Rim one half with Parmesan cheese and the other half with chilli pepper, or use a combination of both for the whole rim. Garnish with a skewer of pepperoni slices, cheese cubes and olives. If you like Hawaiian pizza, then put pineapple and ham cubes on to the skewer.

Bloody Mary Garnishes

- The Bloody Mary has the largest assortment of possible garnishes to choose from.
- Try spearing garnishes on a celery stalk.
- Generally, a Bloody Mary gets a lime wedge, or if it is made with plain tomato juice it gets a lemon wedge.
- Some restaurants set up a self-service Bloody Mary table filled with a wide assortment of garnishes, hot sauces and spices.

Ideas for Bloody Mary Garnishes

Bloody Mary garnishes can include celery, pickles, pickled okra, pickled green beans, olives (green, black, stuffed), peppers (green, yellow, red, pepperoncini), limes, lemons, tomatoes (cherry, grape, plum), onions (green, raw rings, cocktail), asparagus, baby corn, mushrooms, carrot sticks, cucumbers (sticks or rounds), avocado slices, unpeeled prawns, radishes, cheese cubes, salted rim and celery salt rim.

BEER & GLASSWARE

Pull up a stool and learn about the most ancient alcoholic drink of all

As far as historians know, beer was the first documented alcoholic beverage. Archaeologists have found million-year-old grapevine fossils, but unless there is documented proof that someone made wine from them, that simply doesn't count. Recipes for beer have been found on 92 Babylonian stone tablets, in Egyptian and Turkish tombs and on many European cave walls, and beer residue has been found in 9,000-year-old Chinese pottery.

Today beer-drinking vessels are mostly made of glass. The stein is the most decorative beer glass of them all. It was invented in the 1300s, and by the 1500s lids were attached to keep out the flies. Nowadays steins are mostly bought as souvenirs or by collectors. The yard glass is the largest beer glass. Basically, it's one yard (91 cm) in length and can hold 1.14 litres of beer. Beer is the only alcoholic beverage available in many different packages: bottles, cans, kegs or casks.

Beer Glasses

- Beer glasses can vary in size from 35 cl to 1.25 litres.
- Beer has the most types of glassware: around twenty.
- The three most common all-beer glasses are the straight pint glass, the dimpled jug and the pilsner.
- There is a variety of pilsner glasses, but all are thin at the bottom and wider at the top.

Ales

- Ale was the first beer ever recorded.
- The first ales were sweet, murky, thick and warm.
- Hops were not widely used in ales until the 13th century and did not become dominant until the 16th century. Until that time, ales were flavoured with other herbs and plants in a mixture called 'gruit'.
- Ale types include stout, porter, wheat, bitter, lambic, brown, cream and pale.

There are over 20,000 brands of beer worldwide, and all of those beers fall into two categories: ale or lager. Lagers use bottom-fermenting yeast and are brewed at low temperature. Ales use top-fermenting yeast and are brewed at higher temperatures, giving rise to a wide range of secondary flavours and aromas. They are highly regionally distinctive.

ZOOM

The Anchor Brewery in San Francisco makes a unique handmade beer called 'Anchor Steam Beer' using both top- and bottom-fermenting yeasts. The brewery began in 1896, then was consumed by the great San Francisco earthquake and fire, then suffered during Prohibition. After 1933 it reopened and began brewing again. Today it offers seven beers.

Lagers

- The first golden pilsner was invented in Pilzen, in what is now the Czech Republic, by Josef Groll in 1842. It is called 'Pilsner Urquell'.
- The German-born brewer Adolphus Busch introduced his 'Bohemian-style' beer, Budweiser, to the USA in 1876.
- He was the first brewer in America to use pasteurization to keep lager fresh and the first to use refrigerated railroad cars, in which Budweiser was shipped from coast to coast.
- Lager types include bock, dry, light, pilsner, ice, malt, amber and export.

Beer Trivia

- The *Mayflower* pilgrims planned to sail farther but ran out of beer at Plymouth Rock, so the decision was made to disembark.
- The German Oktoberfest was first celebrated in Munich in 1810.
- The New York Public Library has a piece of notebook paper bearing a recipe for small beer written by George Washington in 1757.

RED WINE & GLASSWARE

Learn the basics of red wine through the grapevine

Walking through a forest of wine bottles at your local store can be overwhelming. Yes, there is a lot to know about wine, and entire books have been written on the subject, but I hope to help you understand the basics.

Wine is made from fermented fruit, and the most popular fruit used is grapes. Its history spans thousands of years through every civilization. Today's top wine-producing countries are France, America, Australia, Spain, Italy and Argentina.

All wines basically are in one of two styles: red or white. These styles break down into three body types: full, medium and light. Even though there are over 10,000 varieties of grapes in the world, only about 300 of these are used to make wine commercially. Out of these, 20–30 varieties are used for the most popular wines. In the wine world, you will hear the word 'varietal' often. This refers to wines made from a single variety of grape. Popular red (and black) wine grapes used

Red Wine Glasses

- Red wine glasses have a round, wide bowl. A proper serving is 150–175 ml.
- The largeness of the bowl allows more room for the wine to breathe.
- Some modern red wine glasses offer curvier options, but the rim will never be wider than the bowl.
- A glass of red wine is held with the fingertips touching the bottom of the bowl because warming the wine is not an issue.

Full-bodied Red Wines

- Full-bodied wines are very dark in colour, have a heavy feel on the tongue, and are high in tannins.
- The king grape of heavy-bodied wine is the Cabernet Sauvignon grape.
- Full-bodied red wines include those of Bordeaux, Malbec and Burgundy.
- Full-bodied wines are usually too much for the beginner and are something to be graduated to.

to make red wine include Cabernet Sauvignon, Merlot, Pinot Noir, Sangiovese, Shiraz/Syrah, Zinfandel, Gamay, Grenache, Lambrusco, Pinot Meunier and Tempranillo.

Displays in wine merchants and wine sections in supermarkets are always organized for you (normally by country). After you narrow down the country, then you can narrow down the body type of wine you prefer and/or the grape variety you prefer. Wine labels will give you all the information you need to know about the wine: the location of the vineyard, the vintage (the year the grapes were harvested), the variety (grape type), the producer of the wine or the brand name. Some countries have labelling laws that require a government warning, an indication of the alcohol content, and the list of sulphites used.

Grape varieties are often blended together, so it's not uncommon to find, for example, a Cabernet-Shiraz or a Cabernet-Merlot mix.

Medium-bodied Red Wines

- Medium-bodied red wines will not be as intense as full-bodied red wines in the mouth.
- The colour of a medium-bodied wine will be lighter than that of a full-bodied red wine and darker than that of a light-bodied wine.
- A fruity taste is found with a medium-bodied wine.
- Popular medium-bodied red wines include Merlot, Shiraz/Syrah, Chianti and some Pinot Noirs.

Light-bodied Red Wines

- Light-bodied red wines are ruby red in colour.
- This type of wine is good for beginners, because of its light and fruity taste and feel on the tongue.
- The Gamay grape is a popular grape for light-bodied red wines.
- Popular light-bodied red wines include Beaujolais, Lambrusco and some Pinot Noirs.

WHITE WINE & GLASSWARE

Discover the best butter- and straw-coloured sweet or dry vino

The first thing to know about white wine is that it can be made from white, red, purple or even black grapes. This is because the grape skins are discarded when making white wine. With red wine, the skins are not discarded. And for pink-toned rosé or blush wines, the skins are left on just a little bit to colour the wine.

Just like red wines, white wines will vary in body. They will also vary from dryness to sweetness. Popular grapes used to make white wine include Chardonnay, Sauvignon Blanc, Chenin Blanc, Pinot Gris/Pinot Grigio, Pinot Blanc, Gewürztraminer, Riesling and Viognier. All of these white wine varieties can have a dry or super sweet taste because it all depends on who grows the grapes.

Growing grapes to make wine is indeed an artform. So many elements determined by nature and determined by people come into play. Grapevines love warm, dry summers

White Wine Glasses

- The shape of a white wine glass is narrow. A proper measure is 150–175 ml.
- White wine glasses are held by the stem to avoid warming the wine.
- Restaurants and bars dedicated to the art of wine will carry both a white wine glass and a red wine glass.
- Many establishments will carry an all-purpose wine glass for both types of wine.

Full-bodied White Wine

- The full-bodied Chardonnay grape is the queen of the white grapes.
- Chardonnay is one of the varieties used to make Champagne.
- Chardonnay is heavy, buttery, fruity and oaky.
- Some winemakers don't like the oakiness of Chardonnay, so they age the wine in stainless steel tanks.

and mild winters. Who doesn't? And all grape varieties have a favourite soil. For example, Riesling grapes love a slate-rich soil, and Chardonnay grapes love limestone. Plant each of them in the other's favourite soil, and it would be disastrous! Other factors that come into play are sun exposure, bugs, rainfall, drainage and more.

GREEN LIGHT

Organic wines have become popular, but many aren't entirely organic. In the USA only wines with the USDA organic seal are made from organically grown grapes with only naturally occurring sulphites. If the label says 'made with organically grown grapes' without the seal, sulphites have been added. An equivalent regulation came into force in the European Union in 2005.

Medium-bodied White Wine

- Medium-bodied white wine is a lighter colour than the heavy-bodied Chardonnay.
- Popular medium-bodied white wines include Viognier, Pinot Blanc and Gewürztraminer.
- Sauvignon Blanc is probably the best example of a medium-bodied white wine.
- Sauvignon Blanc has a dry, grassy, citrus, crisp taste.

Light-bodied White Wine

- Light-bodied white wine is the lightest in colour.
- The Riesling grape originated in Germany and is Germany's leading grape variety. Riesling wines are flowery and aromatic, and may be sweet or dry.
- Popular light-bodied white wines include Chenin Blanc and Pinot Gris/Pinot Grigio.
- Light-bodied wines are often drunk in the summer or at a picnic.

CHAMPAGNE & GLASSWARE

Explore the most celebratory liquid of all time

Ironically, in modern times we adore and celebrate the 50 million bubbles in a bottle of Champagne, but until the mid-1600s, bubbles in a bottle of wine meant that the winemaker had failed. The proof was in a wine-soaked cellar full of burst bottles. Locals referred to this wine as 'demon' or 'devil wine'. It's funny how things change with time.

Many people believe that a blind French monk named Dom Pérignon invented Champagne, but the fact is that Champagne invented itself. This is because the Champagne region is in northern France. That means that the region has a short growing season (due to being colder) and that the harvest season ends up being in the late autumn. The coldness of winter stops the fermentation inside the bottles, then when springs rolls around the fermentation picks up where it left off and creates bubbles inside the bottle. Dom Pérignon can most definitely be credited with *improving* Champagne,

Champagne Glasses

- There are basically two types of Champagne glass: the coupe (or saucer) and the flute. A proper serving of Champagne is 150 ml.
- The flute is broken down into two other types called 'trumpet' and 'tulip.'
- The trumpet has a shape that flares up and out, and the tulip has curvy variations.
- The flute-type Champagne glass is meant to keep the bubbles fresher.

Champagne

- Champagnes are named after the houses that produce them, rather than the vineyards where the grapes are grown.
- Champagnes come in levels from sweet to dry: Doux, Demi-Sec, Sec, Extra Dry, Brut, Brut Zero, Ultra Brut, and Extra Brut.
- A good temperature to serve Champagne is 6°C.
- Only three grape varieties are used to make Champagne: Pinot Noir, Pinot Meunier and Chardonnay.

because his passion was to figure out a way to keep the bottles from exploding. And he did. He found thicker and stronger bottles made in England, used Spanish-inspired corks held in place with wire closures, improved pruning and harvesting practices and created a blend, or *cuvée*, of black grapes grown in the Champagne region.

ZOOM

In 1805, 98 years after Dom Pérignon's death, a 27-year-old widow, Madame Barbe-Nicole Clicquot (pronounced clee-KOH), took over her late husband's Champagne business. After eight years of mourning she became extremely interested in improving Champagne and developed the racks that solved the problem of *remuage* or riddling (consolidating the sediment in the bottle for removal).

Sparkling Wine

- The reason why there is even a category of sparkling wine is because of the Champagne Riots in the early 1900s.
- The region's growers rioted against the practice of Champagne houses buying grapes more cheaply from outside the region. The result was a law requiring that only wines made with grapes grown in the Champagne region could bear the word 'Champagne' on their label.
- The words 'sparkling wine' can be seen on all bottles of sparkling wine made after 1927.

Prosecco

- Prosecco is a grape used to make Italian sparkling wine of the same name.
- The Prosecco grape is prized for its delicate and aromatic flavours.
- The most famous cocktail made with Prosecco is the Bellini (white peach purée and Prosecco).
- In 2006, Paris Hilton launched a 'lifestyle' beverage in a can that is a mixture of Prosecco and artificial flavourings called 'Rich Prosecco'.

PORT, SHERRY & GLASSWARE

Learn about the other wine-based choices that are steeped deep in history

Making sherry isn't as cut and dried as making port. With port, winemakers add brandy to prematurely stop the fermentation of the wine, then age it. Sherry is made using the solera system, which is a time-consuming blending of older and younger wines little by little by hand while they're ageing in the barrels. The wines are also exposed to air as they're ageing, which is monitored. Another difference is that sherry is fortified after fermentation, when all the sugar has been converted into alcohol; for sweet styles of sherry sugar is added later.

However, there is one area in which making port is more challenging, and that is the growing conditions of the grapes.

Port and Sherry Glasses

- A proper serving of port or sherry is 75–90 ml.
- A port glass is like a miniature wine glass. It's always stemmed with a nicely shaped bowl.
- Port and sherry glasses are the older siblings of cordial glasses.
- Port is traditionally drunk after dinner, often accompanied by a cigar. Some smokers dip their cigars into the wine.

Port

- True port is made in the Douro River valley in northern Portugal. Today other countries make their own versions of it.
- Port styles include tawny (sweet to medium dry) and ruby (bottle aged, sweet).
- The word 'port' is derived from the name of the port town of Oporto, not Portugal.
- Port was the first fortified wine made by adding brandy to it and then ageing.

The vineyards are located on remote, steep slopes that drop down to the Douro River in Portugal. It is by far the most difficult wine-growing region in the world.

Both sherry and port have a rich history. Port became popular in the 18th century, when the English could not import French wines due to wartime trade embargoes, so they turned to Portugal. The wines were originally fortified so that they would survive the long sea voyage to England.

Madeira, too, has a rich history. Just like port and sherry, it was stocked on ships bound for extended voyages. However, an interesting accident occurred within the barrels of Madeira. The fortified wine was exposed to extreme heat when the ships sailed near the equator, but instead of spoiling it, the heat actually baked a soft, burnt richness into it. At the time, Madeira seemed magical and intriguing. It was the wine used to toast the signing of the American Declaration of Independence, and the USS *Constitution* was christened with a bottle of Madeira. Modern winemakers heat the barrels at 37–60°C for several months to simulate the extreme tropical heat.

Sherry

- Sherry is made only in the triangular area around the town of Jerez in Spain.
- Sherry comes in two types: fino (dry and light) and oloroso (sweet and dark).
- Fino comes in three styles: Fino, Manzanilla and Amontillado. Oloroso also comes in three styles: Oloroso, Cream and Pedro Ximenez.
- Finos are drunk chilled and olorosos at room temperature. Cooking sherry is not for drinking.

Madeira and Vermouth

- Madeira is wine fortified with grape brandy and made on the Portuguese islands of Madeira.
- The four types of Madeira are Malmsey, Bual, Verdelho and Sercial.
- Vermouth is a fortified white wine that has a spirit (usually brandy) added, and is then aromatized with herbs and botanicals such as seeds and flowers.
- Vermouth comes in two types: dry (white, known as 'French') and sweet (red, 'Italian'). For superior cocktails, buy French or Italian vermouths.

BRANDY, COGNAC & GLASSWARE

What do grapes, apples, kings and presidents have in common?

For centuries, the brandy called 'cognac' has been the king of brandies. And cognac has been the choice of kings. The king of cognac is even named after a king. It's called 'Louis XIII,' and Remy Martin produces it. It's aged for 40–100 years in French oak barrels that are several hundred years old, and it's bottled in Baccarat crystal. The price starts at around £1,000.

The term 'angel's share' or 'angel's portion' refers to the annual 3 per cent evaporation of cognac as it ages in wooden casks. They say that when you visit Cognac in France you can actually smell the evaporating cognac in the air. Now, give or take a bottle or two, normally there is enough cognac being aged at all times (in £2,500 oak casks) to fill over a billion bottles. This means that every year almost 200,000 bottles of cognac disappear into thin air. And the angels aren't sharing.

Maurice Hennessey was the first winemaker to begin a grading system for cognac in 1865. Every bottle is graded, and the

Brandy and Cognac Balloons

- Brandy and cognac glasses are called 'balloons'. A proper serving is 60 ml.
- Most balloons are short stemmed and big bowled.
- Balloons are available in sizes of 150–780 ml.
- Usually you can tip a balloon on to its side, then pour brandy to the rim, and that will be a perfect measure.

Cognac

- All cognac is brandy, but not all brandy is cognac.
- Cognac is made only from grapes grown in the Cognac region of France.
- Cognac is distilled twice, then aged in oak casks made from Limousin or Tronçais oak wood from trees that grow in the Cognac region.
- The ageing process is very expensive because 3 per cent of the cognac evaporates each year.

grade is put on the label. The cognac grades are V.S. (very superior or three-star; aged for a minimum of three years), V.S.O.P. (very superior old pale or reserve; aged 4–20 years), and X.O. (extra old; aged 6–40 or more years).

It's interesting how the media can change a spirit's category overnight. For centuries, cognac has been the spirit for the refined. Then around the millennium, rap artists mentioned cognac in their songs, giving it a new demographic.

The name 'cognac' can only be applied to brandy that originates from the Cognac region of France. Armagnac, made in southwest France, also has protected geographical status.

Applejack brandy, distilled from apple cider, is as American as apple pie or cherry trees. Laird's Applejack was the first commercial distillery in America, and records show a written request by the first president, George Washington, asking for the applejack recipe. Calvados, from Normandy, is also made from apples.

Armagnac

- Armagnac is a high-end brandy made from grapes in the Armagnac region of southwest France.
- Armagnac is the oldest distilled spirit in France, dating back to the 1300s.
- It is the only true rival of cognac.
- Only ten varieties of grapes are authorized to be used for Armagnac.

Brandy

- Brandy can be made with any fruits, anywhere in the world.
- The production of brandy dates back to the 12th century, but most historians believe it is much older. Documented proof has not surfaced.
- The word 'brandy' comes from the Dutch *brandewijn*, meaning 'burnt wine'.
- Popular fruit brandy flavours are apple, blackberry, pear, peach and apricot.

VODKA

Possibly the first clear spirit to have been invented

In the simplest terms, distillation is the process by which a liquid is boiled and the condensation of the steam is collected. It's believed that ancient alchemists used this process to make medicine and perfumes. No one knows when distillation was first used to make spirits, but we do know the first names it had: 'ardent waters' (burnt water), 'eau-de-vie' (the water of life), and then 'voda' (vodka). Many believe vodka has been around since the 1300s, but it was not like the clean, clear vodka of today. It's believed that makers infused it with herbs, flowers and fruits.

Smirnoff vodka was the first to use charcoal filtering in 1870. The Smirnoff distillery produced up to 4 million cases of vodka per year, but after the Russian Revolution in 1917 the Bolsheviks confiscated the distillery. Members of the Smirnov family fled for their lives. One of the Smirnov sons, Vladimir, re-established the distillery first in Istanbul and then

The First Vodka in the West

- Piotr Arsenyevitch Smirnov founded his vodka distillery in Moscow in 1860.
- Smirnoff vodka was the first vodka to be introduced to America.
- The Moscow Mule was the first Smirnoff cocktail, introduced in1941 by John G. Martin and Jack Morgan.
- Vodka exploded in popularity when James Bond ordered a Vodka Martini, shaken not stirred, in the 1962 film *Dr No*.

Ultra-premium Vodka

- High-end, boutique and ultra-premium vodkas hit the market around the millennium.
- Master marketer Sidney Frank is responsible for introducing Grey Goose vodka, the first heavily marketed ultra-premium vodka.
- High-end vodkas focus on sleek and modern bottle design and multiple filtering.
- Ketel One vodka has won many blind taste tests.

in Poland. He later settled in Paris, changed his last name to the French form 'Smirnoff', and opened a distillery there. Smirnoff vodka was exported throughout Europe.

After American Prohibition ended in 1933, Vladimir sold the American rights in Smirnoff vodka to a friend, Rudolph Kunett, but Kunett's American vodka adventures were unsuccessful. He sold the rights to John G. Martin. Today Smirnoff is owned by drinks giant Diageo and is the top-selling vodka in the world.

ZOOM

Vodka provides a blank canvas that allows for much experimentation. Companies infuse it with flavours, make it from organic materials, colour it black, or harvest chunks of icebergs to use as their water. College students have even been known to run cheap vodka through a water filter a few times to make it taste like premium vodka.

Flavoured Vodka

- Absolut introduced the first infused/flavoured vodka in 1986, called 'Absolut Peppar'. It's flavoured with three types of pepper, making it perfect for a Bloody Mary.
- Almost every vodka brand has a line of flavoured vodka.
- Absolut Citron exploded the vodka infusion world with Lemon Drops and Cosmopolitans.
- Second to flavour its vodkas was Stolichnaya.

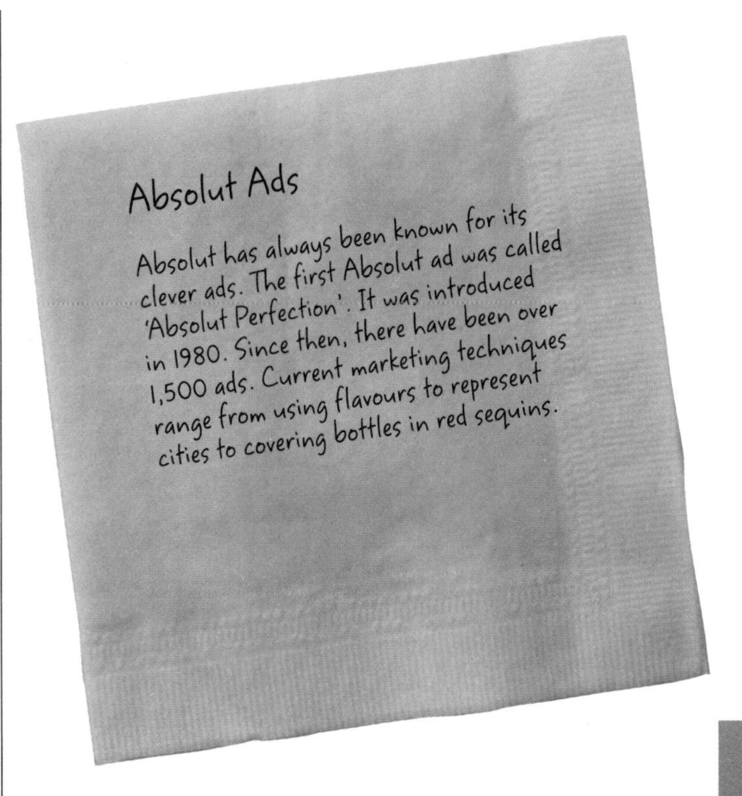

GIN

The clear, historic spirit is distilled with many herbs and botanicals

Gin in its basic form is vodka that has been re-distilled with herbs and botanicals. The main categories of gin are Genever, London Dry, Plymouth and the 2007 American addition, New Western Dry. Gin has been made in Holland, England, Germany, France, America, Spain, Lithuania, Belgium, Canada and Slovakia.

Many people believe that the 17th-century Dutch professor and physician Franciscus Sylvius invented gin for medicinal purposes. Historians have also discovered the first mention of juniper-based, health-related tonics and medicines in a Dutch work called *Der Naturen Bloeme,* by Jacob van Maerlant te Damme, published in 1269. We also know that Holland is credited with making the first commercial gin, which was known as 'Genever', from the French word for 'juniper'.

The taste of Genever is sweet and malty, and there are various types. The word *jonge* ('young') refers to the new way of

Genever

- Genever is considered the first gin.
- Genever is made in Holland, two provinces in West Germany, and two in Northern France.
- The modern categories of Genever are *oude, jonge, graajenever* and *korenwijn*.
- By a European Union declaration of 2008, *jonge* and *oude* Genever may only be labelled and sold as such in Holland and Belgium.

London Dry

- London Dry gin is believed to have originated with British troops who brought Dutch gin back to England after the Third Dutch War in the late 1600s.
- London Dry gin has a crisp, dry taste that mixes well in cocktails.
- This gin is the most common and widely distributed.
- London Dry gin brands include Beefeater, Bombay, Tanqueray, Gordon's and Boodles.

distilling the spirit, *oude* means the old and traditional way, and *korenwijn* is as close to the original recipe as possible.

The first gin made in England was sweet, like Dutch gin. The first popular brand was Old Tom gin, and it's the last remaining sweet English gin on the market today, though it's not widely available. Its name is said to come from a wooden plaque shaped like a black cat (a tom cat), which was mounted on the outside wall of a pub. Patrons would place a penny in the cat's mouth, then put their lips around a small tube between the cat's paws. The tavern keeper inside would then pour a shot of Old Tom gin through the tube and straight into the patron's mouth.

The Plymouth category of gin has one gin – called 'Plymouth.' The gin is fruity and aromatic. It's made in Plymouth, England, and Plymouth Coates & Co. owns all rights.

New Western Dry

- New Western Dry gin is a category coined by master mixologist Ryan Magarian.
- These gins include Aviation, Hendrick's and Martin Miller's.
- New Western Dry gins let juniper take the back seat and focus on the other herbs and botanicals. They also seem to have a delicate and fresh hint of cucumber.

Gin Madness

In the early 18th century, gin was cheaper than ale, and London turned into a slum of poverty and despair. This time in history was called 'Gin Madness'. The Gin Act, passed in 1736, imposed high taxes on the gin shops to try to reduce the trade, but Gin Riots spread through the streets of London, and many people began distilling their own gin, which was often adulterated. Artist William Hogarth captured the atmosphere of the time in his engraving 'Gin Lane', published in 1751.

RUM

Get super sweet on the tropical spirit that is made with sugarcane

Rum can be made from sugarcane or from its by-products: sugarcane juice and molasses. Since the 1600s, rum has been used for trading, drinking, bribing and even paying wages.

Some believe the Dutch first brought sugarcane to Barbados. Others say that sugarcane was first used in China. What we do know is that brothers Don and Jose Bacardi, Spanish businessmen who settled in Cuba, created the first real commercial rum in1862. It took them ten years to perfect the once-crude sugarcane spirit into a smooth, refined drink. Due to wars and other conflicts, Bacardi rum went through many tribulations. Finally, in the 1930s, the company moved to San Juan, Puerto Rico, where it now has its headquarters.

Gold rums have a richer and silkier flavour and texture than light rums. My favourite is Appleton's from Jamaica. In the 19th century, there were almost 150 rum distilleries in Jamaica; today there are five. One of them is Appleton's.

Light Rum

- Light rum is also known as 'silver', 'white' or 'platinum' rum.
- Light rum doesn't require ageing and is usually bottled after distillation.
- Brazil makes a rum from Brazilian sugarcane that is called *cachaça* (pronounced ka-SHAH-sa). The popular cocktail called the Caipirinha (pronounced kai-pee-REEN-ya) is made with it.
- Bacardi is the most popular light rum worldwide.

Gold Rum

- Gold rum is sometimes called 'amber rum'.
- The gold colour comes from the rum's being aged in wooden barrels.
- Some gold rums make great mixing rums, and others are excellent for sipping like a fine cognac. It mostly depends on ageing.
- Some premium gold rums are actually blended rums that have been aged for up to ten years.

Dark rum is usually made with molasses in tropical locations all over the world. Gosling's Black Seal Rum was created by an Englishman, James Gosling, the affluent eldest son of a wine merchant. In the spring of 1806, Gosling set sail for America on a ship named the *Mercury*. The ship carried £10,000 in merchandise with which Gosling intended to open a shop. But sea storms swept him to the port of St George's in Bermuda, and he accepted the detour as a sign that this was where he was meant to be. Eighteen years later he sent for his brother, and they began making rum.

Two other rum categories are over-proof rum and super premium sipping rum. Over-proof rums are used to flame a drink or for culinary purposes. Super premium sipping rums are also called 'añejo rums.'

Dark Rum

- Dark rum is also known as 'black rum'.
- Myers's Original Dark Rum is the most popular dark rum in the world. It's made from 100 per cent Jamaican molasses.
- Two dark rums are used in famous recipes: Gosling's Black Seal Rum in a Dark 'n' Stormy and Myers's Dark Rum in a Planter's Punch.
- Dark rum is often used as a floater on top of a tropical drink.

These rums come in a wide variety of flavours.

Flavoured Rum

- Flavours include coconut, banana, mango, raspberry, vanilla, spiced, pineapple, citron, passion fruit, orange and lime.
- Captain Morgan Spiced Rum was the first flavoured rum to go on sale in America, in 1984.
- Malibu Coconut Rum was released in the early 1980s as well, but it was classified as a liqueur with rum and coconut flavourings. The distillery claims that it's now made with rum.

TEQUILA

Learn about the long history of the national spirit of Mexico

Historians say that the Aztecs were making an alcoholic drink from the agave plant as early as the first century; 1,500 years later the Spanish invaded Mexico and took the agave-type wine and distilled it. One hundred years later the town of Tequila was allowed to make mezcal, a spirit distilled from the agave plant; 150 years after that the Spanish crown granted land and a distillery licence to José Cuervo. Much happened in the next hundred years, due to Mexico trying to gain its independence from Spain, but by the late 19th century both Mexico and tequila had become firmly established.

The *numero uno* thing to know about tequila is that by law it can be produced only in the Tequila region of Mexico. The *numero dos* thing to know is that in order for a label to say 'tequila' it must be made from at least 51 per cent blue agave. If it doesn't meet that standard, then it's called a *mixto* (this is a good example of mezcal).

Blanco Tequila

- Blanco is also called 'silver' or 'white' tequila.
- Most blanco tequila is either bottled straight out of the still or filtered and then bottled.
- If stored, blanco tequila must not be kept longer than 60 days in stainless steel tanks as it is not aged.
- One hundred per cent blue agave blanco tequila is an excellent choice for use in Margaritas.

Reposado Tequila

- Reposado is a blanco that has been aged in white oak casks for 2–12 months. It has a mellow yellow colour and flavour.
- The gold colour of a reposado comes from ageing in the wood casks.
- *Reposado* means 'rested' (as in 'rested in barrels').
- Reposado is the highest-quality tequila that will still taste good in a Margarita. It has a balance between bite and smoothness.

There are over 200 types of agave plants, but the best is the blue agave. An agave plant takes almost ten years to mature. When it matures a flower stalk grows straight up through the plant. If allowed to grow it will produce yellow flowers, but if the agave farmer chops off the stalk, the plant will swell inside, creating a large bulb that will fill with a sweet, juicy pulp. This forms into the *piña*, which is the part of the agave plant that is used to make tequila. The *piña* (which means 'pineapple' because it looks rather like a pineapple) can weigh as much as 45 kg. The piñas are cut, baked, and then crushed to extract the sweet agave juice that is used to make tequila. The worm that is put in mezcal is in fact a moth larva that grows inside agave plants.

Anejos are typically aged between one and eight years.

Añejo Tequila

- Añejo is a blanco tequila that has been aged for more than one year.
- High-quality añejos are aged up to three years.
- Añejo that is aged up to eight years is called 'reserva'.
- There is controversy over letting tequila age this long because the oak begins to overwhelm the flavour of the agave.
- *Añejo* means 'old'.

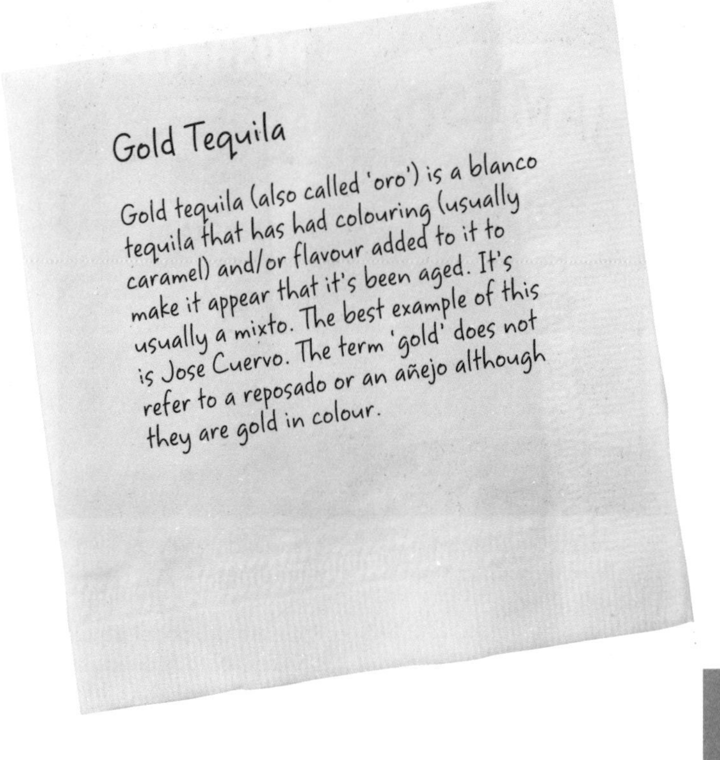

WHISKY/WHISKEY

Amber waves of grain are mashed up, aged and then poured into a bottle

Whisky/whiskey is distilled all over the world, from India and Japan to Germany, France and Russia, but the four countries that have been making it for centuries are Scotland, Ireland, America and Canada. Ireland and Scotland still bicker over who first invented it. By the way, Scotch and Canadian whisky is spelled without an 'e', Irish and American whiskey with an 'e'.

Blended Irish whiskey makes up the majority of Irish whiskey. Single-malt Irish whiskey is made from one whiskey type in either column or pot stills. Grain Irish whiskey is made from 100 per cent Irish grain and is usually used for blends. And pure pot still Irish whiskey is made from a combination of malted and unmalted barley, then distilled in pot stills.

Irish Whiskey

- Ireland makes blended, single-malt, grain and pure pot still whiskey.
- There are only three distilleries in the entire country of Ireland.
- Irish whiskey is made from malt that is dried in sealed ovens and usually distilled three times.
- There are two popular Irish whiskey-based liqueurs: Bailey's Original Irish Cream and Irish Mist.

Scotch Whisky

- Scotland makes single-malt Scotch whisky and blended whisky.
- Scotch whisky is made in four geographical regions, with distinctive flavours: Lowlands, Highlands, Speyside and the Islands.
- Scotch whisky is known for its smoky flavour, which comes from drying malted barley over open peat fires.
- A popular Scotch-based liqueur from Scotland is Drambuie. It's made from heather honey and herbs.

A 15-year-old boy, Johnnie Walker, is credited with first blending Scotch whisky. In 1820, his father died, and Johnnie used the life insurance money to open a small general store. At the time, tea was all the rave, and he got the idea of blending single-malt whiskys in the same way that the tea in his shop was blended. The four whisky-making regions in Scotland each produce different-tasting Scotches.

The term 'bourbon' is derived from the labels on barrels from Bourbon County, Kentucky. Bourbon breaks down into two premium bourbon categories: small batch and single barrel. Small-batch bourbons are bottlings from a batch of barrels, and single-barrel bourbons come from a single barrel of bourbon.

Corn whiskey is basically moonshine, and rye must be made from at least 51 per cent rye. The most popular American blended whiskey is Seagram's 7. Tennessee whiskey is made in Tennessee. The most popular Tennessee whiskeys are Jack Daniel's and George Dickel. You may hear of 'sour mash,' which means that part of a previous batch is used to start a new batch.

Canadian Whisky

- Canada blends its whisky for a smoother taste.
- Often Canada calls its whisky 'rye' but doesn't follow strict laws about how much rye must be in the whisky.
- Crown Royal Canadian whisky was made by Seagram's especially for Queen Elizabeth II's visit in 1939.

American Whiskey

- America produces five kinds of whiskey: bourbon, corn, rye, blended and Tennessee.
- By federal law, bourbon can be made only in the USA and must be made with at least 51 per cent American corn.
- Only bourbon made in Kentucky can have the words 'Kentucky bourbon' on the label.
- In 1964, an act of Congress declared bourbon as 'America's Native Spirit' as well as the country's official distilled spirit.

LIQUEURS

Learn the differences between the many liqueurs made around the world

Who knows what liqueurs ancient alchemists created in their dens? We do know that in the Dark Ages and the Middle Ages monks and physicians experimented with liqueurs to serve medicinal purposes or to find the elixir of life.

By the civilized 19th century, liqueurs were drunk as an apéritif (pre-dinner drink) or as an after-dinner digestive drink. Italians have been known for a long time to drink Sambuca before dinner and shots of Limoncello after a meal. Other popular Italian liqueurs include Tuaca, Galliano, Frangelico, and amaretto di Saronno. Germans are known to drink peppermint schnapps after dinner, but the most popular liqueur from Germany is Jägermeister. Almost every country in the

Liqueurs

- There are over 500 commercial liqueurs in the world.
- Liqueurs are sweet flavour-infused spirits and can also be called 'cordials.'
- Liqueurs can be low-proof, high-proof, cream, crème or schnapps.
- Liqueurs are considered a modifier in the cocktail world. They are used in small quantities to add flavour to a drink.

Cream Liqueurs

- Cream liqueurs are made with dairy cream and a spirit base.
- Baileys Original Irish Cream is the most popular cream liqueur in the world. It was the first cream and paved the way for many others.
- Most cream liqueurs have a shelf life of two years.
- Some bars keep cream liqueurs in the cooler or fridge.

world has at least one liqueur. Popular French liqueurs include Chambord, Cointreau, Chartreuse, St-Germain Elderflower, Grand Marnier, Bénédictine, and the crème family. Spain has Licor 43, Greece has Ouzo, the USA has Southern Comfort, Switzerland has Goldschläger, Jamaica has Tia Maria, Mexico has Kahlúa, Japan has Sakura, South Africa has Amarula, and the list goes on and on.

Today many liqueurs are used to enhance the flavour of a recipe. In most cases, the liqueur is always the smaller portion of alcohol (sometimes called a modifier) that goes into a cocktail.

ZOOM

Baileys Original Irish Cream is a combination of cream from Irish cows, Irish whiskey, chocolate and vanilla. It took the Baileys creators four years of experimenting to find a method to keep the cream from curdling when mixed with Irish whiskey. Finally in 1974 they succeeded.

Crème Liqueurs

- *Crème* is a French word (pronounced 'krem'.)
- Crèmes have a lot of sugar added to them, which results in a syrupy consistency.
- The most popular crèmes are crème de cacao (light and dark) and crème de menthe (white/clear and green).
- Other crèmes include crème de bananes, crème de cassis (blackcurrants), and crème de Yvette (violets).

Schnapps

- The word 'schnapps' is derived from a German word that can refer to any strong alcoholic drink.
- Schnapps is usually a high-proof liqueur because it is made from fermented fruits, grain or herbs, then distilled.
- True German schnapps does not have added sugar.
- American schnapps tends to be very sweet. This is because sugar is added after distillation.

AMERICAN WHISKEY COCKTAILS

Master the cocktails that pioneered the way for all others that followed

As far as we know, the cocktail is an American invention, and American whiskey is believed to have been the fuel that lit the trail into the wide-open spaces of cocktail culture history. Because American whiskey has been around since the late 1700s, it's not surprising that cocktail historians have found recipes in print since the early 19th century. The Mint Julep and the Sazerac tie for the title of first cocktail, but it didn't take long for every spirit to follow suit.

The Mint Julep is steeped in southern American tradition. The recipe is simple, and sometimes simplicity is best. The Sazerac is a perfect example of a balanced cocktail using five distinct flavours, and one can taste and smell each flavour.

Sazerac

Ingredients

7.5 ml absinthe
60 ml rye whiskey
15 ml simple syrup
15 ml filtered water
3 dashes Peychaud's bitters
Ice
Lemon twist for garnish

1. Chill a 120–180-ml rocks glass, then swirl with absinthe.
2. Pour all ingredients except the absinthe into a mixing glass half-filled with ice and stir.
3. Strain into the chilled cocktail glass. Twist garnish but do not drop in.

Mint Julep

Ingredients

Leaves from 3 sprigs of mint, plus a sprig for garnish
1 teaspoon sugar
Ice
60 ml bourbon whiskey
30 ml simple syrup

1. Muddle mint and sugar in a mint julep cup.
2. Fill the cup with crushed ice.
3. Pour in the bourbon and simple syrup and stir until the julep cup is frosty.
4. Add more crushed ice. Add garnish.

It's not unlikely that the Ward Eight and Manhattan, two American whiskey cocktails from the late 1800s, were conceived during political events, because only politicians, men of importance and men of affluence patronized the elegant cocktail bars serving these cocktails. Working-class men mostly drank beer, wine and whiskey shots at local watering holes. And women, well, women were not allowed to patronize any bar at any time, unless they were working girls.

ZOOM

Peychaud's bitters were invented in New Orleans by an immigrant, Antoine Peychaud, in the early 1800s. Antoine was an apothecary, in other words a pharmacist. He owned a pharmacy on Royal Street in the French Quarter and made his own tinctures, balms, potions and even bitters. This led to the creation of the Sazerac cocktail.

Manhattan

Ingredients

Ice
60 ml rye or bourbon whiskey
30 ml sweet vermouth
2 dashes Angostura bitters
Maraschino cherry garnish

1. Chill a 120–180-ml cocktail glass.
2. Half-fill a mixing glass with ice.
3. Pour in the ingredients and stir with ice.
4. Strain into the chilled cocktail glass. Add garnish.

Manhattan by Train

The birth of the Manhattan is believed to have occurred in the 1880s. In the 20th century, the cocktail graced many films and TV shows. One of the most memorable was the 1959 comedy, *Some Like It Hot*, starring Marilyn Monroe and Jack Lemmon. Marilyn's character, Sugar, makes a batch of Manhattans on a train by pouring smuggled ingredients into a hot water bottle.

SCOTCH WHISKY COCKTAILS

Scotland cashes in on the new cocktail culture action

Scotland to this day – and every day forward – takes the credit for having made the first whisky. The Scots will even show you their documented proof from the late 1400s. So, it's no surprise that they would trek to America via stagecoach and a two-month passenger ship voyage across the Atlantic to make their mark in the cocktail world. And that's just what Tommy Dewar, the charming, charismatic son of John Dewar Sr, of Dewar's White Label blended Scotch whisky, set out to do. His efforts proved successful when he became part of the world's first film commercial, which projected his Scotch whisky on to a wall overlooking Herald Square in New York City in 1898. It's believed that shortly after this event, the cocktail called the 'Rob Roy' was created.

The Rob Roy was named after a Scottish folk hero often referred to in Scotland as the 'Scottish Robin Hood'. In the cocktail world, the Rob Roy was often referred to as 'the cousin

Rob Roy

Ingredients

Ice
60 ml blended Scotch whisky
30 ml sweet vermouth
2 dashes Angostura bitters
Lemon twist garnish

1. Chill a 120–180-ml cocktail glass.
2. Half-fill a mixing glass with ice.
3. Pour in the ingredients and stir with ice.
4. Strain into the chilled cocktail glass. Add garnish.

Rusty Nail

Ingredients

Ice
60 ml blended Scotch whisky
30 ml Drambuie
Optional lemon twist garnish

1. Fill a rocks glass with ice.
2. Pour in the ingredients and stir. Add garnish if desired.
3. If a sweeter cocktail is preferred, simply pour equal parts of blended Scotch whisky and Drambuie.

of the Manhattan.' Due to the smoky flavour of Scotch whisky, there weren't as many vintage Scotch-based cocktails created as there were American whiskey cocktails, but there were still enough to suffice.

ZOOM

Drambuie is a Scotch whisky-based heather honey liqueur whose recipe is said to have been a gift from Prince Charles Edward (Bonnie Prince Charlie) to Captain John MacKinnon and his family for hiding and protecting him while in Scotland in 1745. Years later it became a popular local liqueur, but it still took another hundred years of MacKinnon generations to begin to market the liqueur commercially worldwide.

Blood and Sand

Ingredients

Ice
30 ml blended Scotch whisky
15 ml Peter Heering Cherry Liqueur
15 ml sweet vermouth
30 ml fresh blood orange juice
Lime garnish

1. Chill a 200-ml cocktail glass with ice.
2. Shake ingredients with ice.
3. Strain into the chilled cocktail glass. Add garnish.

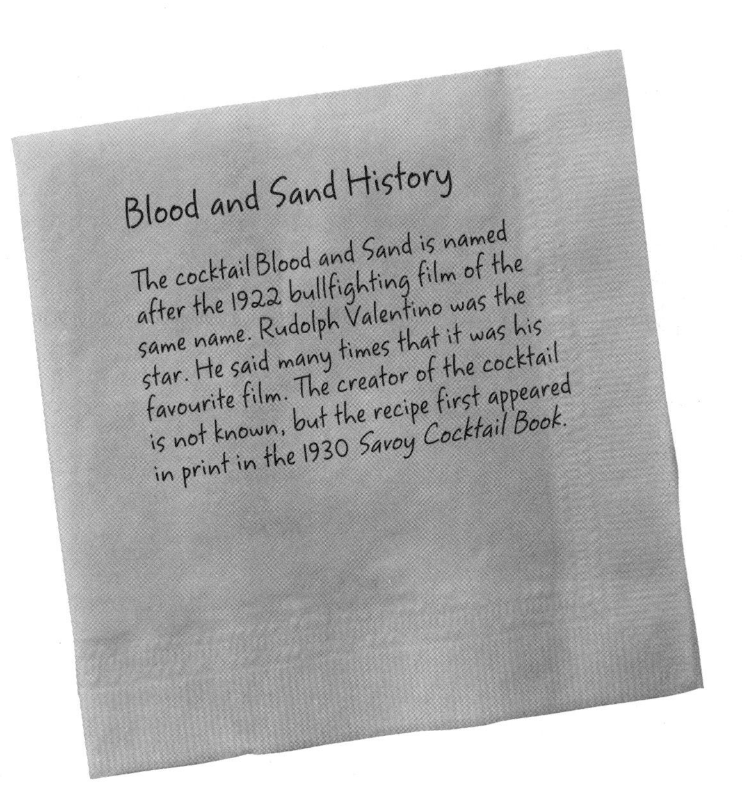

BRANDY COCKTAILS

Brandy was considered dandy for many cocktails far and wide

It might surprise you to learn that the Brandy Alexander was probably the first popular chocolate Martini in cocktail history. It was supposedly created in February 1922 for the wedding of Mary Princess Royal and Viscount Lascelles at Westminster Abbey in London. She was 24 and he was 39. Nonetheless, this sweet, chocolate brandy cocktail garnished with nutmeg was perfect for a winter wedding and became popular thereafter. It even made it to the first episode of the *Mary Tyler Moore* TV show, and is also believed to have been John Lennon's favourite cocktail.

Royalty scores another point because it's strongly believed that Sidecars were served at the spring 1956 wedding of Grace Kelly and Prince Rainier III at the Palace of Monaco.

To hip you up on vintage cocktail lingo, a 'crusta' is a cocktail served in a chilled wine glass with a whole rind of citrus inside. The Brandy Crusta is the granddaddy on this page of

Brandy Alexander

Ingredients

Ice
45 ml brandy
45 ml dark crème de cacao
60 ml cream
Sprinkle of nutmeg for garnish

1. Chill a 200-ml cocktail glass with ice.
2. Shake ingredients with ice.
3. Strain into the chilled cocktail glass. Add garnish.
4. Can be made over ice or blended with vanilla ice cream.

Sidecar

Ingredients

Sugar to rim glass
30 ml brandy
30 ml Cointreau
30 ml fresh lemon juice
Ice

1. Chill a 200-ml cocktail glass, then rim with sugar.
2. Shake ingredients with ice.
3. Strain into the cocktail glass.

vintage brandy cocktails, because it's been around since the 1850s. Joe Santini in New Orleans created it.

The Stinger is a popular, sweet cocktail that really packs a punch. Frank Sinatra, Katharine Hepburn, Grace Kelly and Bette Midler have all drunk it on the silver screen.

ZOOM

Croatian monks on the peninsula of Zadar are known to have first made a liqueur using Marasca cherries in the early 1500s. One hundred years later it was named 'Maraschino liqueur'. It spread to every European port and Britain's King George IV and Queen Victoria ordered shiploads. Others who admired the liqueur were Napoleon Bonaparte, Czar Nicholas I of Russia and Louis XVIII of France.

Brandy Crusta

Ingredients

Sugar to rim glass
60 ml brandy
15 ml Maraschino liqueur
20 ml orange Curaçao
15 ml fresh lemon juice
1 dash Angostura bitters
Whole lemon peel garnish

1. Chill a wine glass, then rim heavily with sugar.
2. Shake ingredients with ice.
3. Strain into the wine glass. Add garnish.

Stinger

Ingredients

Ice
30 ml brandy
15 ml white crème de menthe

1. Fill a rocks glass with ice.
2. Pour in the ingredients and stir.
3. If a sweeter cocktail is preferred, simply pour equal parts of brandy and white crème de menthe.

GIN COCKTAILS

Gin was 'in' for the golden age of vintage to post-Prohibition cocktails

Believe it or not, America's first distillery was built in the 1640s on Staten Island, and it produced gin. It's hard to believe that it took another 200 years for the cocktail to come into vogue. Together with the Gin Martini (found in Chapter 7 on Martinis), these four cocktails best represent the true vintage gin cocktails of days gone by.

Henry C. Ramos invented the Ramos Gin Fizz in 1888 in New Orleans. My guess is that most New Orleans bartenders cursed his name – under their breath, of course – for the next 33 years. My point being that to make the drink took time and effort; liken it to the revived Mojito craze of the millennium. The secret ingredients remained . . . well, secret until Prohibition in 1921:

Ramos Gin Fizz

Ingredients

60 ml gin
15 ml fresh lemon juice
15 ml fresh lime juice
60 ml cream
1 teaspoon sugar
1 organic egg white
3 drops orange flower water
Ice
60 ml soda water

1. Chill a tall glass.
2. Shake ingredients (except soda water) with ice for one minute.
3. Strain into the wine glass.
4. Add soda water.

Nineteen-fourteen

Ingredients

Ice
60 ml gin
15 ml Cointreau
15 ml fresh lemon juice
Half an organic egg white

1. Chill a 200-ml cocktail glass with ice.
2. Shake ingredients with ice.
3. Strain into the chilled cocktail glass.
4. If a sweeter cocktail is preferred, add more Cointreau.

lime and lemon juice, orange flower water, real cream, egg white, and, oh yes, gin. Bartenders had to shake the drink for up to two minutes for the proper chilling and blending of the ingredients. The governor would even take a New Orleans bartender with him on trips to the White House so he could have fresh Ramos Gin Fizzes. As for the obscure ingredient, orange flower water, don't attempt to substitute for it because doing so won't work. This water is made from the flower petals of Mediterranean Seville orange trees. Today you can purchase it at gourmet and Middle Eastern grocery stores.

The Pegu Club was named after the gentlemen's club of the same name in Rangoon, Burma. Travelling British business gentlemen inspired elite private clubs such as this one so they could enjoy the luxuries of home. The original club no longer stands, but New York City built a Pegu Club in its honour. Inside you can order this cocktail as well as many other vintage cocktails, no matter what your sex.

Pegu Club

Ingredients

Ice
30 ml gin
30 ml orange Curaçao
7.5 ml fresh lime juice
1 dash each of orange and Angostura bitters
Lime wedge garnish

1. Chill a 200-ml cocktail glass with ice.
2. Shake ingredients with ice.
3. Strain into the chilled cocktail glass. Add garnish.

Gimlet

Ingredients

Ice
60 ml gin
30 ml Rose's Lime Juice
Lime garnish

1. Chill a 200-ml cocktail glass with ice.
2. Shake ingredients with ice.
3. Strain into the chilled cocktail glass. Add garnish.
4. Can be made on the rocks as well.

WINE & LIQUEUR COCKTAILS

Sweet, bitter, strong and weak play a part in these cocktails

The Absinthe Drip is the best example of 'what was old is new again'. It was illegal nearly everywhere from 1915 to 2007. Why? The nutshell version is that it was drunk in the early to mid-19th century by high society during the Belle Époque in France. In 1863, France imported American grapes in the hope of hybridizing and creating a new grape variety, but the grapevines contained a disease called phylloxera, which destroyed nearly all of France's vines (as well as most of Europe's). The price of wine skyrocketed, but absinthe remained available for everyone. Many artists, such as Picasso, Van Gogh and Manet, drank and painted absinthe.

Once the grapevines recovered, members of the wine industry put together a fierce marketing plan to demonize absinthe so that they could win back their wine consumers. They spread gossip and lies about absinthe worldwide through posters and newspapers. Though the propaganda

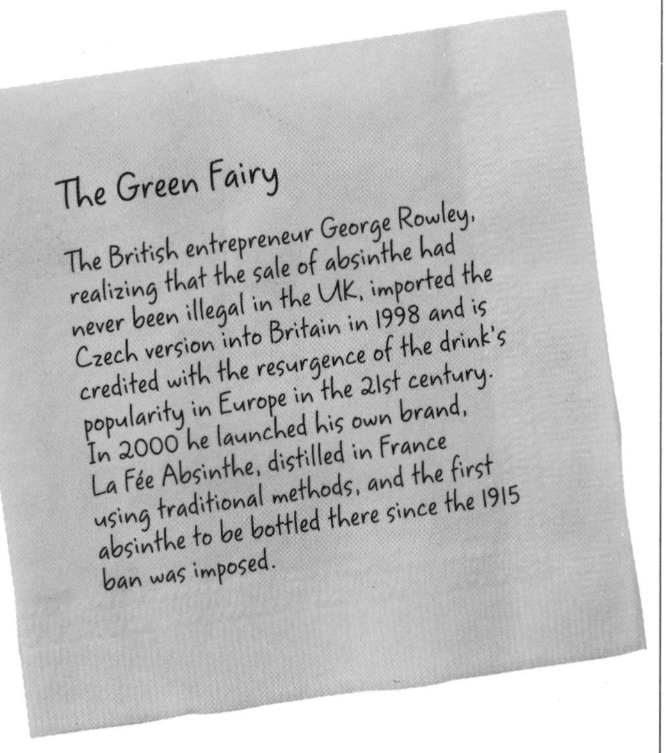

Absinthe Drip

Ingredients

45 ml absinthe
Sugar cube
15 ml ice cold water

1. Pour absinthe into the glass.
2. Set an absinthe spoon with a sugar cube on top of the glass.
3. Slowly drip ice cold water over the sugar cube. The cube will melt into the glass.
4. Stir.

was later disproved, most people believed it, and by 1915 absinthe had been banned in many countries, though one notable exception was Britain.

While the French were enjoying their absinthe, one of the cocktails the Italians were drinking was called a 'Milano-Torino'. Visiting Americans took a liking to it, so it was renamed 'Americano'. The cocktail was first served in Caffè Campari in Milan in the 1860s.

GREEN LIGHT

The Sherry Cobbler is the perfect choice if you want to enjoy a vintage cocktail that has a low alcohol content. Over the years, sherry has acquired the reputation of being a little old lady's drink served in tiny glasses, but the Sherry Cobbler is light, icy and fruity. It tastes best when served over crushed ice rather than cubed ice.

Americano

Ingredients

Ice
30 ml sweet vermouth
30 ml Campari
30 ml soda water
Lemon twist garnish

1. Chill a 200-ml cocktail glass with ice.
2. Stir ingredients with ice.
3. Strain into the chilled cocktail glass. Add garnish.
4. Can be made on the rocks as well. Some like to add more soda water.

Sherry Cobbler

Ingredients

Ice
1 tablespoon sugar
150 ml sherry
Seasonal fruit garnish

1. Fill a tall glass with ice.
2. Add sugar.
3. Pour in sherry and stir.
4. Garnish with fresh seasonal fruit and berries.

RUM COCKTAILS

Island-inspired rum cocktails prove that what was old is new again

Did you think that the Mojito was a new cocktail creation? Yes, it's true that James Bond ordered one with Halle Berry in 2002, but this minty fresh cocktail has been around a long time. In fact, many believe that it derived from African slaves working the fields in Cuba in the 1800s. What we know for sure is that the mojito is mentioned in the Key West, Florida, *Sloppy Joe's Bar Manual* from the early 1930s. America was under Prohibition until 1933, so the affluent would make their way down to Havana to party. One place in particular was La Bodeguita del Medio. This is where famous writers, artists, musicians and soon-to-be famous starlets gravitated. And they all drank Mojitos. The bar is still there.

The term *Cuba libre* means 'free Cuba', and that's the cry that was heard throughout the Battle of Santiago de Cuba in 1898 during the Spanish-American War. It's believed that the drink Cuba Libre was created around that time. Legend

Mojito

Ingredients

Leaves from 3 sprigs of mint, plus a sprig for garnish
½ a lime, cut
Ice
45 ml Cuban light rum
30 ml simple syrup
120 ml soda water

1. Muddle the mint leaves and limes in a double old-fashioned glass.
2. Fill with crushed or cracked ice.
3. Pour in the rum, simple syrup and soda water.
4. Stir and add garnish.

Cuba Libre

Ingredients

Ice
2 lime wedges for garnish
180 ml cola
60 ml light rum

1. Fill a tall or highball glass with ice.
2. Squeeze one juicy lime wedge over the ice and discard.
3. Add the cola and rum.
4. Squeeze the second lime wedge and drop into the drink. Stir.

has it that Teddy Roosevelt and his Rough Riders were drinking Cuba Libres and brought the drink back to New York. The drink had another resurrection during World War II when the Andrews Sisters' hit song 'Rum & Coca-Cola' was heard on radios everywhere.

MAKE IT EASY

When making these vintage rum cocktails, feel free to experiment with different kinds of rum. A gold or aged rum will give the Mojito more depth. Flavoured rums such as vanilla, coconut, spiced or banana can add a nice modern twist to a milk punch. And you can follow the same rule for the simple Cuba Libre as well.

Milk Punch

Ingredients

Ice
60 ml light rum
30 ml simple syrup
120 ml whole milk
Nutmeg and cinnamon for garnish

1. Fill a 350-ml glass with ice.
2. Add ingredients and stir.
3. Garnish with nutmeg and cinnamon.
4. For more flavour, you can replace the light rum with dark rum.

Guys and Dolls

In the 1955 film *Guys and Dolls*, Marlon Brando takes church lady Jean Simmons to Cuba on a date. At dinner, he orders Milk Punches. Jean asks about the flavouring in the Milk Punch, and he tells her that at night they put a preservative called 'Bacardi' in the milk. She drinks several of them.

CLASSIC MARTINIS

Master these for a solid Martini-making foundation

The Martini is without doubt the king of cocktails. It's an icon in modern society as well as in the cocktail culture worldwide. Since the mid-1800s, the Classic Martini has risen and fallen in popularity and has gone through many ingredient changes, but the common denominator has always been gin. Some say making a Martini is simple, whereas others believe it's an artform. A Classic Martini should always be stirred and never shaken, because shaking a cocktail adds air, resulting in a light and bubbly feel on the tongue. In addition, it dilutes the cocktail with water. Stirring a Martini keeps the alcohol smooth and silky, yielding a perfect proportion of dilution from the ice. To reach a chilled temperature, stir 20 times clockwise, then 20 times counterclockwise.

You should always pre-chill a cocktail glass when making a Classic Martini. The Martini is all about being very cold. You can have glasses ready from the freezer or pre-chill by

Classic Martini

Ingredients

Ice
60 ml gin
7.5 ml dry vermouth
2 large olives and/or a lemon twist garnish

1. Chill a 120–180-ml cocktail glass.
2. Half-fill a mixing glass with ice.
3. Pour in the ingredients and stir with ice.
4. Strain into the chilled cocktail glass. Add garnish.

Gibson

Ingredients

Ice
60 ml gin
7.5 ml dry vermouth
2 cocktail onions to garnish

1. Chill a 120–180-ml cocktail glass.
2. Half-fill a mixing glass with ice.
3. Pour in the ingredients and stir with ice.
4. Strain into the chilled cocktail glass. Add garnish.

putting ice and water into a glass while you're making the cocktail. It's also recommended that you use smaller, vintage-sized glasses (120–180 ml) to keep the Martini cold longer. There's nothing more undesirable than a warm Martini half-way down the glass.

MAKE IT EASY

Of course, you can make a Martini in a jam jar with holes punched in the lid for straining, and you can even use an iced teaspoon to stir it! But make it easy for yourself and invest in the proper bar tools needed for making this classic drink. You'll need a mixing glass, julep strainer and a bar spoon. Using a disc-ended bar spoon works the best.

Dirty Martini

Ingredients

Ice
60 ml gin
7.5 ml dry vermouth
15 ml olive brine
2 large olives and/or a lemon twist garnish

1. Chill a 120–180-ml cocktail glass.
2. Half-fill a mixing glass with ice.
3. Pour in the ingredients and stir with ice.
4. Strain into the chilled cocktail glass. Add garnish.

Decoding the Classic Martinis

- Dry means having less vermouth.
- Extra dry means having no vermouth.
- In and out means to swirl the vermouth inside the glass, then dump the remains.
- Perfect means to use half dry vermouth and half sweet vermouth, as in a Perfect Manhattan.
- Mist means to spray a layer of vermouth across the top of the drink with a small atomizer or mister.
- Dirty can have many levels of dirtiness.

THE FIRST VODKA MARTINIS

These classics shook things up for every vodka-based Martini that followed

In 1953, Ian Fleming wrote the first known dry Martini into literature. Not only that, but it was shaken, not stirred. The novel is *Casino Royale*, the chapter is seven, and the handsome spy who ordered it is James Bond. Bond named the Martini after his love interest in the book, Vesper. In 1962, the first James Bond film, *Dr No*, hit the screen and showed Bond ordering and shaking a Vodka Martini made with Smirnoff vodka. The interesting fact is that vodka was new to Americans in the 1950s, and they didn't take a liking to it until the debonair James Bond endorsed it. Today it is the USA's number one spirit.

The birth of the Cosmopolitan took place in Miami in 1988 when Absolut released its second flavoured vodka, Citron.

Vesper

Ingredients

Ice
60 ml gin
30 ml vodka
15 ml Lillet blanc
Lemon twist garnish

1. Chill a 120–180-ml cocktail glass.
2. Half-fill a mixing glass with ice.
3. Pour in the ingredients and stir with ice.
4. Strain into the chilled cocktail glass. Add garnish.

Vodka Martini

Ingredients

Ice
60 ml vodka
15 ml dry vermouth
2 large olives and/or a lemon twist garnish

1. Chill a 120–180-ml cocktail glass.
2. Half-fill a mixing glass with ice.
3. Pour in the ingredients and stir with ice.
4. Strain into the chilled cocktail glass. Add garnish.

However, like most things, it took ten years for the scarlet libation served in a cocktail glass to spread to the masses. In the mid-1990s, it was available at posh bars and lounges in the shiny cities, but the brightest lights shone in 1999 during the second season of a little TV show entitled *Sex in the City*. From there, what is now nicknamed the 'Cosmo' ignited worldwide, opening the floodgates for the vodka-based Martinis of today.

ZOOM

James Bond's exact words to the bartender in Ian Fleming's novel when ordering a Martini are, 'Three measures of Gordon's, one of vodka, half a measure of Kina Lillet, shake it very well until it's ice cold, then add a large thin slice of lemon peel. Got it?' The Kina Lillet is extinct, so Lillet Blanc is acceptable in its place.

Original Cosmopolitan

Ingredients

Ice
60 ml Absolut Citron vodka
15 ml triple sec
15 ml lime cordial
30 ml cranberry juice
Lime wedge garnish

1. Chill a 200-ml cocktail glass with ice.
2. Shake ingredients with ice.
3. Strain into the chilled cocktail glass. Add garnish.

Cosmopolitan

Ingredients

Ice
60 ml citrus vodka
15 ml Cointreau
15 ml fresh lime juice
30 ml cranberry juice
Lemon twist garnish

1. Chill a 200-ml cocktail glass with ice.
2. Shake ingredients with ice.
3. Strain into the chilled cocktail glass. Add garnish.

LEMON DROP MARTINIS

Your troubles will melt like lemon drops when you master these treats

Lemon Drop shots and shooters began surfacing at the beginning of the 1990s. The Lemon Drop Martini followed the Cosmopolitan as another citrusy girly drink to be shaken and then strained in a seductively sexy cocktail. The sweet twist is that the rim was frosted with sugar, turning the Lemon Drop Martini into grownup lemonade. The combination of the sour following the sweet on the tongue is a delectable taste, so it's no surprise that this Martini spread pretty fast. However, it was shot into orbit after Rachael Ray and Oprah Winfrey prepared it together on Oprah's TV show in 2006.

To make the best Lemon Drop Martini, you must use freshly squeezed lemon juice and simple syrup, not a shop-bought

Lemon Drop Martini

Ingredients

Sugar to rim glass
Ice
60 ml citrus vodka
15 ml Cointreau
30 ml fresh lemon juice
30 ml simple syrup
Lemon wedge/wheel garnish

1. Rim a chilled cocktail glass with sugar.
2. Shake the ingredients with ice.
3. Strain into the chilled sugar-rimmed glass. Add garnish.

Raspberry Lemon Drop Martini

Ingredients

Sugar to rim glass
Ice
30 ml citrus vodka
30 ml raspberry vodka
15 ml Chambord
30 ml fresh lemon juice
30 ml simple syrup
Lemon wedge/wheel garnish

1. Rim a chilled cocktail glass with sugar.
2. Shake the ingredients with ice.
3. Strain into the chilled sugar-rimmed glass. Add garnish.

sweet-and-sour mix. You can purchase simple syrup, but it's better to make your own (see Chapter 19). Every lemon yields a different amount of juice, so always squeeze with a hand juicer or other juicer, then measure out the amount you need. You'll get the most juice from a heavy room-temperature lemon. Roll the lemon with your palm on the worktop first to break up the tiny membranes inside, then cut in half and squeeze. Strain through a sieve or a mesh strainer to remove the seeds and pulp.

GREEN LIGHT

To bump up the fun a bit, use different types of sugar or sugar tinted in different colours to rim your lemon drop Martinis. You can colour sugar by putting it into a jar or plastic bag with a few drops of food colouring, then shaking. Kitchen shops and cake decorating suppliers sell a wide range of colours – try the new neons.

Blueberry Lemon Drop Martini

Ingredients

Blue sugar to rim glass
Ice
30 ml citrus vodka
30 ml blueberry vodka
15 ml Cointreau
30 ml fresh lemon juice
30 ml simple syrup
Lemon wheel and 3 blueberries for garnish

1. Rim a chilled cocktail glass with sugar.
2. Shake the ingredients with ice.
3. Strain into the chilled blue sugar-rimmed glass. Add garnish.

Banana Drop Martini

Ingredients

Yellow sugar to rim glass
Ice
30 ml citrus vodka
30 ml banana vodka
15 ml Cointreau
30 ml fresh lemon juice
30 ml simple syrup
Lemon wheel garnish

1. Rim a chilled cocktail glass with sugar.
2. Shake the ingredients with ice.
3. Strain into the chilled yellow sugar-rimmed glass. Add garnish.

CHOCOLATE MARTINIS

Make these decadent drinks to be the envy of all your friends

The basics of a Chocolatini are simple: vodka and chocolate liqueur shaken with ice, then strained into a chilled cocktail glass. The beautiful thing is that chocolate goes well with so many other flavours, so you can introduce a whole range of ingredients into a chocolate Martini.

Chocolate complements orange, lemon, mint, banana, strawberry, raspberry, cream, vanilla, nuts, butterscotch, pepper, cinnamon, whisky, Champagne, cherry, clove, coconut, coffee and pear. All of these possibilities make the shaking field wide open. You can see that by incorporating different-flavoured spirits, liqueurs and mixers, Chocolatinis are limited only by your imagination.

The three base vodkas you can use in a Chocolatini are plain, vanilla or chocolate vodka. If you introduce another flavoured vodka in addition to the base vodka, use a half measure of each. Flavoured vodka choices could be raspberry, strawberry,

Chocolatini

Ingredients

Grated dark chocolate for garnish
Ice
60 ml vodka
60 ml white crème de cacao

1. Rim a chilled cocktail glass with grated chocolate.
3. Shake the ingredients with ice.
4. Strain into the chilled chocolate-rimmed glass.

White Chocolatini

Ingredients

Chocolate syrup for garnish
Ice
30 ml vanilla vodka
15 ml white crème de cacao
15 ml Godiva white chocolate liqueur
30 ml single cream

1. Rim a chilled cocktail glass with chocolate syrup.
2. Shake the ingredients with ice.
3. Strain into the chocolate syrup-rimmed glass.

banana, cherry, coconut, lemon or orange. Liqueur choices are plentiful. A trip to the liqueur section of your local store will open up a world of possibilities. Simply pick out flavours you like, but bear in mind that there will be a range of prices and choices for every flavour.

Chocolate begins as a bean picked from the tropical cacao (pronounced ka-COW) tree. After being fermented, roasted and ground, it's mixed with other ingredients such as sugar, lecithin and cocoa butter to create chocolate bars, chocolate powder, alcohol and syrups. This variety leads to the fun part of dressing up and garnishing a Chocolatini. You can rim a glass with cocoa powder, hot chocolate powder, grated chocolate and so forth. The inside of the glass can be coated in chocolate syrups, and the garnishes can range from filled chocolates or chocolate curls to bite-sized chocolate cakes, brownies, cookies and more!

Strawberry Chocolatini

Ingredients

Chocolate and strawberry syrup
Ice
30 ml vanilla vodka
30 ml strawberry vodka
30 ml white crème de cacao
30 ml single cream
Chocolate-dipped strawberry garnish

1. Crisscross the chocolate and strawberry syrups in a cocktail glass.
2. Shake the ingredients with ice.
3. Strain into the chocolate and strawberry syrup cocktail glass and garnish with a chocolate-dipped strawberry.

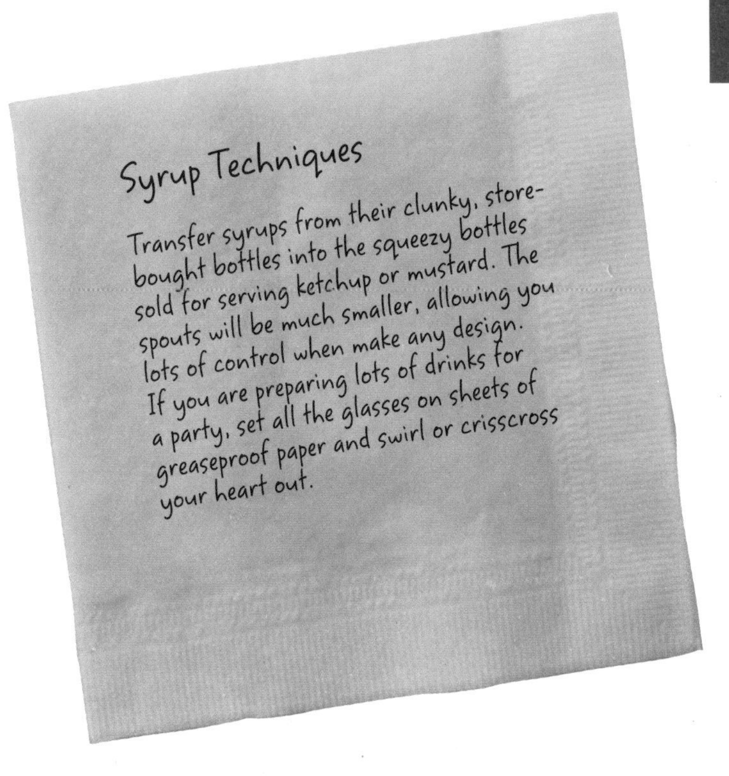

Syrup Techniques

Transfer syrups from their clunky, store-bought bottles into the squeezy bottles sold for serving ketchup or mustard. The spouts will be much smaller, allowing you lots of control when make any design. If you are preparing lots of drinks for a party, set all the glasses on sheets of greaseproof paper and swirl or crisscross your heart out.

APPLETINIS

Sweet-and-sour liquid goodness may be just what the doctor ordered

If Eve had owned a cocktail shaker, these Martinis are what she would have served to Adam. Most definitely, the number one ingredient you'll need for an Appletini is apple schnapps – but it must be sour apple schnapps. The Appletini hit the trendy wet spots of the world immediately after the Lemon Drop Martini, because it was about that time that sour apple schnapps was introduced to the market. It was an overnight sensation.

Garnishes for the Appletini family are mostly simple, and some Appletinis are not garnished at all. This fact does not limit you; in fact, you are free to apply your imagination. Ideas could include sticking a piece of caramel on the rim

Appletini

Ingredients

Ice
30 ml citrus vodka
30 ml sour apple schnapps
30 ml fresh lemon juice
30 ml simple syrup
Cherry or Granny Smith apple slice garnish

1. Chill a 200-ml cocktail glass with ice.
2. Shake ingredients with ice.
3. Strain into the chilled cocktail glass. Add garnish.

Washington Appletini

Ingredients

Ice
30 ml whisky
30 ml sour apple schnapps
60 ml cranberry juice

1. Chill a 200-ml cocktail glass with ice.
2. Shake ingredients with ice.
3. Strain into the chilled cocktail glass.

of a Caramel Appletini or swirling caramel inside the glass. A Washington Appletini could be garnished with a slice cut from a red Washington apple, and any Appletini could be garnished with a crisp slice of Granny Smith apple. And on the wild side, you could drop green apple-flavoured jelly beans into your cocktails.

Caramel Appletini

Ingredients

Caramel syrup
Ice
30 ml apple vodka
30 ml sour apple schnapps
30 ml butterscotch schnapps
30 ml fresh lemon juice
30 ml simple syrup
Green apple slice garnish

1. Swirl caramel into a cocktail glass.
2. Shake ingredients with ice.
3. Strain into the cocktail glass. Add garnish.

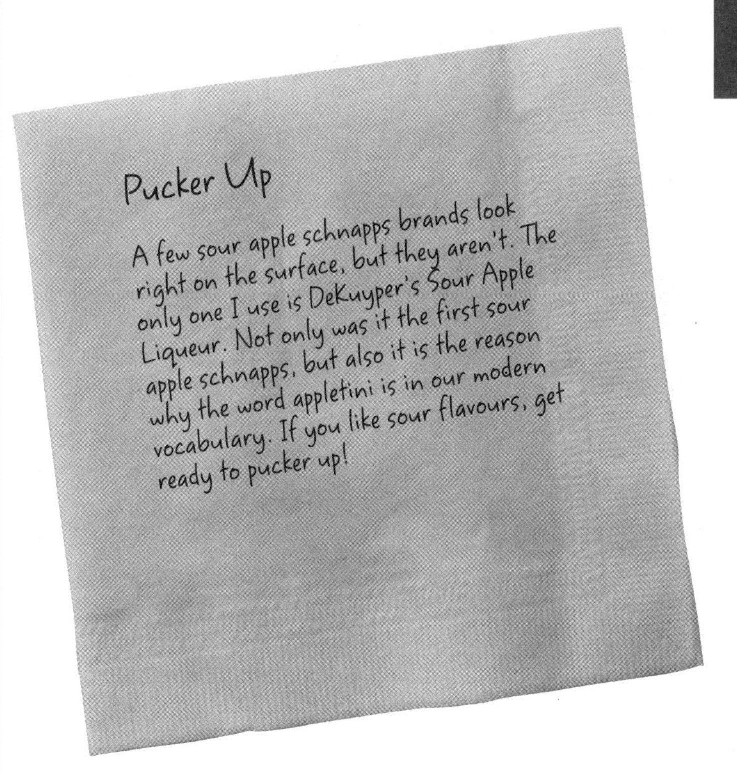

Pucker Up

A few sour apple schnapps brands look right on the surface, but they aren't. The only one I use is DeKuyper's Sour Apple Liqueur. Not only was it the first sour apple schnapps, but also it is the reason why the word appletini is in our modern vocabulary. If you like sour flavours, get ready to pucker up!

DESSERT MARTINIS

With imagination, you can turn any dessert into a delicious cocktail

Do you have a favourite dessert or sweet indulgence? Simply match up the flavours and make a cocktail. The sky's the limit! Almost every flavour imaginable can be represented in a drink. Don't limit yourself to flavoured spirits; make sure you look at the many flavours available in the form of liqueurs and mixers as well. Need inspiration? Walk down your local supermarket's sweets and cakes aisle. To determine what proportions you'll need to match up to a cake or dessert, simply look at the ingredients on the packaging. The ingredients are always listed from the largest amounts to the least.

Cream liqueurs and cream-based mixers are excellent to use for cake- or nougat-type dessert cocktails. Chocolate liqueurs, of course, are perfect for anything that needs chocolate. If you want a nutty flavour, try hazelnut liqueur or amaretto.

Garnishing a dessert drink can be fun. If it's a spinoff of a cake or pie, then take inspiration from the way these desserts

Pineapple Upside-down Cake

Ingredients

30 ml vanilla vodka
30 ml Irish cream
60 ml pineapple juice
Ice
15 ml grenadine
Pineapple ring, whipped cream, and a cherry garnish

1. Shake the vodka, Irish cream and pineapple juice with ice.
2. Strain into a chilled cocktail glass.
3. Pour in the grenadine: it will sink to the bottom. Add garnish.

Almond Joy-tini

Ingredients

Chocolate syrup and grated coconut garnish
Ice
30 ml vanilla vodka
30 ml crème de cacao
30 ml coconut rum
30 ml single cream

1. Rim a cocktail glass with chocolate syrup and coconut flakes.
2. Shake ingredients with ice.
3. Strain into the chilled cocktail glass.

are normally garnished. Add special touches with creative rims made of crushed Oreos or ginger cookies, sprinkles and more! While you're wandering down the sweet, cake and spice aisles you'll begin to notice all the possibilities.

MAKE IT EASY

You can easily make many non-alcoholic dessert versions using flavoured extracts such as vanilla and almond. There is also an incredible choice of flavours available in cocktail syrups. You'll find an assortment of exotic and unique flavours such as kiwi, mango, blueberry, tiramisù and lemongrass.

Key Lime Pie-tini

Ingredients

Digestive biscuit crumbs to rim glass
Ice
60 ml lime vodka
30 ml simple syrup
15 ml lime cordial
30 ml single cream
Whipped cream and lime garnish

1. Rim a cocktail glass with biscuit crumbs.
2. Shake ingredients with ice.
3. Strain into the chilled cocktail glass. Add garnish.

Key to Stability

Have you ever squirted whipped cream into a drink and found that it flopped over? That's because the liquid doesn't provide stability. The trick is to anchor the whipped cream to the side of the glass. You'll find this tip especially helpful for hot drinks, because the heat accelerates the melting process. The cream on the Pineapple Upside-down Cake is stabilized by the pineapple.

THE TYPES OF MARGARITAS

Learn the four main ways to make Mexico's national drink

With many things in life, simpler is better. And this holds true for the Margarita. As a matter of fact, the Margarita is the most popular cocktail in the world. A true Margarita is simply tequila, orange liqueur and fresh lime juice, shaken and then strained into a cocktail glass. That's it. Using these three ingredients at a ratio of 3:2:1 is ideal.

The orange liqueur should be all the sweetness a true Margarita needs, but a laid-back singer named Jimmy Buffett had a hit song in the 1970s entitled 'Margaritaville', which led to the launch of a lot of sweet fake lime Margarita mixes to meet consumer demand. In the mixer aisle today, you can choose from sour mix, sweet-and-sour mix, limeade and Margarita mix, but the very best mix is homemade. Learn to make it in Chapter 19.

As for orange liqueur, you can use triple sec or Curaçao. Triple sec is an orange liqueur that has been distilled three

Original Margarita

Ingredients

Ice
60 ml 100 per cent agave blanco tequila
45 ml triple sec
30 ml fresh lime juice

1. Chill a 120–180-ml cocktail glass with ice.
2. Shake ingredients with ice.
3. Strain into the chilled cocktail glass.

Classic Margarita

Ingredients

Salt to rim glass (optional)
Ice
60 ml 100 per cent agave tequila of choice
30 ml triple sec
30 ml fresh lime juice
30 ml simple syrup
Lime garnish

1. Chill a 200-ml cocktail glass with ice.
2. Shake ingredients with ice.
3. Strain into the chilled cocktail glass. Add garnish.

times (hence 'triple'), and *sec* is French for 'dry'. A high-end French triple sec is Cointreau (pronounced QWAN-twoh). Curaçao (pronounced cure-uh-SOW, to rhyme with now) is made on the Caribbean island of the same name and comes in three colours: orange, blue and green.

ZOOM

Cocktail researchers say that a salted rim was never part of the original Margarita recipe, but was probably used later to mask the taste of cheap tequila being added to the drink. Rimming half the glass can cater for all preferences. Use coarse sea salt or rock salt for rimming a Margarita glass, not ordinary table salt.

Margarita on the Rocks

Ingredients

Salt to rim glass (optional)
Ice
60 ml 100 per cent agave tequila of choice
30 ml triple sec
30 ml fresh lime juice
30 ml simple syrup
Lime garnish

1. Rim a Margarita glass with salt if desired.
2. Fill the glass with ice.
3. Shake ingredients with ice.
4. Strain into the glass. Add garnish.

Frozen Margarita

Ingredients

Salt to rim glass (optional)
Ice
60 ml tequila of choice
30 ml triple sec
30 ml fresh lime juice
30 ml simple syrup
Lime garnish

1. Rim a Margarita glass with salt if desired.
2. Put ingredients in a blender with half a cup of ice. Blend, adding more ice if needed.
3. Pour into Margarita glass. Add garnish.

PREMIUM MARGARITAS

Raise the bar with some high-end Margaritas to really taste the difference

Everything in life has levels from low to high, and the Margarita is no exception. By bumping up the quality of tequila and orange liqueur, you'll create a taste with depth and character. The first thing to look for on the tequila label is '100 per cent blue agave'. (The label may read just '100 per cent agave'.) Next, you want it to be either a blanco or a reposado. The blanco also uses the marketing terms 'silver' or 'white'. An añejo will be more expensive because it is aged longer and filtered more times, but it will have too smooth a taste, causing it to blend instead of balance the acid of the lime. The blanco or reposado will provide the bite to balance the flavours. Save the añejo for sipping.

Gold Margarita

Ingredients

Salt to rim glass (optional)
Ice
60 ml reposado tequila of choice
30 ml Cointreau
30 ml fresh lime juice
30 ml simple syrup
Lime garnish

1. Straight up: Shake ingredients with ice. Strain into a chilled cocktail glass.
2. Rocks: Shake ingredients with ice. Strain into a Margarita glass filled with ice.
3. Frozen: Blend juice and syrup with half a cup of ice. Pour into a Margarita glass. Top with the alcohol. Stir.

Top-shelf Margarita

Ingredients

Salt to rim glass (optional)
Ice
60 ml reposado tequila of choice
15 ml Cointreau
15 ml Grand Marnier
30 ml fresh lime juice
30 ml simple syrup
Lime garnish

1. Straight up: Shake ingredients with ice. Strain into a chilled cocktail glass.
2. Rocks: Shake ingredients with ice. Strain into a Margarita glass filled with ice.
3. Frozen: Blend juice and syrup with half a cup of ice. Pour into a Margarita glass. Top with the alcohol. Stir.

Basically, 'gold tequila' is a marketing term that covers a category of tequila called *joven*. Jovens are just blanco tequilas that have had fake colouring added to make them look gold. Consumers are supposed to think they are purchasing aged tequila, because ageing in barrels is what turns spirits amber gold. The most popular joven is José Cuervo.

Cointreau is the best orange liqueur. Grand Marnier is also an orange liqueur but has a cognac base.

GREEN LIGHT

If you love your Margarita frozen/blended, the best way to make it is to blend only the non-alcoholic ingredients, pour it into the glass leaving room at the top, then pour the alcohol over it. Blending requires ice, which is just frozen water, so the flavour of good-quality tequila gets watered down when you blend it.

Millionaire Margarita

Ingredients

Edible gold flakes mixed with salt to rim glass
Ice
60 ml Clase Azul Ultra Tequila
30 ml Grand Marnier Cuvée Speciale Cent Cinquantenaire
30 ml fresh organic lime juice
30 ml simple syrup

1. Straight up: Shake ingredients with ice. Strain into a chilled cocktail glass.
2. Rocks: Shake ingredients with ice. Strain into a Margarita glass filled with ice.
3. Frozen: Blend juice and syrup with half a cup of ice. Pour into a Margarita glass. Top with the alcohol. Stir.

The Ultimate Margarita

Clase Azul Ultra Tequila could prove elusive: launched in 2007 in Mexico and the USA, in a limited edition of 100 bottles, it sells for around $1,200. Grand Marnier Cuvée Speciale Cent Cinquantenaire is made with 50-year-old cognac sealed by hand in a handpainted bottle. It sells for about £125. Not in your budget? Then buy the Cuvée du Centenaire. It's made with 25-year-old cognac and costs about £80. You can buy edible 22-carat gold flakes from cake-decorating suppliers.

FRUITY MARGARITAS

Incorporate flavoured liqueurs, purées and more in a basic Margarita for fruity versions

Adding an extra flavour to the simple and basic recipe of a Margarita adds fun and flair. These fruity flavours are found in almost every bar, and injecting the extra fruitiness can be done in many ways. Flavours that work well in a Margarita are strawberry, raspberry, melon, peach, mango, coconut, orange and pineapple.

The flavour can come from juices, fruits, purées, nectars, liqueurs and even flavoured tequilas. If you are using a fruit liqueur as your flavouring agent, you can simply replace the orange liqueur in the basic recipe with the flavoured liqueur. When using any other flavourings, keep the orange liqueur in the recipe.

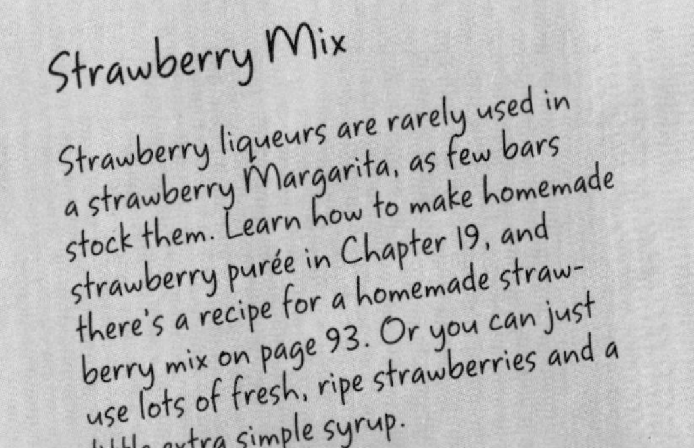

Strawberry Margarita

Ingredients

Ice
60 ml 100 per cent blanco tequila of choice
30 ml triple sec
30 ml fresh lime juice
30 ml simple syrup
60 ml strawberry mix or purée
Lime and strawberry garnish

1. Blend ingredients with half a cup of ice. Add additional ice if needed.
2. Pour into a Margarita glass. Add garnish.

If you use a flavoured liqueur, flavoured tequila or juice in fruity Margaritas, you have the option of serving them straight up, on the rocks or frozen. When using purées and nectars, you can still make them up or on the rocks, but they work best when made frozen because they are thicker.

Normally you wouldn't salt the rim on a fruity Margarita, though some people like salt on a sweeter Margarita. Some people rim the glass in sugar, and others make a 1:1 mixture of salt and sugar to rim with. The bottom line is preference.

ZOOM

For every liqueur on the market, there are low-end and high-end choices. Sometimes you can get by with the lower end if you are on a budget. However, when it comes to melon liqueur, it's best to go with Midori. It's been around since 1978 and comes from Japan. The word *midori* is Japanese for 'green'.

Melon Margarita

Ingredients

Ice
60 ml 100 per cent blanco tequila of choice
30 ml melon liqueur
3 ml fresh lime juice
30 ml simple syrup
Lime garnish

1. Blend ingredients with half a cup of ice. Add additional ice if needed.
2. Pour into a Margarita glass. Add garnish.

Peach Margarita

Ingredients

Ice
60 ml 100 per cent blanco tequila
30 ml triple sec
3 ml fresh lime juice
30 ml simple syrup
60 ml peach purée
15 ml grenadine
Peach and lime garnish

1. Blend ingredients (except the grenadine) with half a cup of ice.
2. Pour the grenadine into the bottom of the glass.
3. Pour the blended mixture into the glass. Add garnish.

UNIQUE FRUITY MARGARITAS

Combine fruity flavours that complement each other for extra flavour and fun

Certain flavours simply blend together well. A great example is chocolate and peanut butter, but don't worry: you won't be making a chocolate and peanut butter Margarita! Combining complementary flavours is the next step in creating unique fruity Margaritas. Don't limit yourself to the recipes on this page, because so many flavours go well together in a Margarita. Some examples are strawberry with kiwi, peach with papaya, blueberry with mint, mandarin with coconut, watermelon with pepper and raspberry with lemon.

You can also find an assortment of infused and flavoured tequilas: these include coconut, pomegranate, citrus, coffee, chilli, mango, almond and berry. Of course, you can always

Blue Coconut Margarita

Ingredients

Grated coconut to rim glass
Ice
60 ml coconut tequila
30 ml blue Curaçao
3 ml fresh lime juice
30 ml simple syrup

1. Rim a Margarita glass with grated coconut.
2. Blend ingredients with half a cup of ice. Add additional ice if needed.
3. Pour into the Margarita glass.

Pomegranate and Mango Margarita

Ingredients

Ice
60 ml reposado tequila
30 ml triple sec
30 ml fresh lime juice
30 ml simple syrup
30 ml mango purée
15 ml pomegranate juice

1. Blend ingredients with a cup of ice. Add additional ice if needed.
2. Pour into a Margarita glass.

infuse your own tequila with your favourite flavouring – you can learn how to do this in Chapter 19.

As for unusual rims for Margaritas, you can make coloured salt and flavoured salt. To colour salt, simply put half a cup of coarse salt and one drop of food colouring into a plastic bag, then shake. Flavours can be added the same way by using extracts, syrups, juice or citrus zest. Other dry ingredients can be mixed with the salt, too, such as chilli powder, cinnamon, ground coffee, ground peppercorns or edible gold and silver flakes.

MAKE IT EASY

Rimming with coconut flakes requires a little more sticking power than just rubbing a lemon or lime around the rim and then dipping. And even though simple syrup is very sticky, it's just not quite sticky enough. You'll need to use golden syrup. Pour a little syrup into a saucer, add a squeeze of lime juice and mix together.

Sunrise Margarita

Ingredients

Ice
60 ml reposado tequila
30 ml triple sec
30 ml fresh lime juice
30 ml orange juice
30 ml simple syrup
15 ml grenadine

1. Fill a Margarita glass with ice.
2. Shake all ingredients except the grenadine with ice.
3. Strain into the glass.
4. Add the grenadine.

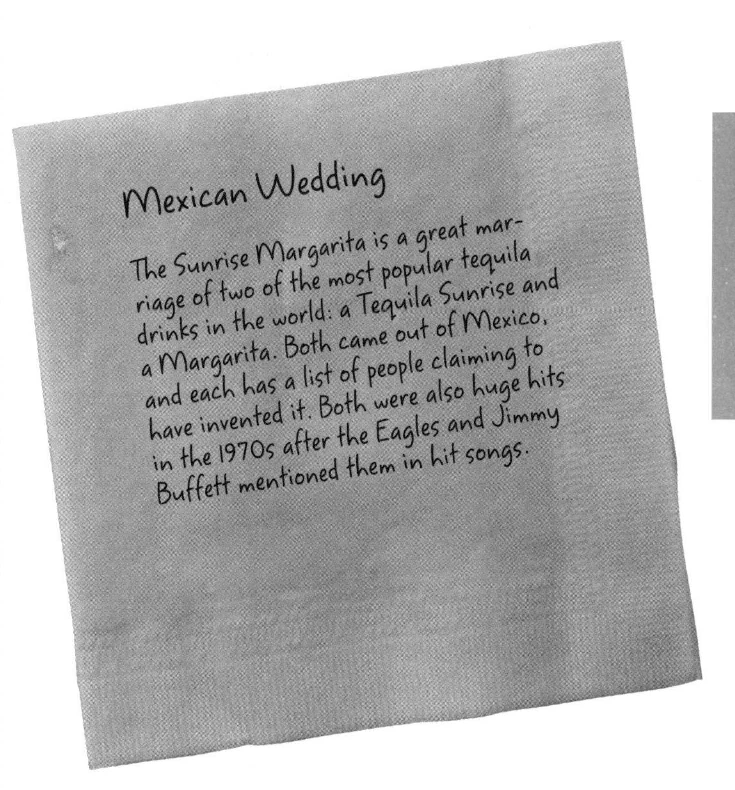

MARGARITAS

AROUND-THE-WORLD MARGARITAS

Sip your Margarita with flavours and liqueurs that can be found around the globe

Global-themed Margaritas can be great to serve at themed parties, and you can have fun creating new ones. Basically, you are adding an ingredient that represents a country, city, state, province, region, town, county, village, district, borough, hamlet, kingdom . . . well, you get the point.

What makes a Hawaiian Margarita Hawaiian is the pineapple and papaya, because both are grown in Hawaii. You can replace the papaya with other Hawaiian fruits such as banana, coconut or mango. Feel free to garnish the drink with plenty of edible flowers and paper parasols.

The Italian Margarita uses the very sweet and romantic Disaronno Originale. What makes it so romantic? Well, in 1525

Hawaiian Margarita

Ingredients

Ice
60 ml 100 per cent blanco tequila
30 ml triple sec
30 ml fresh lime juice
30 ml pineapple juice
30 ml papaya purée
15 ml simple syrup
Pineapple garnish

1. Straight up: Shake ingredients with ice. Strain into a chilled cocktail glass.
2. Rocks: Shake ingredients with ice. Strain into a Margarita glass filled with ice.
3. Frozen: Blend ingredients with a half cup of ice. Pour into a Margarita glass.

Italian Margarita

Ingredients

Ice
60 ml 100 per cent tequila of choice
30 ml Disaronno Originale amaretto
30 ml fresh lime juice
15 ml simple syrup
Pineapple garnish

1. Straight up: Shake ingredients with ice. Strain into a chilled cocktail glass.
2. Rocks: Shake ingredients with ice. Strain into a Margarita glass filled with ice.
3. Frozen: Blend all but amaretto with half a cup of ice. Pour into a Margarita glass. Top with amaretto. Stir.

an artist who studied under Leonardo da Vinci was commissioned to paint a fresco in the Basilica of Santa Maria delle Grazie in Saronno, Italy. His name was Bernardino Luini, and the fresco is entitled *The Adoration of the Magi*. Luini chose a beautiful Italian girl to model for the Madonna in the fresco. She fell in love with Luini and created a liqueur made with brandy, apricot kernels, and other secret spices as a gift. She had created amaretto di Saronno.

ZOOM

Many people will find it interesting to know that there is not one drop of whiskey in Southern Comfort. It's a high-proof liqueur made from peach, apricot and secret spices. It was invented by a New Orleans bartender, Martin Wilkes Heron, in 1874. It won a gold medal at the 1904 St Louis World's Fair.

Southern Margarita

Ingredients

Ice
60 ml reposado tequila
30 ml Southern Comfort
30 ml fresh lime juice
30 ml simple syrup
Lime garnish

1.Straight up: Shake ingredients with ice. Strain into a chilled cocktail glass.
2. Rocks: Shake ingredients with ice. Strain into a Margarita glass filled with ice.
3. Frozen: Blend all but Southern Comfort with half a cup of ice. Pour into a Margarita glass. Top with the Southern Comfort. Stir.

French Margarita

Ingredients

Ice
60 ml reposado tequila
30 ml Chambord raspberry liqueur
30 ml fresh lime juice
30 ml simple syrup
Lime garnish

1. Straight up: Shake ingredients with ice. Strain into a chilled cocktail glass.
2. Rocks: Shake ingredients with ice. Strain into a Margarita glass filled with ice.
3. Frozen: Blend ingredients with half a cup of ice. Pour into a Margarita glass. Add more Chambord if desired.

CREATIVE MARGARITAS

Get more creative to bump up the 'wow' factor

After you've mastered the basic – but still yummy – Margarita, you can add flair with fun fruit flavours. But don't stop there! You can bump it up a notch by making some creative Margaritas. You know it's a creative Margarita when you look at the name and do a double-take: 'Huh? A Jalapeño Marmalade Margarita?' The double-take reaction in your friends when you tell them about it is all the confirmation you need that you're being creative.

Here are some creative Margarita ideas to provide a springboard. Make a Mango Key Lime Pie Margarita using mango tequila and Key lime juice. Make a Beer Belly Margarita using beer. Make a Watermelon Mojito Margarita using mint and pieces of frozen watermelon, an Apple Pie Margarita using Tuaca and apple juice, an Apricot Prickly Pear Margarita using prickly pear juice, a Blood Orange Cinnamon Margarita, a Banana Flambé Margarita using a banana or banana liqueur

Bed of Roses Margarita

Ingredients

Ice
30 ml reposado tequila
60 ml Tequila Rose liqueur
30 ml fresh lime juice
15 ml simple syrup
Rose petals and lime garnish

1. Blend ingredients with half a cup of ice.
2. Pour into a Margarita glass. Add garnish.
3. You can also rim the glass with finely shredded rose petals if you wish.

and then lighting the floating Grand Marnier (drink only when the flame dies down), or a Piñata Margarita that's layered with three different-coloured Margaritas (try regular/lime, peach and strawberry) and garnished with an assortment of fun fruits to carry on the piñata theme. Perfect for your next fiesta!

RED ● LIGHT

It's best to wear gloves when handling jalapeños. If you don't have gloves, then pay special attention at all times because their oil can be hot. The most common mistake is forgetting you've touched a cut jalapeño then rubbing your eye. Wash your hands thoroughly after preparing them, especially around children.

Guacamole Margarita

Ingredients

Salt to rim glass
Ice
60 ml reposado tequila
30 ml Cointreau
15 ml fresh lime juice
15 ml fresh lemon juice
30 ml simple syrup
½ ripe avocado
Avocado slice and coriander sprig garnish

1. Rim a Margarita glass with salt.
2. Blend ingredients with half a cup of ice.
3. Pour into the Margarita glass. Add garnish, which can include a lime slice as well if you like.

Jalapeño Marmalade Margarita

Ingredients

Ice
60 ml reposado tequila
30 ml Grand Marnier or Cointreau
30 ml fresh lime juice
30 ml orange marmalade
½ jalapeño (or a whole one if you like the heat)
Whole jalapeño garnish

1. Blend ingredients with a cup of ice. Add additional ice if needed.
2. Pour into a Margarita glass. Add garnish.
3. You can add more fresh lime juice to taste.

DAIQUIRIS

Learn the foundation of a daiquiri, then build upon it to create your own

Like the Margarita, the Daiquiri has a simple foundation based on minimal ingredients: rum, fresh lime juice and simple syrup. The Daiquiri is of Cuban descent (there's a place named Daiquirí) and, as you might have guessed, many people claim to have invented the drink. As far as we know the term was first seen in print in 1898.

Today many people think that the definition of Daiquiri is 'frozen drink', but this isn't true. Yes, a Daiquiri can be made frozen, and often is, but to be a Daiquiri it must contain all three of the base ingredients. So, for example, you can never define a Piña Colada as a Daiquiri because it does not contain lime juice.

Classic Daiquiri

Ingredients

Ice
45 ml light Cuban rum
30 ml fresh squeezed lime juice
15 ml simple syrup
Lime garnish

1. Chill a 120–180-ml cocktail glass with ice.
2. Shake ingredients with ice.
3. Strain into the chilled cocktail glass and garnish.

Frozen Daiquiri

Ingredients

Ice
60 ml light Cuban rum
60 ml fresh squeezed lime juice
60 ml simple syrup
Lime garnish

1. Blend ingredients with half a cup of ice. Add additional ice if needed.
2. Pour into a stemmed glass.
3. Add garnish.

To make flavoured mixes, all you need are five things: the fruit (or fruits) of your choice, water, sugar, lime juice and a blender. It's easy! Let's say you want to make Strawberry Daiquiri mix. (1) Take 400 g sugar and 500 ml lukewarm water and shake in a jar. Let the cloudiness clear, then shake again until all the sugar has dissolved in the water. Set aside. (2) Squeeze 250 ml lime juice and set aside. (3) Cut the tops off 450 g ripe strawberries and wash well (you can also use frozen strawberries). (4) Everyone has a different-size blender, so you may have to make the mix in batches. Fill your blender with half the strawberries, then pour in half the lime juice and half the sugar water and blend. Your goal is to keep adding and blending ingredients to make a pourable mix. Taste as you go. You may not need all the sugar water, depending on the ripeness of the strawberries. These quantities make about 2 litres. Pour the mix into a container and chill it in the fridge until you're ready to make your Strawberry Daiquiris.

Strawberry Daiquiri

Ingredients

Sugar to rim glass (optional)
Ice
60 ml light rum
120 ml strawberry Daiquiri mix
Choice of lime, strawberry, or whipped cream garnish

1. Rim a stemmed glass with sugar if you wish.
2. Blend ingredients with half a cup of ice. Add additional ice if needed.
3. Pour into stemmed glass.
4. Add preferred garnish.

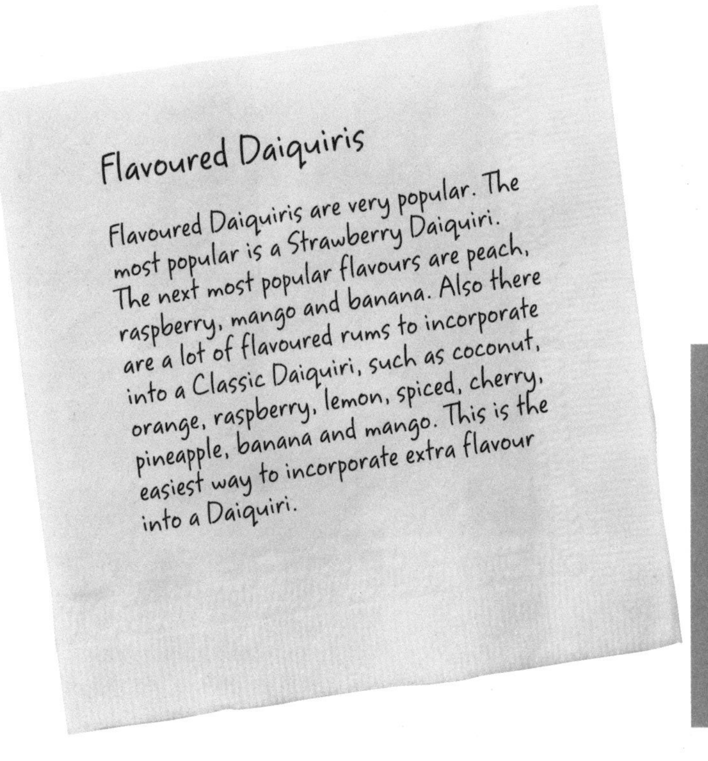

Flavoured Daiquiris

Flavoured Daiquiris are very popular. The most popular is a Strawberry Daiquiri. The next most popular flavours are peach, raspberry, mango and banana. Also there are a lot of flavoured rums to incorporate into a Classic Daiquiri, such as coconut, orange, raspberry, lemon, spiced, cherry, pineapple, banana and mango. This is the easiest way to incorporate extra flavour into a Daiquiri.

PIÑA COLADAS

Make the creamy, dreamy drink that instantly conjures a tropical state of mind

Mexico has the Margarita, Cuba has the Daiquiri, and Puerto Rico has the Piña Colada. This frozen confection is sung about, seen in films and dreamt about by nine-to-five workers on a daily basis.

The term *piña colada* is Spanish for 'strained pineapple'. And of course, as you suspected, there's a line of people claiming to have invented the drink. The name was first seen in print in 1920, but the creamy version we have today wasn't available until the early 1950s, when Coco López coconut cream was invented. Before that, bartenders used coconut milk and shook and strained the drink (usually into coconut shells for tourists). The invention of the coconut cream allowed the

Piña Colada

Ingredients

Ice
60 ml Puerto Rican rum
30 ml coconut cream
90 ml pineapple juice
Pineapple flag garnish

1. Blend ingredients with half a cup of ice. Add more ice if needed.
2. Pour into a tropical glass.
3. Add garnish.

Miami Vice

Ingredients

Ice
60 ml light rum
30 ml coconut cream
90 ml pineapple juice
120 ml strawberry Daiquiri mix
Pineapple and strawberry garnish

1. Blend the first three ingredients with half a cup of ice.
2. Pour into a tropical glass.
3. Blend the strawberry daiquiri mix with half a cup of ice.
4. Pour into the glass. Add garnish.

Piña Colada to be blended. Tip: shake a can of coconut cream before opening, because the solids and liquids separate.

You can compare the basic Piña Colada with the Margarita and Daiquiri, because its simplicity allows an imaginative use of extra flavours to enhance it. For example, just using different rums introduces a depth of flavour. Dark rums that contain molasses make the Piña Colada taste like heaven. Many people like to float the dark rum on top or just add it to the blending process. There are many gold, aged and flavoured rums to substitute for the light rum.

MAKE IT EASY

If you plan to make a few Piña Coladas for friends and family, make it easy by preparing a Piña Colada mix. All you need is a jug, some pineapple juice and a can of coconut cream. Fill the jug three-quarters full with pineapple juice, then top it up with coconut cream and stir.

Melon Colada

Ingredients

Ice
30 ml light rum
30 ml melon liqueur
30 ml coconut cream
90 ml pineapple juice
Pineapple and cherry garnish

1. Blend ingredients with half a cup of ice. Add more ice if needed.
2. Pour into a tropical glass.
3. Add garnish.

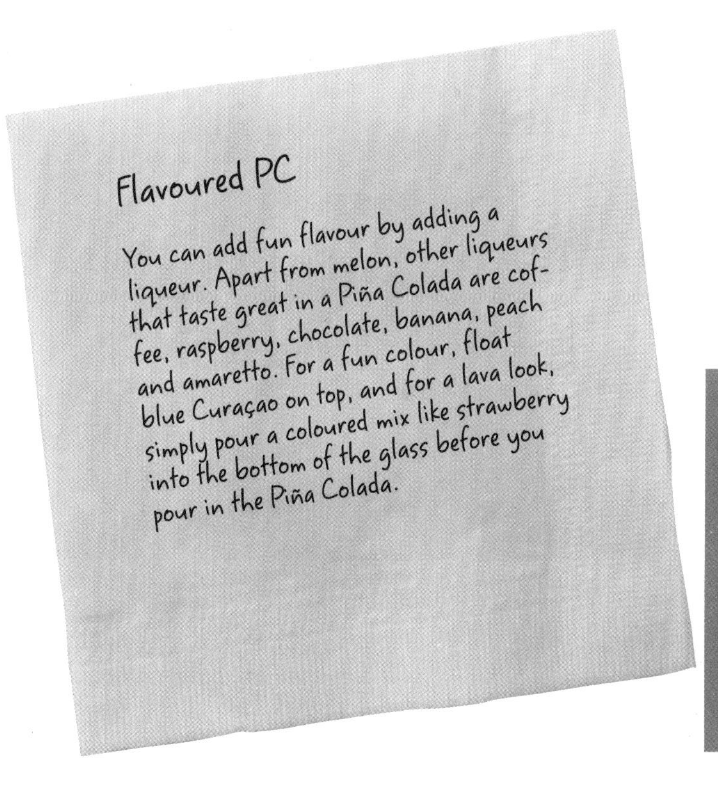

POST-PROHIBITION TROPICAL DRINKS

Try making some world-renowned drinks that will live on forever

Prohibition in America ended on 5 December 1933, at 3:32 p.m. Wow, what a party that must've been! One New Orleans speakeasy owner, Pat O'Brien, closed down his speakeasy, moved ten blocks to the French Quarter, and opened his doors for business. A major issue at this time was that whiskey was in short supply, because the whiskey distilleries had been closed for 13 years and whiskey takes time to age. Rum was abundant, however, and if a bar owner wanted a case of whiskey he had to buy up to 50 cases of rum. That's how the Hurricane was born: huge hurricane glasses were filled with lots of rum and juices for tourists and sailors.

Donn the Beachcomber, a bootlegger in New Orleans during Prohibition, decided to leave Cajun country to open the first tiki bar in Hollywood. He invented the 'pu pu platter' (a lazy Susan with a small Hibachi grill and an assortment of Polynesian or Asian-style appetizers) and many tiki drinks, of which the

Hurricane

Ingredients

Ice
60 ml light rum
60 ml dark rum
60 ml red passion fruit syrup
30 ml orange juice
30 ml pineapple juice
30 ml fresh lime juice
Pineapple or orange flag garnish

1. Fill a hurricane glass with ice.
2. Shake ingredients with ice.
3. Strain into the glass. Add garnish.

Zombie

Ingredients

30 ml gold rum
30 ml 151 Demerara rum
30 ml light rum
30 ml lemon juice
30 ml lime juice
30 ml pineapple juice
30 ml passion fruit syrup
1 teaspoon brown sugar
1 dash Angostura bitters
Ice
Mint sprig garnish

1. Pour everything into a shaker tin without ice and stir until the sugar dissolves. Add ice, then shake and strain into the glass – a tiki mug or tall glass.
2. Add garnish.

Zombie was the most popular. The Zombie was served at the 1939 New York World's Fair.

Trader Vic owned a small grocery in San Francisco and worked as a waiter. He opened a tiki bar across the street from his grocery store, where he invented the Mai Tai, and went on to open a chain of tiki bars around the world.

ZOOM

The term *mai tai* is Tahitian for 'out of this world'. The original recipe is slightly different from the recipe created for the Trader Vic's chain, due to the availability of ingredients. When bartenders not working at Trader Vic's are asked to duplicate the recipe, they are limited to the standard ingredients behind their bars, a limitation that gave rise to the Copycat Mai Tai.

Trader Vic Mai Tai

Ingredients

Ice
30 ml aged Jamaican rum (such as Appleton's)
30 ml amber Martinique rum (such as St James or Clément)
15 ml orange Curaçao
15 ml orgeat syrup (French almond syrup)
15 ml fresh lime juice
30 ml Trader Vic's rock candy syrup (or commercial simple syrup)
Mint sprig garnish

1. Fill a double old-fashioned glass with ice.
2. Shake ingredients with ice.
3. Strain into the glass. Add garnish.

Copycat Mai Tai

Ingredients

Ice
15 ml triple sec
15 ml amaretto
60 ml sweet-and-sour mix
60 ml pineapple juice
30 ml light rum
30 ml dark rum
Pineapple and cherry garnish

1. Fill a tropical glass with ice.
2. Shake ingredients (except the dark rum) with ice.
3. Strain into the glass.
4. Float the dark rum on top. Add garnish.

GLOBAL TROPICAL DRINKS

Make frozen and tropical drinks from popular tourist destinations

In the 1950s, Hawaii went through a phase of exotic paradise construction to attract tourists. Tropical getaways were being built on every island, and the largest of these was the Hawaiian Village on the island of Oahu. Harry Yee, a veteran bartender working at the Hawaiian Village, was asked by Bols to help promote its blue Curaçao, and the Blue Hawaii was born. When asked about the orchid garnish, his answer was, 'We used to use a sugarcane stick, and people would chew on the stick, then put it in the ashtray. When the ashes and cane stuck together it made a real mess, so I put the orchids in the drink to make the ashtrays easier to clean.'

Yee was not only the first to put an orchid into a drink but also the first to put a paper parasol into a drink; he even put a Chinese back scratcher into a drink, which he called a 'tropical itch'. There are just too many of his drinks to mention, but at that time there weren't any 'Hawaiian drinks', so he was the

Blue Hawaii

Ingredients

Ice
20 ml Puerto Rican rum
20 ml vodka
15 ml Bols blue Curaçao
90 ml pineapple juice
30 ml sweet-and-sour mix
Orchid garnish

1. Fill a tropical glass with ice.
2. Shake ingredients with ice.
3. Strain into the glass.
4. Add garnish.

Blue Hawaiian

Ingredients

Ice
30 ml light rum
15 ml blue Curaçao
90 ml pineapple juice
30 ml sweet-and-sour mix
Pineapple flag garnish

1. Fill a tropical glass with ice.
2. Shake ingredients with ice.
3. Strain into the glass.
4. Add garnish.

one responsible for lighting this fire. The Blue Hawaiian is a spinoff from Harry's Blue Hawaii, minus the orchid and the vodka. If you ask for this drink in any bar today, this is the version you will be given.

The Singapore Sling was created in the Long Bar of Raffles Hotel in Singapore at the turn of the 20th century by Chinese bartender Ngiam Tong Boon to attract women, so it was 100 years ahead of the Cosmopolitan in that respect.

No one knows who invented the Bahama Mama, but it came from the Bahamas in the 1980s. It can be made in many different ways with many ingredients, as long as you keep the same flavour profile, which is a cross between a Piña Colada and a Rum Punch.

Singapore Sling

Ingredients

Ice
45 ml gin
15 ml Peter Heering Cherry Liqueur
7.5 ml Cointreau
7.5 ml Bénédictine
60 ml pineapple juice
1 dash Angostura bitters
7.5 ml grenadine
15 ml lime juice
60 ml soda water
Pineapple or orange flag garnish

1. Fill a tropical glass with ice.
2. Shake ingredients (except soda water) with ice.
3. Strain into the glass. Add soda water.
4. Add garnish.

Bahama Mama

Ingredients

Ice
30 ml coconut rum
30 ml light rum
60 ml orange juice
60 ml pineapple juice
15 ml grenadine
Pineapple or orange flag garnish

1. Rocks: Shake ingredients with ice. Strain into a tropical glass filled with ice. Add garnish.
2. Frozen: Blend ingredients with half a cup of ice. Pour into a tropical glass. Add garnish.

ANIMAL-INSPIRED TROPICAL DRINKS

These concoctions are guaranteed to be more fun than a barrel of monkeys

Animal names for drinks have always been very popular. With a little research one can find names such as Grasshopper, Moscow Mule, Horse's Neck, Monkey Gland, Greyhound, Salty Dog and Scorpion.

It's safe to assume that any drink with the word 'monkey' in its name will involve banana. The Chocolate Monkey is a base recipe for you to start with. Much can be substituted, just as long as you keep the banana/chocolate balance. For example, in place of the vanilla vodka you could use chocolate vodka, banana vodka or banana rum. Let your imagination go wild! For a garnish, you could use chocolate whipped cream, chocolate vermicelli, grated chocolate or a banana-shaped sweet.

Chocolate Monkey

Ingredients

Chocolate syrup
30 ml vanilla vodka
30 ml banana liqueur
30 ml white crème de cacao
120 ml single cream
Ice
Whipped cream garnish

1. Squirt some chocolate syrup into a tall glass.
2. Blend ingredients with half a cup of ice. Add more ice if needed.
3. Pour into the glass. Add garnish.

Frog in a Blender

Ingredients

Chocolate syrup
15 ml grenadine
30 ml white crème de cacao
30 ml green crème de menthe
120 ml single cream
Ice
Whipped cream garnish

1. Squirt some chocolate syrup into a tall glass.
2. Pour grenadine into the glass.
3. Blend remaining ingredients with half a cup of ice.
4. Pour into the glass. Add garnish.

So far there's no solid evidence for the origin of the Yellowbird. What we do know is that in 1957 Alan and Marilyn Bergman wrote the lyrics for the song 'The Yellow Bird' to a Haitian tune of 1883. Now let's fly to Hawaii, where Arthur Lyman – king of tiki lounge exotica music – recorded the song (which shot to No 4 on the Billboard charts in 1961). Well, it just so happens that Lyman played weekly in the Shell Bar at the Hawaiian Village (think bartender Harry Yee/Blue Hawaii). So it's possible that the drink was invented in Hawaii.

GREEN LIGHT

The Frog in a Blender is a novelty frozen drink. It tastes like a fresh chocolate peppermint cream, but it can easily jump all the way to the other end of the spectrum if you insert a rubber frog halfway into the drink and then serve. It's perfect to serve at Halloween! To bump up the alcohol level, add vodka or chocolate vodka.

Yellowbird

Ingredients

Ice
30 ml light rum
30 ml Galliano
15 ml banana liqueur
60 ml pineapple juice
60 ml orange juice

1. Fill a tall glass with ice.
2. Shake ingredients with ice.
3. Strain into the glass.

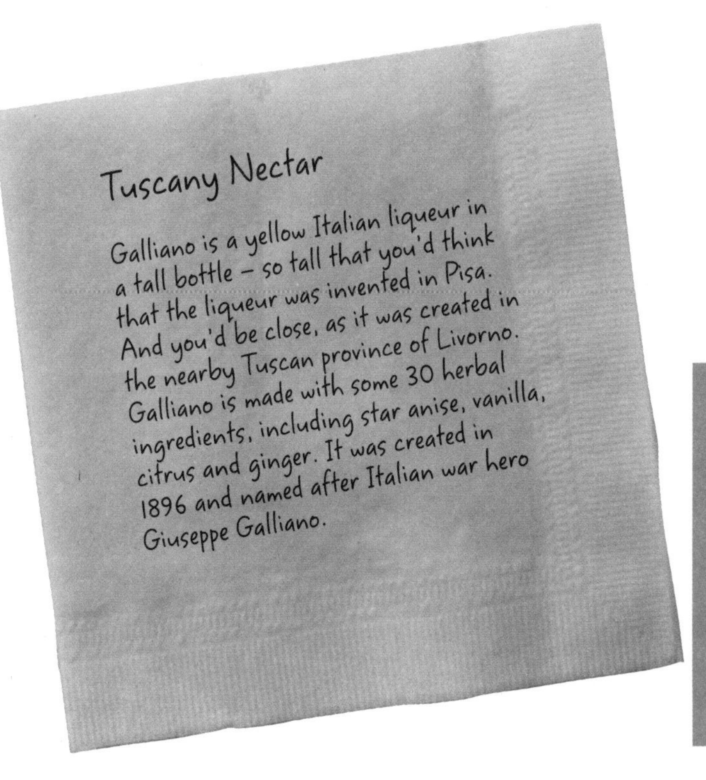

Tuscany Nectar

Galliano is a yellow Italian liqueur in a tall bottle – so tall that you'd think that the liqueur was invented in Pisa. And you'd be close, as it was created in the nearby Tuscan province of Livorno. Galliano is made with some 30 herbal ingredients, including star anise, vanilla, citrus and ginger. It was created in 1896 and named after Italian war hero Giuseppe Galliano.

FROZEN DESSERT DRINKS

Trade your spoon for a spoon straw and enjoy a favourite dessert in a glass

This is where you can really have some fun. The first question to ask is, 'What are my favourite desserts?' because practically any dessert can be turned into a dessert drink. So what is it? Maybe the thought sent your brain on a sugar rush, and it's spinning a little right now, so take a breath and break it down. How about cakes? Do you like any of these: devil's food, red velvet, carrot, black forest, pineapple upside-down or wedding cake?

What about pie flavours such as lemon meringue, pecan, pumpkin, custard, coconut cream, lime or peach? Maybe you're a cookie person: how about chocolate chip, oatmeal, apple and cinnamon, macaroons, Oreos, gingernuts or mint crisps?

Banana Cream Pie

Ingredients

Golden syrup to paint glass
Digestive biscuit crumbs
30 ml vanilla vodka
30 ml banana liqueur
15 ml butterscotch schnapps
Half a banana
120 ml single cream
Ice
Whipped cream garnish

1. Paint half the inside of a tall glass with golden syrup.
2. Sprinkle the syrup with biscuit crumbs.
3. Blend ingredients with half a cup of ice.
4. Pour into the glass. Add whipped cream garnish.

Strawberry Shortcake

Ingredients

2 tablespoons whipped cream
30 ml vodka
30 ml amaretto
60 ml single cream
60 ml strawberry mix
Ice
Strawberry garnish

1. Drop a tablespoonful of whipped cream into the bottom of a tall glass.
2. Blend ingredients with half a cup of ice.
3. Pour into the glass. Garnish with remaining whipped cream and a strawberry.

The whole point is to spark your imagination. With all the flavoured spirits, liqueurs and mixers available, the possibilities are endless. You simply break down the key elements of a recipe. For example, if you read a recipe for Banana Cream Pie, you'll see that the recipe calls for bananas, milk, sugar, butter, vanilla and a whipped cream topping. So you can use vanilla vodka, banana liqueur, butterscotch schnapps, cream and some fresh banana to give it some body. Blend it up, then top it with whipped cream. *Voilà!*

ZOOM

Strawberry shortcake is a classic American dessert. Quite unlike British shortbread, it's a scone-like cake that is split and filled with fruit and whipped cream. In the mid-19th century strawberries – like many other things – were available only seasonally and locally, and Americans held strawberry shortcake parties to celebrate the beginning of their brief season.

German Chocolate Cake

Ingredients

Chocolate syrup and grated coconut
30 ml coconut rum
30 ml dark crème de cacao
15 ml hazelnut liqueur
1 scoop chocolate ice cream
30 ml single cream
Ice
Whipped cream and chocolate shavings garnish

1. Rim a tall glass with chocolate syrup and grated coconut.
2. Blend ingredients with half a cup of ice.
3. Pour into the glass. Add garnish.

Place Your Bet

If you bet that German Chocolate Cake originated in Germany and was created by a stout German woman in her kitchen, well, you'd lose. A Texas housewife created it in 1957, and sent the recipe to her local newspaper. It got its name because her recipe used German's Sweet Chocolate, a brand created by Sam German, an Englishman, in 1852.

TEQUILA-BASED SHOTS

Here are the shots that will shoot you to Mexico the fastest

Before cocktails, there were shots. It was simple, really: a shot of hard liquor alongside a beer. And even though things change over time it's funny how they stay the same. I bet those cowboys sitting at dusty tables in local saloons didn't think it was hip to order a bottle for the table. Today they call it 'bottle service', and it can be found in trendy nightclubs the world over. And although shots have changed in flavour, colour and names, their purpose remains the same.

A plain old Shot of Tequila will probably never go out of style. There will just be new ways of shooting it. The most common way today is the lick it, slam it, suck it method. You lick some salt, then drink the tequila and suck on a lime. A lemon can be used instead, if that's your preference. Using salt and lime to help you get the tequila down your throat is often referred to as using 'training wheels'. In some countries, people substitute cinnamon for the salt and orange for

Shot of Tequila

Ingredients

Lime (or lemon) wedge
Salt to rim glass
45 ml tequila of choice

1. Wet part of a shot glass with a lime wedge, then dip it in salt.
2. Pour tequila into the glass.
3. Lick the salt, drink the tequila, then bite into the flesh of the lime.

Prairie Fire

Ingredients

45 ml tequila of choice
5 dashes Tabasco

1. Pour the tequila into a shot glass.
2. Dash in five hard jerks of Tabasco.

the lime when shooting aged tequila. And around the millennium, the trendy way to shoot tequila was chilled, which is another way to avoid actually tasting the tequila.

ZOOM

Tequila passion shots have been popular since the 1980s. To set one up, you lick part of another person's body (hopefully a person you've known for a bit), then sprinkle salt on the moist patch. Next, place a lime wedge flesh side out in the person's mouth. Now you're ready to lick the salt, drink the shot and suck the lime.

A dash of Tabasco helps mask the taste of tequila.

Bull Fight

Ingredients

30 ml coffee liqueur
15 ml Sambuca
15 ml gold tequila
2 dashes Tabasco

1. Slowly layer the first three ingredients in order into a shot glass.
2. Dash the Tabasco.

Flat Tyre

Ingredients

20 ml black Sambuca
20 ml tequila of choice
Ice

1. Shake the black Sambuca and tequila with ice.
2. Strain into a shot glass.

VODKA-BASED SHOTS

Make some bursting-with-flavour citrus shots that satisfy all

Everyone seems to like citrus-based shots, so you can't go wrong here. All these need to be super-chilled by shaking with ice; however, if you'd rather experience a fuller flavour, keep the citrus vodka in the freezer and then just pour it when you're ready.

If you want to add a fun twist to a Lemon Drop Shot, dip half of a lemon wheel in sugar and the other half in ground espresso. Here's a top-shelf Lemon Drop Shot spinoff that you can serve to your special guests. For each one, you'll need 45 ml chilled citrus vodka, 15 ml Grand Marnier, a lemon slice, a teaspoon of sugar, a match, a saucer and a shot glass. To start, lay the lemon slice on the saucer and cover with the sugar. Pour some Grand Marnier over the sugar to make it flammable, then light it. As the sugar is being crystallized into the lemon, pour a shot of chilled citrus vodka into the shot glass. By the time you're done, the flame will have died

Lemon Drop Shot

Ingredients

Sugar to rim glass
45 ml citrus vodka
Ice

1. Rim a shot glass with sugar.
2. Shake vodka with ice.
3. Strain into the glass.

Russian Roulette

Ingredients

45 ml vodka
Ice
Orange slice
Sugar
7.5 ml 151 rum or Grand Marnier

1. Shake the vodka with ice and strain into a shot glass.
2. Place an orange slice on top of the glass with sugar and rum on top of the orange.
3. Light the orange, then wait until the flame dies down.
4. Pick up the orange, drink the shot, and then bite the sugary, warm orange.

down. Now drink the chilled shot, then bite into the warm, sugary lemon. Pick up the saucer and pour the leftover Grand Marnier into the shot glass and drink it, too. It's a very decadent taste experience.

RED LIGHT

Always be very careful when using fire. Long sleeves, long hair and paper napkins nearby are just a few of the things people forget about. Always think ahead, as if you're child-proofing the area, and never let flames get out of control. When lighting alcohol, avoid butane lighters because they spray chemicals. A match is better.

Chocolate Cake

Ingredients

Ice
30 ml lemon vodka
15 ml Frangelico hazelnut liqueur
Sugared lemon wedge garnish

1. Shake the ingredients with ice.
2. Strain into a shot glass.
3. Drink, then bite into the lemon dipped in sugar.

Weird Cake

There's no chocolate in the Chocolate Cake shot, but it tastes like chocolate. This shot showed up around the millennium. It's one of those weird 'Twilight Zone' mouth sensations. It uses citrus vodka and hazelnut liqueur and ends with a sugared lemon. The strange part is that when you bite into the lemon, it tastes like chocolate cake. Weird.

LIQUEUR-BASED SHOTS

Try some sweet and creamy shots that pack a punch

The B-52 shot was named after the B-52 Stratofortress bombers built for the United States Air Force in 1954. President George H. W. Bush took them off alert duty in 1991. Many people have claimed that they created the B-52 shot, but the only hard fact agreed upon so far is that its birth must have been some time in the 1970s. Grand Marnier was born in 1880, Kahlúa was born in 1936, but Baileys Original Irish Cream was not born until 1974.

The names of shots were always pretty tame up until the 1980s. America had just come out of the wild and free rock/disco explosion that followed the ending of the Vietnam War, but then in 1981 a disease that no one had ever heard of permeated the world. It was called AIDS and it was frightening because no one knew what was causing it. Finally it was found to be a sexually transmitted disease. For the bar scene, this was a huge concern. Ever since women had been

B-52

Ingredients

15 ml Kahlúa coffee liqueur
15 ml Baileys Original Irish Cream
15 ml Grand Marnier

1. Layer the liqueurs in the order given into a shot glass.

Whipped Cream Shot

Ingredients

20 ml coffee liqueur
20 ml Irish cream
Whipped cream garnish

1. Slowly layer the two ingredients in order into a shot glass.
2. Top with whipped cream.
3. Drink without using your hands.

allowed in in the 1920s, bars had had sexual undertones. Public anxiety grew, and many people were frustrated by not knowing what to do now that having sex – the way they were used to – could mean dying. It was the collective frustration of not being able to act out sexually that led to the provocative names given to newly conceived drinks. Bartenders were just providing what the public desired at that time. If people couldn't have sex, then, by golly, they would enjoy playful substitutions for it.

You can adjust liqueur measures to the size of the shot glass you are using.

Buttery Irishman

Ingredients

20 ml butterscotch schnapps
20 ml Irish cream

1. Pour the butterscotch schnapps into a shot glass.
2. Slowly layer the Irish cream on top of the schnapps.

Irish Cream Shots

Irish cream shots first appeared in 1974 and there are many other liqueurs that mix well with it. In the same way you layer the Irish cream on top of butterscotch schnapps to make a Buttery Irishman, you can layer it on top of Sambuca, crème de banane or cinnamon schnapps.

WHISKEY-BASED SHOTS

Try some whiskey shots made from the Earth's amber waves of grain

The Three Wise Men shot was more than likely created by men tired of the sweet, girly shots from the 1980s and 1990s. The novelty of the shot strictly plays off the names of the particular whiskies used. This foundation recipe is pretty solid, because a tower of shots can be built on top. For example, if you add Wild Turkey bourbon, the shot is called Three Wise Men Go Hunting.' Add José Cuervo into the mix, and it turns into Three Wise Men Go to Mexico. You begin to see the pattern pretty quickly.

Here are more to try: Three Wise Men Go Bananas = add banana liqueur; Three Wise Men Go Sailing = add Captain Morgan spiced rum; Three Wise Men Love Chocolate = add

Three Wise Men

Ingredients

15 ml Jack Daniel's Tennessee whiskey
15 ml Johnnie Walker Scotch whisky
15 ml Jim Beam bourbon
Ice

1. Shake the three whiskeys with ice.
2. Strain into a shot glass.
3. Can be served neat as well.

Monkey on Jack's Back

Ingredients

20 ml banana liqueur
20 ml Jack Daniel's Tennessee whiskey

1. Pour the banana liqueur into a shot glass.
2. Slowly layer the Jack Daniel's on top of the liqueur.
3. Can be served chilled and straight up as well.

chocolate liqueur; Three Wise Men Go Nutty = add amaretto; Three Wise Men Go Goose Hunting with a Friend = add Greygoose vodka and George Dickel bourbon; Three Wise Men Triple Date = add brandy, ginger liqueur and Tia Maria; and Three Wise Men Strike Gold in Germany = add Goldschläger and Jägermeister. You can insert an adjective as well, such as Three Bitter Wise Men = add a dash of bitters. Other words to try are 'buttery', 'blue', 'fuzzy' and 'hot'.

ZOOM

Jack Daniel was the youngest of 13 children. His mother died when he was two, and after a few years he felt neglected and ran away to the neighbours, where he learned how to make whiskey. By the age of 13 he owned his own distillery. He never married or had children, and died in 1911, aged 65.

Snowshoe

Ingredients

Ice
20 ml Wild Turkey bourbon
20 ml peppermint schnapps

1. Shake the ingredients with ice.
2. Strain into a shot glass.

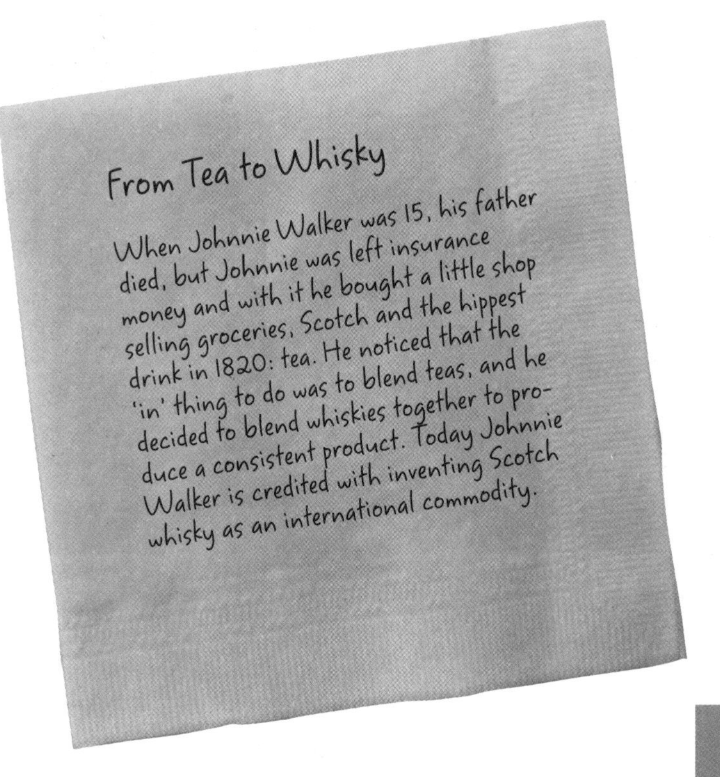

FLAG SHOTS

Test your layering skills with shots inspired by national flags

Some people may think it's disrespectful to marry flags and alcohol together, but it's not like we're burning any of these flags. And most countries seem to have an alcoholic drink that they're particularly associated with, so it can be fun to match those up with appropriately coloured liqueurs and see which combinations taste the best.

There are many possibilities. Mexico has tequila, the USA has bourbon, Scotland has Scotch whisky, Ireland has Irish whiskey, England has gin, Portugal has port, Russia has vodka, Greece has ouzo, France has cognac, Norway has akvavit, and many Caribbean islands have rum. So, *salud*, cheers, *à sua saúde*, *à votre santé* and *skaal*!

The American Flag shot can also be called by either of the flag's two nicknames, 'Old Glory' and 'Star-Spangled Banner'. If you like the latter, cut a star fruit and set it on the rim just for fun. This shot – when it's drunk in one gulp – tastes exactly like

American Flag

Ingredients

40 ml white crème de cacao
Few drops of grenadine
7.5 ml blue Curaçao

1. Pour the white crème de cacao into a shot glass.
2. Pour in the grenadine, and it will sink to the bottom.
3. Slowly layer the blue Curaçao on top.

Mexican Flag

Ingredients

15 ml grenadine
15 ml green crème de menthe
15 ml single cream

1. Pour the grenadine into a shot glass.
2. Slowly layer the green crème de menthe on top of the grenadine.
3. Slowly layer the cream on top of the crème de menthe.

a chocolate-covered cherry. If you stir the layers together with a cocktail straw it turns purple.

The Irish Flag shot is perfect for celebrating St Patrick's Day. Some people use orange liqueur for the top layer, but Irish whiskey is appropriate to the theme and tastes better with the Irish cream.

MAKE IT EASY

When making the Alaskan Flag shot, it's best to have the ingredients chilled beforehand, but don't shake them with ice. Simply put the bottles of Goldschläger and blue Curaçao in the freezer until you are ready to make the shot. Also, having the alcohol freezing cold will really make you feel as if you are in Alaska.

Irish Flag

Ingredients

15 ml green crème de menthe
15 ml Irish cream
15 ml Irish whiskey

1. Pour the green crème de menthe into a shot glass.
2. Slowly layer the Irish cream on top.
3. Slowly layer the Irish whiskey on top of the Irish cream.

Alaskan Flag

Ingredients

20 ml chilled Goldschläger cinnamon schnapps
20 ml blue Curaçao

1. Pour the Goldschläger into a shot glass.
2. Slowly layer the blue Curaçao on top.

NOVELTY SHOTS

Create some out-of-the-box shots to impress your friends

You can purchase pricey chocolate shot glasses, but why do that when you can make your own? You must use very good-quality dark chocolate, though, or they won't set with a beautiful crisp, glossy finish. Also you want them to taste fantastic. To mould the chocolate you will need some small 90-ml and 30-ml plastic or paper cups, which you can buy from baking and sugarcraft suppliers. Oil the cups to stop them sticking, three-quarters fill the larger cups with melted chocolate, then push in the smaller cups to mould the inside of the glass. Leave them in the freezer until set, then pop off the moulds. Start with small batches to get the hang of the technique: if they don't work first time, at least you can eat the failures.

You can fill these delectable edible glasses with any of your favourite shots, but here they're used to make a cocktail version of S'mores, a traditional campfire treat beloved by all

Pirate Treasure

Ingredients

20 ml chilled Goldschläger
20 ml chilled Captain Morgan spiced rum

1. Pour the Goldschläger into a shot glass.
2. Slowly layer the Captain Morgan spiced rum on top.

S'mores

Ingredients

15 ml vanilla vodka or rum
7.5 ml butterscotch schnapps
7.5 ml Irish cream
Chocolate shot glass
1 Teddy Grahams biscuit for garnish
Splash 151 rum
2 mini-marshmallows on a cocktail stick

1. Pour the first three ingredients into a chocolate shot glass.
2. Set the Teddy Grahams biscuit on top, then top with 151 rum. Set light to the rum.
3. Roast the marshmallows, blow out the flame.
4. Drink, then eat chocolate glass and marshmallows.

American and Canadian scouts, which consists of chocolate and freshly toasted hot marshmallow sandwiched between two Graham crackers. Here the recipe's re-created in miniature, with mini-marshmallows and a tiny biscuit: look out for Teddy Grahams in large supermarkets, or buy them from online suppliers of American foods.

Twist it up by using coloured marshmallows and white chocolate glasses.

MAKE IT EASY

Many shots just taste better ice cold, and the Pirate Treasure is an example, so be sure to chill the bottles in the freezer first. Also, the novelty of the shot is that the Captain Morgan spiced rum is amber in colour, to represent sand, and the pirate gold is buried under the sand.

Flu Shot

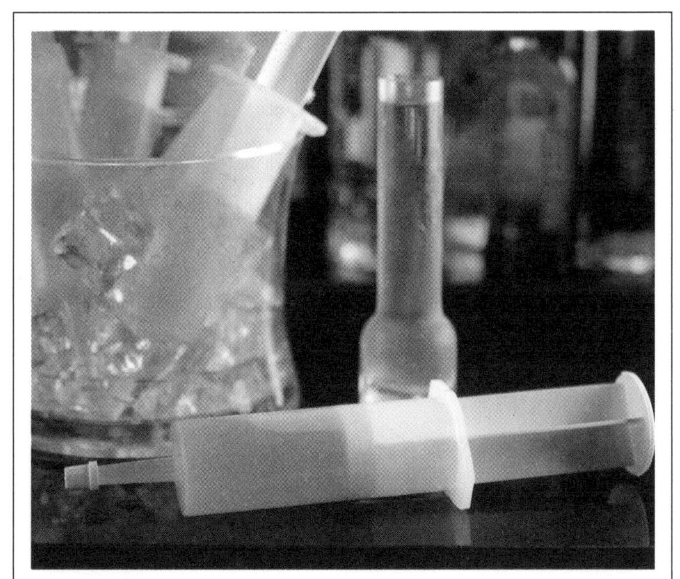

Ingredients

20 ml melon liqueur
20 ml Jägermeister
Ice

1. Shake the ingredients with ice.
2. Pour into a shot glass or syringe.

Give Your Best Shot

Be the life of the party or impress your friends by investing in some plastic shooter syringes. Of course, you can fill a syringe with any shot, but the flu shot fits the bill perfectly. Make a batch by multiplying the recipe. Place them in a bowl or bucket of ice so they stay chilled.

CLASSIC SHOOTERS

Add a little mixer to your shots and feel your taste buds jump for joy

Shots and shooters have two things in common: both are meant to be drunk in one gulp, and both have the same alcohol content. The difference is that while shots are 100 per cent alcohol, shooters have a mixer added to them. So shooters require a slightly larger glass, and they fit best in 90–150-ml glasses.

Tip: at a nightclub, it's best to order shots, not shooters (unless money is no object). For some reason, in the last few years nightclub bartenders have begun shaking up shooters and pouring them into shot-sized glasses. The alcohol measure for a shot or shooter should be 30–45 ml. So these bartenders are pouring a measure of alcohol into the shaker tin, adding a lot of mixer, shaking, then straining out – and charging for – five to eight shots from that one measure! It was never this way in the 1960s–90s.

Lemon Drop Shooter

Ingredients

Ice
Sugar to rim glass
30 ml citrus vodka
15 ml triple sec
15 ml lemon juice
15 ml simple syrup
Sugared lemon (optional)

1. Rim a 90–150-ml shooter glass with sugar.
2. Shake the ingredients with ice and strain into the sugar-rimmed glass.
3. Garnish with sugared lemon if you wish.

Melon Ball

Ingredients

Ice
30 ml vodka
15 ml melon liqueur
30 ml orange juice

1. Shake ingredients with ice.
2. Strain into a 90–150-ml shooter glass.

ZOOM

It's rumoured that this way of serving shooters evolved after the 'Martini craze' of the late 1990s. Before that, bartenders would sometimes serve rounds of shooters in cocktail/Martini glasses (mostly to women). So, really, the flavoured sipping Martinis of today are just the gulping shooters of yesterday.

Some people like to replace the orange juice with pineapple juice.

SoCo Lime

Ingredients

Ice
45 ml Southern Comfort
15 ml Rose's lime cordial

1. Shake ingredients with ice.
2. Strain into a 90–120-ml shooter glass.

Old Is New

Members of the millennium J-Lo generation may have thought they were being hip and trendy by combining Southern Comfort and lime juice and naming the result 'SoCo Lime', but if Janis Joplin were alive today she'd have a few things to say about that. She was drinking Southern Comfort and Lime in the 1960s and made it well known that it was her drink of choice.

KAMIKAZES

Learn to make this Japanese-inspired shooter, then add your own twist

Kamikaze is a Japanese word. *Kami* means 'God' or 'divine' and *kaze* means 'wind'. In the late 13th century, the Mongolians tried to conquer Japan, but a typhoon destroyed the Mongolian fleet and thwarted the invasion. The Japanese interpreted the typhoon as a gift from the gods. The Kamikaze shooter, however, did not get its name from the typhoon.

In 1944, almost 700 years later during World War II, the Japanese used the word again to describe the suicide missions of their pilots deployed to attack the Allied fleet in the Pacific. Young kamikaze pilots would steer their explosives-filled planes straight down into Allied ships. In the end, Japan lost around 2,800 pilots, who sank 34 ships and damaged

Kamikaze

Ingredients

Ice
30 ml vodka
15 ml triple sec
15 ml Rose's lime cordial

1. Shake ingredients with ice.
2. Strain into a 90–150-ml shooter glass.

Blue Kamikaze

Ingredients

Ice
30 ml vodka
15 ml blue Curaçao
15 ml Rose's lime cordial

1. Shake ingredients with ice.
2. Strain into a 90–150-ml shooter glass.

368. Almost 5,000 Allied sailors were killed and about the same number were wounded.

Today many things are named 'kamikaze'. There are video games, flying carnival rides, record labels, underground bands, Japanese comic books and, of course, the Kamikaze shooter. No one knows who invented it, or when or where. Basically it's just a vodka Gimlet with the addition of triple sec. And if you add cranberry juice, then you can call it a Cosmopolitan. These modern Kamikaze versions bump up the flavour value in a big way.

MAKE IT EASY

Kamikazes offer lots of possibilities because so many flavours go well with lime. and there are many flavoured vodkas to choose from. You can also make Rainbow Kamikazes by secretly dropping one drop of food colouring into glasses. As you strain the Kamikazes into the glasses, your friends will be amazed that each drink comes out a different colour.

Raspberry Kamikaze

Ingredients

Ice
30 ml raspberry vodka
15 ml Chambord
15 ml Rose's lime cordial

1. Shake ingredients with ice.
2. Strain into a 90–150-ml shooter glass.

Cherry Kamikaze

Ingredients

Ice
30 ml cherry vodka
15 ml triple sec
15 mlm Rose's lime cordial
Cherry garnish

1. Shake ingredients with ice.
2. Strain into a 90–150-ml shooter glass. Add garnish.

RASPBERRY-BASED SHOOTERS

Go razzle-dazzle and shake up some delectable raspberry goodness

Raspberries have a decadent taste, and their price throws them into the delicacy category. Simply put, raspberries don't taste sweet unless they are fully ripe. But soft and ripe don't travel well. The very best raspberries are the ones you grow in your own garden, or find on a bush while strolling through the countryside.

There are a lot of raspberry liqueurs on the market, but Chambord Liqueur Royale de France is the ultimate raspberry liqueur. No other raspberry liqueur can compare with its taste. It has been made in the Loire Valley in France since the late 17th century, using black raspberries, Madagascan vanilla, Moroccan citrus peel, honey, cognac and, of course, some secret ingredients. It's said to have been drunk by Louis XIV during a royal visit to the Château de Chambord.

The bottle is unlike any other liqueur bottle in the world: it's shaped like a royal orb, adorned with a gold band and

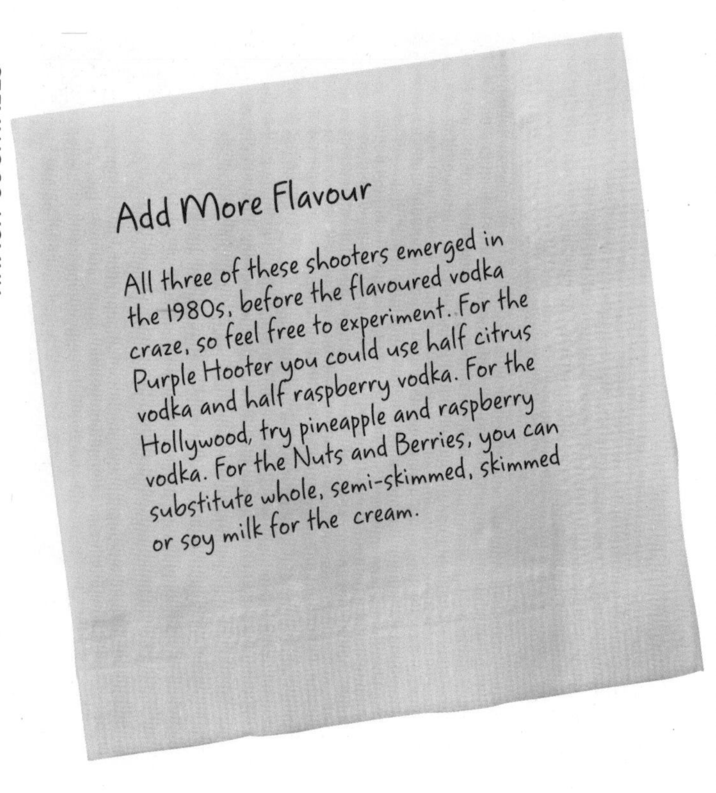

Purple Hooter

Ingredients

Ice
30 ml vodka
15 ml Chambord raspberry liqueur
15 ml lemon juice
15 ml simple syrup

1. Shake ingredients with ice.
2. Strain into a 90–150-ml shooter glass.

topped with a golden crown. On the company's website, chambordonline.com, you can find several wonderful recipes for drinks. The site also has some Chambord cuisine recipes for hors d'oeuvres, salads, appetizers, entrées and desserts.

MAKE IT EASY

If these shooters sound as if they'd make a nice, tall, cool cocktail, you're right! All you have to do is fill a tall glass with ice, add the alcohol, fill with the mixer, and stir. It works the other way, too. Have a favourite cocktail? Well, make a shooter out of it by reducing the amount of mixer.

Hollywood

Ingredients

Ice
30 ml vodka
15 ml Chambord raspberry liqueur
30 ml pineapple juice

1. Shake ingredients with ice.
2. Strain into a 90–150-ml shooter glass.

Nuts and Berries

Ingredients

Ice
30 ml Chambord raspberry liqueur
30 ml Frangelico hazelnut liqueur
30 ml single cream

1. Shake ingredients with ice.
2. Strain into a 3–5-ounce shooter glass.

CRANBERRY-BASED SHOOTERS

Whip up some sweet and tart shooters using a mixer born in the USA

Cranberries are the fruits of low-growing shrubs that are indigenous to North America. Native Americans made a sweet sauce using cranberries and maple syrup. Although Cape Cod is known for its cranberries, it's Wisconsin that produces half of the annual crop. Other states that grow cranberries include New Jersey, Oregon and Washington.

Cranberries have been around a long time, but it wasn't until 1930 that the first cranberry juice was marketed. The juicer was invented in the 1920s, so that invention may have played a part. In 1930, Ocean Spray introduced the commercial cranberry juice cocktail, and today every supermarket sells cranberry juice drinks, straight or blended with other

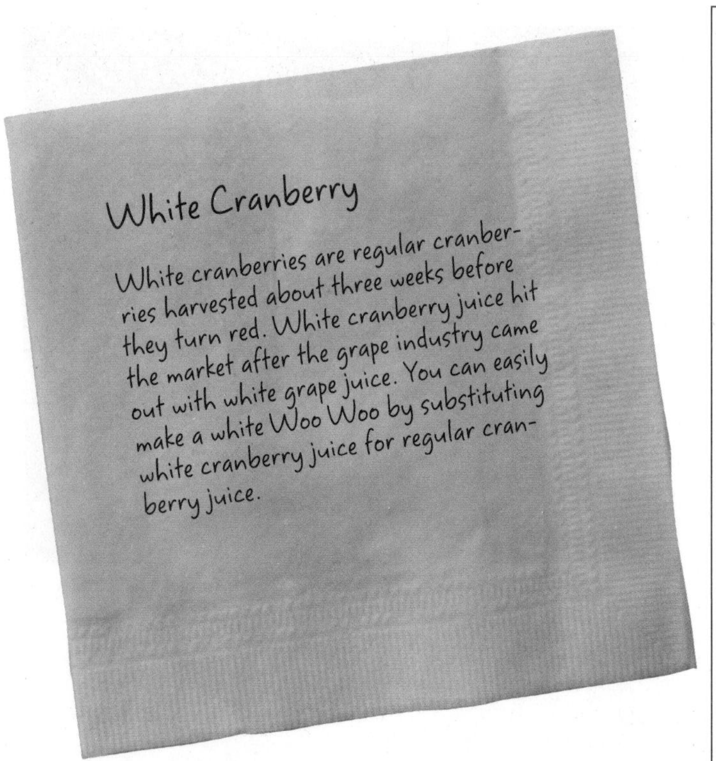

Woo Woo

Ingredients

Ice
30 ml vodka
30 ml peach schnapps
30 ml cranberry juice

1. Shake ingredients with ice.
2. Strain into a 90–150-ml shooter glass.
3. You're supposed to drink this shooter, then yell 'Woo woo!'

fruits such as raspberry and orange. This opens up new possibilities for substituting regular cranberry juice with blends in any of the shooter recipes on these pages.

The Scarlett O'Hara (Southern Comfort and cranberry juice with a lime) was the first popular cranberry cocktail. It was created for the 1939 film *Gone with the Wind*. The next popular cranberry cocktails didn't gain recognition until the 1970s: the Cape Codder, Sea Breeze and Bay Breeze. The reason for this delay was that the cranberry industry collapsed when the US Department of Health announced that cranberry crops were tainted with toxic herbicides in 1959. By the 1980s, cranberry juice had recovered and breathed new life into the cocktail world, spawning the Sex on the Beach and the Woo Woo. In the 1990s, cranberry juice hit a ball out of the park with the Cosmopolitan, and the new millennium brought us the Red Snapper and Red-Headed German.

Red Snapper

Ingredients

Ice
30 ml Crown Royal whiskey
30 ml amaretto
30 ml cranberry juice

1. Shake ingredients with ice.
2. Strain into a 90–150-ml shooter glass.

Red-Headed German

Ingredients

Ice
30 ml Jägermeister
30 ml peach schnapps
30 ml cranberry juice

1. Shake ingredients with ice.
2. Strain into a 90–150-ml shooter glass.

LIQUEUR-BASED SHOOTERS

Surf your way to lunch with a monkey, and it will erase your mind

If not for Sidney E. Frank, the word 'Jägermeister' would probably not be part of modern bar vocabulary. He was the genius who marketed this German herbal liqueur during the 1970s. And what better way to sell a lot of a product than to create a novelty machine to go with it! That's when the Jägermeister tap machine was born. This machine chills the Jäger to –2°C. It has been a huge success internationally and is still going strong.

Oh, Sidney didn't stop there. Even though he was in his sixties during the 1980s, he knew that the key to marketing is to target pop culture. So he promoted Jäger by becoming the tour sponsor for Mötley Crüe, Metallica and a list of underground bands. He then started the annual Jägermeister Music Tour.

In the 1990s, Sidney promoted Jäger by hiring models to become his Jägerdudes and Jägerettes. They rode

Surfer on Acid

Ingredients

Ice
30 ml Jägermeister
15 ml coconut rum
30 ml pineapple juice

1. Shake ingredients with ice.
2. Strain into a 90–150-ml shooter glass.

Monkey's Lunch

Ingredients

Ice
30 ml banana liqueur
30 ml coffee liqueur
30 ml single cream

1. Shake ingredients with ice.
2. Strain into a 90–150-ml shooter glass.

around America on a fleet of Jäger Buses. He even created Jägermeister Trikes (Jäger Harley-Davidsons) to tour with the Jägermeister Music Tour and Band Program.

In 2000, Sidney was 81 years old, but that still didn't stop him. He lived long enough to promote the most explosive shooter of the millennium, the Jäger Bomb. He died in 2006.

ZOOM

Jägermeister was created in 1934 to serve medicinal purposes and to honour the German forestry administration. This is why there is the head of a deer and a poem in German on the label. The word *Jägermeister* means 'hunt-master' (Jäger = hunter, and meister = master). Jägermeister is made with 56 herbs, and most people think it tastes like cough medicine.

Mind Eraser

Ingredients

Ice
30 ml coffee liqueur
15 ml vodka
120 ml soda water

1. Fill a highball glass with ice.
2. Pour the ingredients in order into the glass.
3. Drink fast with a straw.

Clean Slate

The Mind Eraser has been around since the 1980s. Its novelty lies in the fact that you drink it really fast through a straw. Some people put two straws together. You can give it a modern update by using flavoured vodkas such as vanilla, chocolate, orange or raspberry. You could also substitute the coffee liqueur for espresso liqueur to give it an extra kick.

BOILERMAKERS

Pour, drop, splash and drink your way through the most popular Boilermakers

The Boilermaker started with two simple parts: a shot of whiskey followed by a chaser of beer. Then one day some man somewhere – presumably after a hard day's work as a boilermaker – sat in the local bar and thought to himself, 'I'm so tired that it would be much less trouble to just drop the shot in the beer, then drink the lot.' And the Boilermaker was born. American travellers now had a neat little bar-room trick to show off while they made their way by train and stage-coach from coast to coast. Of course this is all speculation, because no one knows the origin of the Boilermaker.

Today a Boilermaker has turned into a type of drink, the type in which you drop one liquid into another liquid, then drink

Car Bomb

Ingredients

20 ml Irish whiskey
20 ml Baileys Original Irish Cream
180 ml Guinness stout

1. Pour the first two ingredients into a shot glass.
2. Pour the stout into a pint glass.
3. Drop the shot into the pint glass and drink immediately.

Lunch Box

Ingredients

20 ml Southern Comfort
20 ml amaretto
90 ml lager beer
90 ml orange juice

1. Pour the first two ingredients into a shot glass.
2. Pour the beer and juice into a pint glass.
3. Drop the shot into the pint glass.

them both together. The most popular drinks in this category are represented on this page.

The Car Bomb is a yummy Boilermaker with an unfortunate and controversial name, and for this reason some bartenders refuse to serve it. It's said to have been developed in the 1970s from a shot called the Grandfather (a mixture of Irish cream and Kahlúa) to which Irish whiskey was added making it bubble up explosively.

Other Boilermakers you can try are a Sake Bomb (a shot of sake dropped into Japanese beer), a Jackknife (Jack Daniel's dropped into beer), and a Russian Ruffe (vodka dropped into beer).

In New Orleans, Tulane University students have been known to drop a shot of half citrus vodka and half blue Curaçao into a pilsner beer. The beer turns green, which matches the nickname of their sports team, the Green Wave.

Flaming Dr Pepper

Ingredients

180 ml lager beer
30 ml amaretto
15 ml 151 rum

1. Pour the beer into a pint glass.
2. Pour the other ingredients in order into a shot glass. Light.
3. Drop the flaming shot into the pint glass.

Jäger Bomb

Ingredients

45 ml Jägermeister
120 ml Red Bull energy drink

1. Pour the Red Bull into a highball glass.
2. Pour the Jägermeister into a shot glass.
3. Drop the shot into the pint glass.

CLASSIC CHAMPAGNE COCKTAILS

Pop your way back in time by trying some historic champagne cocktails

The Champagne cocktail appeared in the very first cocktail recipe book to be published, *How to Mix Drinks* by Jerry Thomas, which appeared in 1862. There are now dozens of variations, and the cocktail has featured in many films, including *Casablanca* in 1942, *An Affair to Remember* in 1957 and *Blast from the Past* in 1999.

Kir (rhymes with 'ear') is made with crème de cassis (blackcurrant liqueur) and white wine with a lemon twist. If you replace the white wine with Champagne, it's called a Kir Royale. It was named after a Frenchman, Félix Kir, who was mayor of Dijon in Burgundy after World War II, and popularized the drink in order to promote local products to help

Champagne Cocktail

Ingredients

1 sugar cube
5 dashes Angostura bitters
180 ml brut Champagne
Lemon twist garnish

1. Soak a sugar cube with the bitters.
2. Drop the cube into a Champagne glass.
3. Pour in the Champagne. Add garnish.

Kir Royale

Ingredients

15 ml crème de cassis
180 ml brut Champagne
Lemon twist garnish

1. Pour the crème de cassis into a Champagne glass.
2. Pour in the Champagne. Add garnish.

revive the economy. He served it at every official event, especially when he had international guests. Crème de cassis had been around since 1841, but the cocktails were simply known as 'crème de cassis and white', or 'crème de cassis and Champagne'. It took 100 years for them to get their names.

The French 75 first appeared in 1930, in *The Savoy Cocktail Book* by Harry Craddock. It was named after a French 75-mm gun used in World War I.

MAKE IT EASY

When making cocktails with Champagne, it's important to chill as many ingredients as possible before they go into the glass – especially the Champagne. You can even chill the glasses ahead of time if you want. Also, because you are adding sweetness to the drinks with juices, liqueurs, and purées, it's best to use a dry Champagne to balance.

French 75

Ingredients

Ice
45 ml gin
15 ml lemon juice
15 ml simple syrup
90 ml brut Champagne
Lemon twist garnish

1. Shake the first three ingredients with ice.
2. Strain into a Champagne glass.
3. Pour in the Champagne. Add garnish.

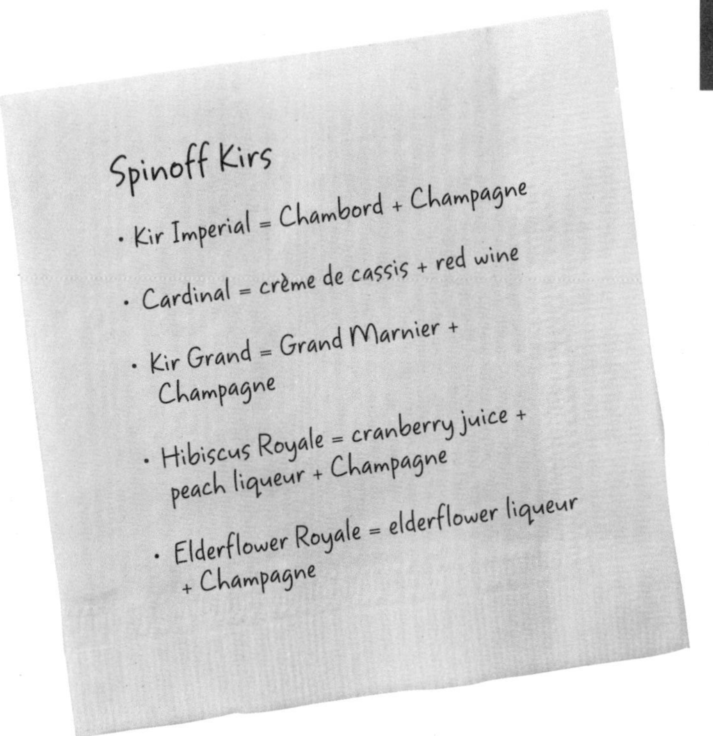

FRUIT CHAMPAGNE COCKTAILS

Adding fresh fruit juice, liqueur or purée to champagne is always a hit

The two most popular brunch cocktails are the Bloody Mary and the Mimosa. The Mimosa is believed to have been invented at the Ritz Hotel in Paris in the 1920s. One of the world's most famous hotels, the Paris Ritz has been visited by royalty and celebrities (Ernest Hemingway stayed there so much that the hotel named one of its bars after him), was home to Coco Chanel for 30 years, and was the building that Diana, Princess of Wales, left minutes before her death.

Owner and bartender Arrigo Cipriani invented the Bellini at Harry's Bar in Venice in the 1930s, and named it after Italian artist Giovanni Bellini. Harry's is another bar frequented by celebrities, again including Hemingway! The Bellini was

Mimosa

Ingredients

60 ml freshly squeezed orange juice
120 ml Champagne
Strawberry garnish

1. Pour the juice into a Champagne glass.
2. Pour in the Champagne. Add garnish.

Hibiscus

Ingredients

60 ml cranberry juice
120 ml Champagne

1. Pour the juice into a Champagne glass.
2. Pour in the Champagne.

invented for special occasions, but when it became a big hit Cipriani had white peaches shipped in specially. Of course, at a pinch you can make some yellow peach purée, but don't ever replace the fresh peach with peach liqueur. And don't replace the Prosecco with Champagne. Prosecco is an Italian sparkling wine with its own flavour. French Champagne does not pair well with the light, fruity flavour of the Bellini.

ZOOM

In the TV show *Sex and the City* the Flirtini is mentioned at a New York City rooftop party, when Samantha asks Carrie what she's drinking. Today you can twist it up by using pineapple vodka. One thing you don't want to do is shake and strain the vodka and pineapple juice first, because the pineapple juice is too frothy.

Bellini

Ingredients

60 ml white peach purée
120 ml Prosecco

1. Pour the puree into a Champagne glass.
2. Pour in the Prosecco.

Flirtini

Ingredients

15 ml vodka
30 ml pineapple juice
120 ml Champagne

1. Pour the vodka and juice into a Champagne glass.
2. Pour in the Champagne.

CELEBRITY CHAMPAGNE COCKTAILS

These famously fun concoctions will tickle your taste buds

American novelist Ernest Hemingway accomplished a lot in his lifetime. He won a Pulitzer Prize and a Nobel Prize. He also married four times and had three sons, as well as travelling extensively. And while travelling he visited every famous bar along the way. And if the bar wasn't famous when he got there, it was by the time he left.

While living in Key West, Hemingway had the chance to visit Cuba many times and created his own twisted Daiquiri, appropriately named the Hemingway Daiquiri (grapefruit juice and Maraschino was added), which he drank at the historic bar Sloppy Joe's. While in England he created a Champagne cocktail. It was called the Hemingway Champagne, but it had another name as well: Death in the Afternoon – the title of his 1932 book about bullfighting.

Admiral Nelson made such a name for himself that he's still commemorated every year on Trafalgar Day on 21 October.

Hemingway Champagne

Ingredients

60 ml absinthe
120 ml Champagne

1. Pour the absinthe into a Champagne glass.
2. Pour in the Champagne.

Admiral Nelson's Blood

Ingredients

30 ml ruby port
120 ml Champagne

1. Pour the port into a Champagne glass.
2. Pour in the Champagne.

He joined the navy at the age of 12, in 1771, and by the time he was 20 years old, he had worked his way up to the rank of captain. The Battle of Trafalgar was his decisive, and final, victory. He was shot by sniper fire on the deck of his ship.

The crew preserved his body in a barrel of rum so it would survive the voyage back to England. It's been said that by the time the ship made it back, the barrel was half empty because the crew kept taking sips of the rum. The rum in that barrel was dubbed Nelson's blood, a term that later lent itself to a Champagne cocktail.

If certain berries aren't in season yet, use some frozen berries.

Marilyn Merlot

Ingredients

Ice
30 ml Maraschino liqueur
90 ml Merlot wine
90 ml Champagne
Maraschino cherry garnish

1. Half-fill a wine glass with ice.
2. Pour in the ingredients. Add garnish.

Halle Berry Bubbles

Ingredients

Ice
15 ml blueberry vodka
15 ml Chambord
150 ml Champagne
Berries garnish

1. Half-fill a wine glass with ice.
2. Pour in the ingredients. Add garnish.

UNIQUE CHAMPAGNE COCKTAILS

Combine yummy ingredients to add some uniqueness to your glass of bubbles

One of the things that everyone should know about Champagne is that you can't call it or label it 'Champagne' unless it's made from grapes grown in the Champagne region of France. This is because of the 19 years of Champagne Riots between 1908 and 1927. Basically, the issue was about cheaper grapes being imported into the region by the Champagne houses so they could make more wine and therefore more money. The region's growers had suffered years of difficult vintages due to rain, hail and frost, and their crops had been devastated by the phylloxera epidemic when it eventually reached Champagne. Meanwhile, the market for Champagne was growing and the producers bought in

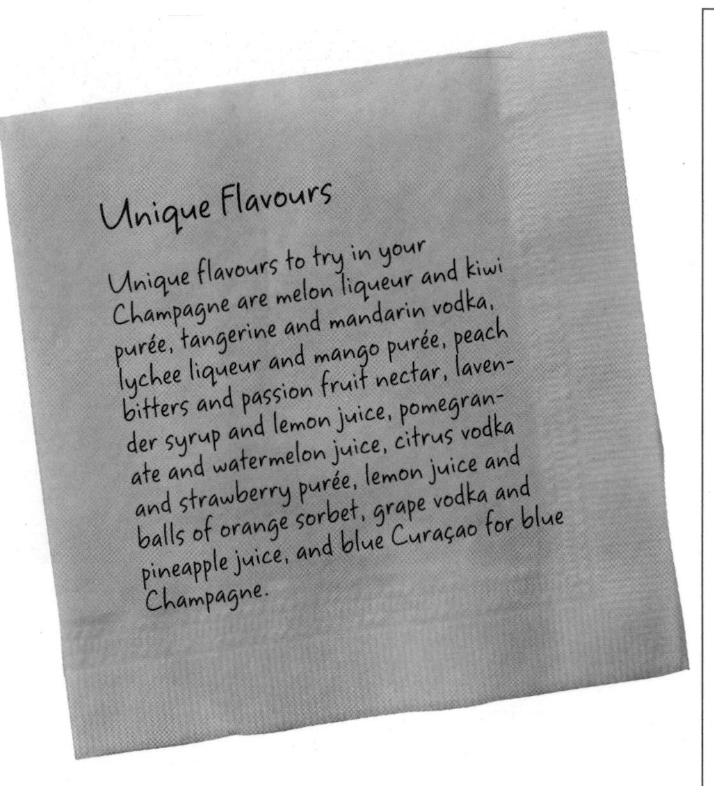

Cherry Vanilla Fizz

Ingredients

Sugar to rim glass
Ice
15 ml vanilla vodka
15 ml grenadine
15 ml lemon juice
150 ml brut Champagne
Cherry garnish

1. Rim a Champagne glass with sugar.
2. Shake the first three ingredients with ice.
3. Strain into a Champagne glass.
4. Pour in the Champagne. Add garnish.

grapes to meet the demand. The rioters (5,000 of them at times) rampaged and destroyed the imported grapes and everything else in their path. Finally, in the summer of 1927, a law was passed in France decreeing that all Champagne must be made in the Champagne region.

MAKE IT EASY

You can easily make your own candied ginger garnishes. All you need is 250 ml water, 200 g sugar, and 200 g peeled and chopped fresh ginger. Put them in a pan and simmer for 30 minutes. Drain the ginger pieces and lay them out to dry for 30 minutes, then sprinkle with more sugar.

Violet Pear Sparkle

Ingredients

30 ml Parfait Amour
30 ml lemon pear purée
120 ml brut Champagne
Edible flower garnish

1. Pour the first two ingredients into a coupe Champagne glass.
2. Pour in the Champagne. Add garnish.

Blood Orange Ginger Champagne

Ingredients

Ice
30 ml Domaine de Canton ginger liqueur
30 ml blood orange juice
180 ml brut Champagne
Candied ginger skewer garnish

1. Half-fill a wine glass with ice.
2. Pour in the ingredients. Add garnish.

PINK CHAMPAGNE COCKTAILS

Explore some fun, pretty-in-pink possibilities

Pink Champagne is a very romantic drink and can be very girly. Regular Champagne is made from only three grapes. No, one of them is not the adorable little Champagne grapes seen in the greengrocer's. The three grapes used are Pinot Noir, Pinot Meunier and Chardonnay. The Pinot Noir and Pinot Meunier are red, and the Chardonnay is white. All grape juice is white: even inside the red ones, the juice is clear. Only the skins have colour. So when making pink Champagne, winemakers leave the skins on a little longer to get a pink colour, much as they do when making blush and rosé wines.

Even though pink Champagne had been around a long time, not until the 1950s did it explode (no pun intended). The reason was that until that time the colour pink hadn't been used in fashion culture. All of a sudden there were pink Cadillacs, pink pumps, pink poodle skirts, pink lipstick, pink dresses, and even pink refrigerators and appliances. One icon

Bubblegum Bubbly

Ingredients

Ice
30 ml banana liqueur
15 ml peach schnapps
150 ml brut rosé Champagne
Bubblegum lollipop garnish

1. Half-fill a wine glass with ice.
2. Pour in the ingredients. Add garnish.

Tickled Pink

Ingredients

Pink sugar to rim glass
Organic rose petals
30 ml raspberry vodka
15 ml lemon juice
15 ml rose syrup
150 ml brut rosé Champagne

1. Rim a Champagne glass with pink sugar. Then drop in rose petals.
2. Shake the next three ingredients with ice.
3. Strain into a Champagne glass.
4. Pour in the Champagne.

from the 1950s, Elvis Presley, wore a pink shirt. It has been said that he had the shirt specially made because, well, quite frankly, there weren't any pink shirts for men at Sears and Roebuck. He was a true fashion trendsetter.

ZOOM

Pink Champagne is seen in the 1957 film *An Affair to Remember* starring Cary Grant and Deborah Kerr. They drink pink Champagne, then decide it's best not to be together (he's engaged, and she has a boyfriend). Later, arriving separately at the bar, each orders a pink Champagne cocktail without knowing the other's order until the drinks are on the bar.

Princess for a Day

Ingredients

Edible gold glitter or flake
15 ml blueberry vodka
30 ml strawberry-flavoured white cranberry juice
150 ml brut rosé Champagne

1. Rim a Champagne glass with edible gold.
2. Pour in the vodka and juice.
3. Pour in the Champagne.

Royal Treatment

You can have fun with the Princess for a Day at special occasion parties. You could provide tiaras or drop very large plastic jewels into the drink (large because you don't want anyone to accidentally swallow one). And on a romantic note, you could drop in a pink diamond engagement ring as part of your proposal.

FRENCH-INSPIRED CHAMPAGNE

Mix up these bubbly concoctions that are based on some fun French icons

The term *moulin rouge* translates as 'red windmill' (hence the red windmill on the building that houses the Parisian cabaret of the same name). Fox Studios gave us an idea of what the Moulin Rouge cabaret is all about when they released a film of the same name in 2001. Today the cabaret offers three shows daily. For the evening shows, you have an option to purchase a show ticket, a dinner ticket or a Champagne ticket. Champagne has been a staple at the Moulin Rouge since its opening in 1889.

Marie Antoinette was married at the age of 14 and became queen of France at the age of 19 in 1770. It is sometimes said that the coupe style of Champagne glass was created to

Moulin Rouge

Ingredients

Ice
150 ml sweet vermouth
15 ml sloe gin
150 ml Champagne
Mini-windmill cherry garnish

1. Half-fill a wine glass with ice.
2. Pour in the ingredients. Add garnish.

Marie Antoinette

Ingredients

20 ml St-Germain elderflower liqueur
150 ml Champagne
White edible flower garnish

1. Pour liqueur into a coupe Champagne glass.
2. Pour in the Champagne Add garnish.

replicate her breasts. Her husband, King Louis XVI, certainly hosted excessive parties at Versailles. Others dismiss this theory, because glasses of that shape were not used until the mid-19th century. Nonetheless, it makes a great story.

Bollinger Champagne is dubbed the 'James Bond Champagne', as it has featured in nine Bond films to date. Bollinger is one of the few Champagne houses that is family owned and managed, handed down from generation to generation since 1829.

ZOOM

The Champagne coupe was used for many vintage cocktails. You can see the saucer-shaped cocktail glass in films of the 1920s–50s. Martinis can be seen in glasses of this shape in several films, including *The Thin Man*, *After Office Hours*, *My Man Godfrey* and *The Philadelphia Story*. Set designers today often use incorrect glassware for period films.

007

Ingredients

Black sugar to rim glass
30 ml Blavod black vodka
15 ml lemon juice
15 ml simple syrup
90 ml Bollinger Champagne

1. Rim a Champagne glass with black sugar.
2. Shake the first three ingredients.
3. Strain into the Champagne glass.
4. Pour in Champagne.

Bond Drinking Habits

It's no secret that James Bond and alcohol, well . . . have a bond. To date, believe it or not, Bond has drunk 431 drinks on film. Sixty-five of them are Champagne. Some others include bourbon (57), Scotch (42), Vodka Martini (41), sake (37), brandy and cognac (24), gin (21), red wine (21), white wine (9), Americano (6), Vesper (4), Old Fashioned (4), ouzo (3), Stinger (3), Mint Julep (1), Mojito (1), Negroni (1), Rum Collins (1), and pink gin (1).

SUGAR-FREE CLASSICS

Make classic cocktails that are 100 per cent free of sugar

Are you tired of drinking your favourite alcohol with diet cola or plain soda water to avoid the sugar? It doesn't have to be that way. You can make practically every cocktail (and your favourites) without sugar. One trick is to replace the sugar with sugar-free simple syrup. You can learn to make your own in Chapter 19. Many restaurants and bars seem to offer only diet cola. But when you're in the supermarket looking for ideas, well, your head will spin with the flavour choices.

There are also some great sugar-free syrups on the market. They are available in many flavours so it will open up a world of ideas. For example, let's say you like Blackberry Mojitos; all you have to do is replace the simple syrup with sugar-free blackberry syrup and *voilà*! Maybe you like Strawberry Margaritas? Just make them with sugar-free simple syrup.

You can also try flavour extracts, used for flavouring cakes and desserts. Because they don't contain sugar, you can use

Skinny Mojito

Ingredients

Handful of mint leaves, plus a mint sprig garnish
30 ml lime juice
Ice
45 ml light rum
30 ml sugar-free simple syrup
Soda water

1. Muddle the mint and lime juice in a tall glass.
2. Fill with cracked or crushed ice.
3. Pour in the next two ingredients, then stir.
4. Top with soda water and stir. Add garnish.

Skinny Margarita

Ingredients

Salt to rim glass (optional)
Ice
45 ml tequila
Cap of orange extract
30 ml lime juice
30 ml sugar-free simple syrup

1. Straight up: Shake ingredients with ice. Strain into a chilled cocktail glass.
2. Rocks: Shake ingredients with ice. Strain into a Margarita glass filled with ice.
3. Frozen: Blend ingredients with half a cup of ice. Pour into a Margarita glass.

them to add flavour. Orange extract takes the place of the triple sec that would normally be in the Margarita and Long Island Iced Tea.

MAKE IT EASY

It's quite possible to order a sugar-free Long Island at the bar. Simply ask the bartender for the triple sec and sweet-and-sour to be omitted and replace the cola with diet cola. For the sour mix, ask for three lemon wedges, two packets of Splenda, and a rocks glass of water. Mix and pour into the drink.

Skinny Long Island Iced Tea

Ingredients

Ice
15 ml vodka
15 ml gin
15 ml rum
15 ml tequila
Cap of orange extract
30 ml lemon juice
30 ml sugar-free simple syrup
Splash of diet cola
Lemon garnish

1. Fill a tall glass with ice.
2. Shake all the ingredients (except the cola) with ice.
3. Strain into the glass.
4. Top with diet cola. Add garnish.

Skinny Whiskey Sour

Ingredients

Ice
45 ml whiskey
30 ml lemon juice
30 ml sugar-free simple syrup
Orange flag garnish

1. Fill a highball glass with ice.
2. Shake all the ingredients with ice.
3. Strain into the glass. Add garnish.

LOW-CARB COCKTAILS

Learn about the wide range of low-carb drink choices

Here are three low-carb cocktails to help springboard some ideas of your own. You should know that there are carbohydrates in fruits, vegetables, bread, rice, beans, pasta, grains and sugar, sugar, sugar. So that leaves proteins. But don't worry, you won't find any steak and egg Daiquiris. There is one liquid protein you can incorporate into a cocktail, and it's cream. Of course, the fat content is high because it's an animal product, but it contains zero carbs.

Fruit and vegetable juices sound healthy, and they are, but they are loaded with carbs. And fruit juice is loaded with sugar – natural sugar, but it's still sugar to your body. Any mixer you use for a low-carb cocktail will have to be sugar free. But you're in luck because there are so many choices! There are loads of sugar-free soda flavours. Just walk down the soft drinks aisle of your local supermarket, and you'll see plenty of possibilities.

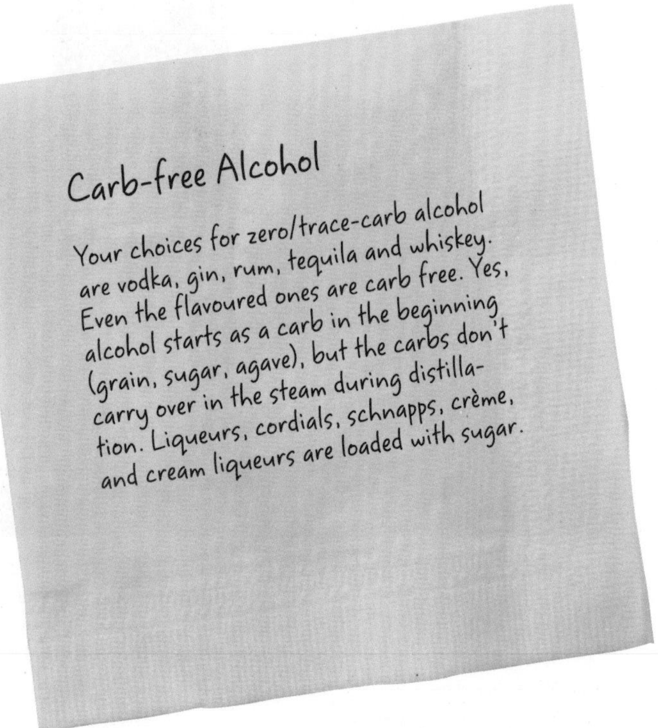

Skinny Raspberry Lemonade

Ingredients

Ice
20 ml raspberry vodka
20 ml citrus vodka
180 ml sugar-free lemonade
Lemon and raspberry garnish

1. Fill a tall glass with ice.
2. Shake all the ingredients with ice.
3. Strain into the glass. Add garnish.

YELLOW ● LIGHT

A lot of flavoured soda waters have hit the market recently and can be a little deceiving. The label may promise that it's 'Fat Free', because all sugar is fat free, but your body converts the sugar into fat. Always turn the bottle round and read the label to see if there's sugar in it.

Dip rim in the sugar-free syrup first so that the crumbs will stick.

Skinny Chocolatini

Ingredients

Crushed Oreo to rim glass
Ice
60 ml vanilla vodka
30 ml sugar-free chocolate syrup
60 ml single cream

1. Rim a cocktail glass with crushed Oreo.
2. Shake all the ingredients with ice.
3. Strain into the glass.

Skinny Pirate

Ingredients

Ice
45 ml Captain Morgan spiced rum
150 ml diet cola

1. Fill a highball glass with ice.
2. Pour in the ingredients.

ORGANIC VODKA & GIN DRINKS

Drinking green is easy when you have many organic spirit and mixer choices

Rain is organic American vodka that was ahead of its time. It hit the market in 1996 when people were walking around with pagers in their pockets and most didn't have a computer at home. Rain is made in small batches from 100 per cent organic white corn in Kentucky. The packaging is made from 100 per cent recyclable materials, and for every purchase the company donates money to the Wilderness Society. It has won several gold awards. Other brands have since followed its lead, and the organic spirits market is growing fast.

In Britain, the Organic Spirits Company produces Utkins UK5 vodka, using pure spring water and organically grown grain. The same company makes the world's only organic

Mary Me

Ingredients

Filtered ice
45 ml organic vodka
150 ml organic Bloody Mary mix
Variety of organic garnishes

1. Fill a tall glass with filtered ice.
2. Pour in the organic vodka and organic Bloody Mary mix. Stir.
3. Add organic garnish.

Day at the Spa

Ingredients

30 ml organic lemon juice
Chunk of organic cucumber peeled and sliced
3 sprigs organic mint leaves
Filtered ice
60 ml organic vodka
30 ml organic honey syrup
120 ml organic ginger soda
Mint sprig garnish

1. Muddle the first three ingredients in a tall glass.
2. Add filtered cracked or crushed ice.
3. Add the last three ingredients and stir. Top with garnish.

London dry gin, Juniper Green (which is also the only gin that is now actually distilled and bottled in London). The botanicals used in the recipe – such as juniper, coriander, angelica and savoury – are all organically grown.

GREEN LIGHT

Stay green and recycle the spirit bottles. All are beautiful and can be reused for a multitude of things. Make sure your cocktail glasses don't have chemical residue on them. Rinse them in vinegar and allow to air dry. And make sure your ice maker has a filter to eliminate chlorine.

Liquid Herb Garden

Ingredients

Filtered ice
45 ml gin
30 ml lavender organic simple syrup
15 ml organic lime juice
15 ml organic lemon juice
120 ml organic tonic water
Organic mint sprig and sprinkle of dried lavender garnish

1. Fill a tall glass with filtered ice.
2. Add the first four ingredients and stir.
3. Top up with tonic. Add garnish.

Juniper Treehugger

Ingredients

Filtered ice
45 ml organic gin
30 ml organic maple simple syrup
15 ml organic lime juice
15 ml organic lemon juice
2 dashes orange bitters
60 ml sparkling spring water

1. Fill a tall glass with filtered ice.
2. Shake the first five ingredients with filtered ice.
3. Strain into the glass.
4. Top up with sparkling water.

ORGANIC RUM & TEQUILA DRINKS

The tropics give a green light to eco-drinking set in a tropical paradise

A few organically produced rums are on the market: Papagayo Organic Spiced rum (from Paraguay), Matraga white rum (from southern Brazil), Utkins Fairtrade white rum (Paraguay) and Rivers Royal (Grenada). As for tequila, look for 4 Copas Tequila. No pesticides or chemicals are used in farming the agave plants, and the maker uses only organic yeast in fermentation.

Don't forget that you can infuse organic spirits with organic products. For example, for the Fresh Funky Monkey, you could make infused banana rum. Or chocolate rum. Vanilla rum would be yummy, too, by using organic vanilla pods. Also available is organic chocolate soy milk. For the Blueberry Eco-Mojito, you could make infused mint rum. If you don't

Fresh Funky Monkey

Ingredients

60 ml organic chocolate syrup
Filtered ice
60 ml organic rum
1 organic banana
90 ml organic soy milk
Organic shaved chocolate garnish

1. Squirt 30 ml of the organic chocolate syrup into one side of a tall glass.
2. Pour the rest of the ingredients into a blender with a cup of ice and blend.
3. Pour into the glass. Add garnish.

Blueberry Eco-Mojito

Ingredients

Handful of organic mint leaves
Handful of organic blueberries
30 ml lime juice
Ice
45 ml organic rum
30 ml organic raw simple syrup
Filtered sparkling water or organic soda water
Organic blueberry and mint garnish

1. Muddle mint, blueberries and lime juice in a tall glass.
2. Fill with cracked or crushed ice.
3. Pour in the next two ingredients, then stir.
4. Top up with sparkling water. Add garnish.

care for blueberries, simply replace them with another fruit such as organic strawberries, blackberries, peaches or black cherries. It's all up to you!

The Natural SeñoRita is basically an organic Margarita made with organic orange juice instead of the orange liqueur. You can also use other organic juices in its place. Pomegranate would be nice. While you're at it, you can infuse the tequila with many flavours, too!

GREEN LIGHT

Investing in a soda siphon will enable you to make your own sparkling water. You've seen such siphons in the old movies where people walk up to the home bar and squirt soda water into their drink. Even green bars are using them. Simply fill with filtered water.

Natural SeñoRita

Ingredients

Ice
45 ml organic tequila
30 ml organic orange juice
30 ml organic lime juice
30 ml organic raw simple syrup
Optional organic sea salt rim and lime garnish

1. Straight up: Shake ingredients with ice. Strain into a chilled cocktail glass.
2. Rocks: Shake ingredients with ice. Strain into a Margarita glass filled with ice.
3. Frozen: Blend ingredients with a half cup of ice. Pour into a Margarita glass.

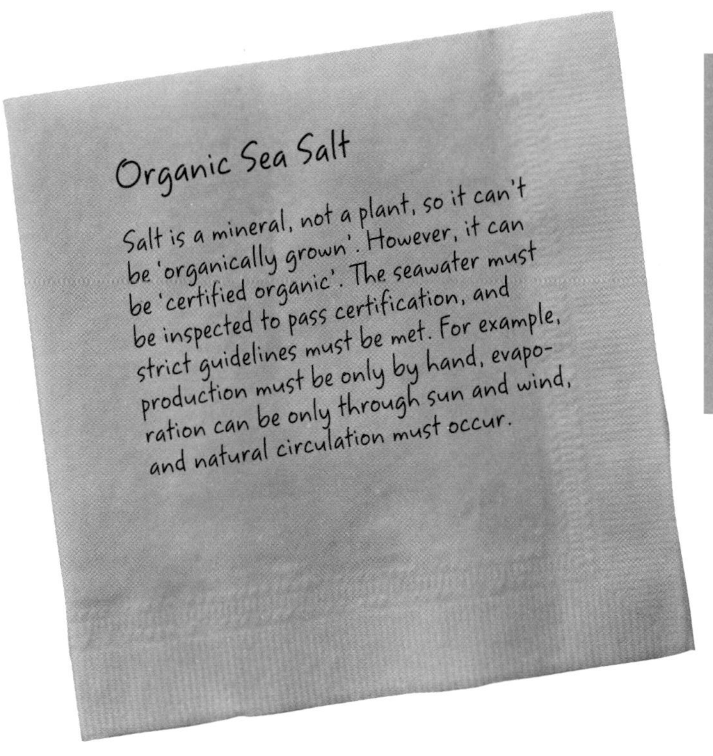

ORGANIC WHISKEY & BRANDY DRINKS

Pour, shake, and stir up some classic spin-offs with a green influence

Whiskeys and brandies are coming up behind in the organic race, but it's not because they aren't making an effort. There is more involved in these spirits. For starters, they are aged. Vodka, gin, rum and tequila can be distilled and poured straight into the bottle. Not whiskey or brandy.

So far the United States, Canada and Ireland haven't produced any organic whiskey, but Scotland has. The first is called Benromach, and it was the first single-malt whisky to be fully certified organic by the Soil Association. It's produced entirely by hand using traditional methods, pure spring water and organic barley and yeast. As for the casks used for ageing, the company imports American virgin oak casks made of wood that is harvested from environmentally managed forests. Two more Scotches are Highland Harvest and Da Mihle.

As for organic brandy and cognac, there are L&L, Guy Pinard and Lafragette.

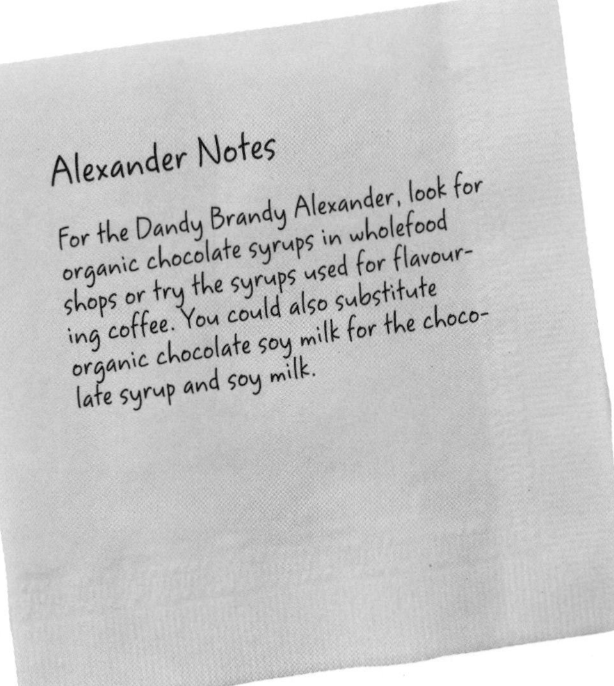

Bee Natural

Ingredients

60 ml organic single-malt Scotch whisky
30 ml organic raw honey syrup
Filtered ice
Organic lemon twist garnish

1. Pour the ingredients into a rocks glass and stir until honey is dissolved.
2. Add filtered ice. Add garnish.

If you're not able to find any of these organic whiskeys and brandies, focus on the organics of the mixers because you have a few decisions to make. For example, for the Bee Natural, the organic lemon is a no-brainer, but there will be a large assortment of organic honeys to choose from.

GREEN LIGHT

For the Radical Raspberry Sidecar recipe, you're not limited to that flavour. Look for other fruits you can make syrup or purée from. Flavourwise, the best choices are strawberries, blackberries, blueberries and peaches. Or you can leave the flavour out altogether and replace the fruit syrup with organic raw simple syrup.

Radical Raspberry Sidecar

Ingredients

Raw organic sugar to rim glass
Filtered ice
60 ml organic cognac
15 ml organic raspberry syrup
30 ml organic lemon juice

1. Rim a cocktail glass with organic raw sugar.
2. Shake all the ingredients with filtered ice.
3. Strain into the glass.

Dandy Brandy Alexander

Ingredients

Filtered ice
60 ml organic cognac or brandy
30 ml organic chocolate syrup
60 ml organic soy milk
Organic nutmeg sprinkle garnish

1. Chill a cocktail glass with filtered ice.
2. Shake all the ingredients with filtered ice.
3. Strain into the glass. Add garnish.

ANTIOXIDANT DRINKS

These drinks contain ingredients that are actually good for you!

What is so great about antioxidants? Well, antioxidants are found in all fruits, vegetables and things grown in the earth. Some foods are richer in antioxidants than others. When antioxidants enter our body they act like little doctors, running around repairing damage from the free radicals that have entered our system. Free radicals come from pesticides, pollution, cigarette smoke, and all the other things that aren't meant to be there. Doctors have long lists of the benefits of antioxidants. A few benefits include improved immune system, better vision, liver cleansing, cancer prevention and lower blood pressure.

Some ingredients on this page may be new to you. So, let's briefly go over some of them. Kefir is a cultured, enzyme-rich food filled with friendly micro-organisms that help balance your inner ecosystem. It's actually more nutritious than yogurt.

GSE (grapefruit seed extract) is a highly concentrated liquid made from the seeds of grapefruit. It has a multitude of uses.

Mean Green Tea

Ingredients

Filtered ice
60 ml organic vodka
30 ml organic raw honey syrup
60 ml organic lemon juice
60 ml organic green tea
1 teaspoon Spirulina powder (or 15 ml wheatgrass juice)
5 drops GSE
90 ml organic ginger ale
Organic lemon garnish

1. Fill a tall glass with filtered ice.
2. Shake the next six ingredients with filtered ice.
3. Strain into the glass.
4. Top with organic ginger ale. Add garnish.

Down the Rabbit Hole

Ingredients

Filtered ice
60 ml organic vodka
60 ml organic carrot juice
30 ml pomegranate juice
30 ml organic runny honey
120 ml organic yogurt
60 ml kefir
Handful of organic blueberries
Organic carrot stick and blueberries garnish

1. Blend ingredients with a cup of filtered ice. Add additional ice if needed.
2. Taste to determine sweetness and add more honey to taste.
3. Pour into a stemmed glass. Add garnish.

It should always be diluted with water and at full-strength should not come in contact with your skin. You can gargle with it, purify water with it, or clean anything with it (hospitals use it in operating rooms).

Spirulina comes from blue-green algae and contains many disease-preventive nutrients.

ZOOM

Many foods have antioxidant properties. Here are some juices at the top of the list that you can mix into a cocktail: blueberry, pomegranate, blackberry, raspberry, strawberry, fresh cranberry, apple, prune, plum, black cherry, red grape, carrot, wheat grass, and açaí. Other liquids include soy milk, kefir, green tea, white tea, aloe, GSE and red wine.

Fountain of Youth

Ingredients

Filtered ice
60 ml organic black cherry-infused organic vodka
30 ml açaí juice
15 ml aloe juice
30 ml organic cherry juice
30 ml organic lemon juice
90 ml organic pear cider
Organic cherry garnish

1. Shake all the ingredients (except the pear cider) with filtered ice.
2. Strain into a large stemmed glass.
3. Top with pear cider. Add garnish.

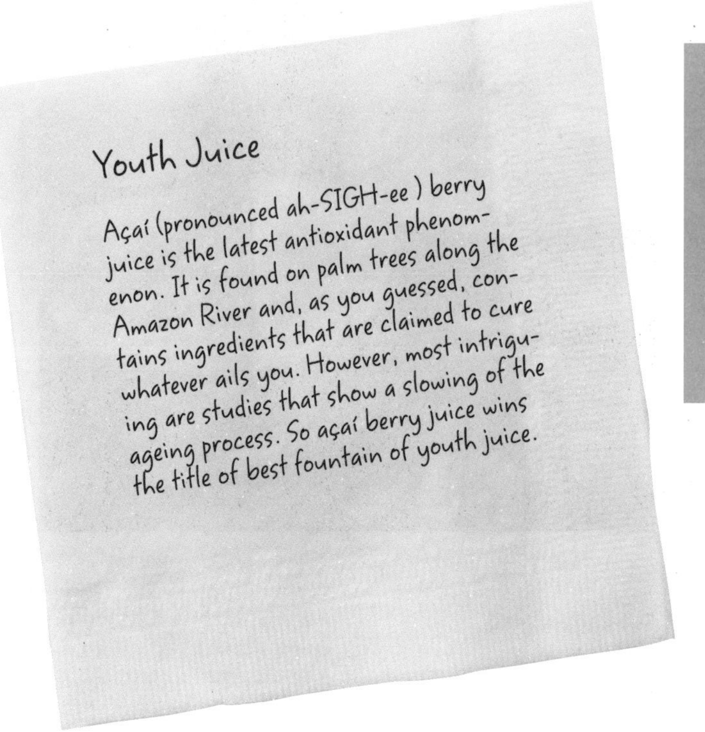

VALENTINE DRINKS

Shake up some love potions for the most romantic day of the year

Whether you're planning an intimate evening with someone you love or getting together with friends you love, these potions will melt your beating heart.

The Kama Sutra is made with cherry vodka, but that can easily be replaced with raspberry or strawberry vodka if that suits your taste buds better. The most important ingredient is the lemon juice, because you need the citrus to balance out the sweetness of the sugar rim. The Alizé liqueur is available in several flavours and colours; make sure you get the red passion flavour.

To notch up the fun with the Pucker Up, why not lipstick kiss the outside of the glass? If you can't find red candy lips for the garnish you could use fresh deep red rose petals.

Valentine's Day on 14 February is the traditional time for romantic declarations and over-the-top celebrations of love. There were two early Christian martyrs called Valentine,

Kama Sutra

Ingredients

Sugar to rim glass
Ice
30 ml cherry vodka
30 ml Alizé Red Passion liqueur
30 ml fresh lemon juice
60 ml Smirnoff Ice
Cherry garnish

1. Rim a cocktail glass with sugar.
2. Shake the first three ingredients with ice.
3. Strain into the glass.
4. Top with Smirnoff Ice. Add garnish.

Pucker Up

Ingredients

Ice
30 ml sour apple vodka
30 ml watermelon pucker schnapps
30 ml lime juice
Candy lips garnish

1. Chill a cocktail glass with ice.
2. Shake the ingredients with ice.
3. Strain into the glass. Add garnish.

and neither had a particular association with romantic love, but 14 February does coincide with the Roman festival of Lupercalia, which had connections with fertility. By the Middle Ages, when the rituals of courtly love were established, St Valentine's Day was firmly associated with lovers, and the tradition shows no sign of fading away.

ZOOM

Do you love those little sweets called 'love hearts'? They've been made in England since 1933. They carry many different messages (like 'Say yes', 'Be mine' or 'Kiss me'), so it's unusual to find any repeats in a packet. Americans have similar sweets called 'conversation hearts,' which have printed rather than embossed messages and have been manufactured since the 1860s.

Box of Chocolates

Ingredients

Chocolate syrup
Ice
30 ml vanilla vodka
30 ml butterscotch schnapps
30 ml Irish cream
30 ml single cream
Chocolate candy garnish

1. Swirl chocolate syrup into cocktail glass.
2. Shake the ingredients with ice.
3. Strain into the glass. Add garnish.

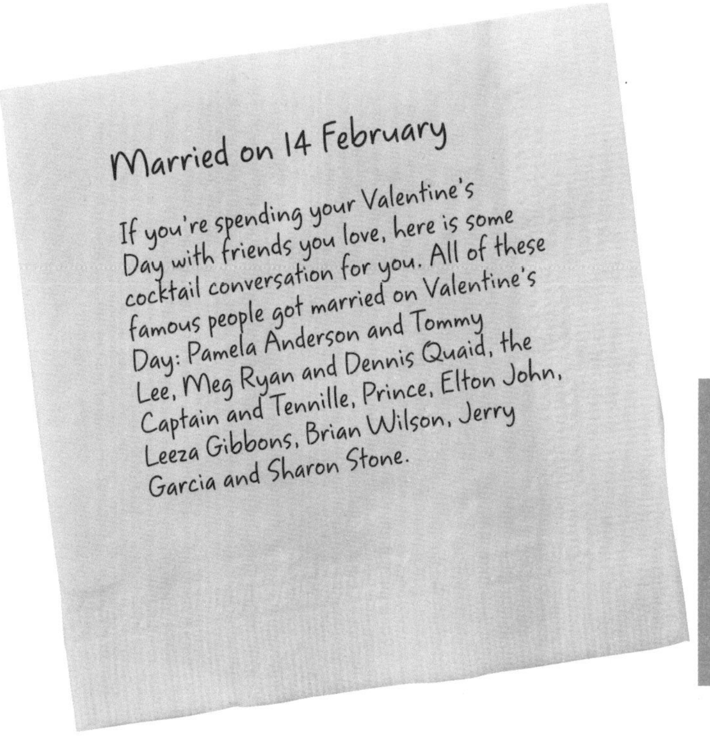

ST PATRICK'S DAY DRINKS

May the road (and these Irish drinks) rise up to meet you

A bar in San Francisco claims to make 2,000 Irish coffees a day. It's true! The bar is the Buena Vista Café, and it's been sitting at the corner of Hyde and Beach Street since the early 1900s. So how did Irish Coffee become famous in California when it's an Irish drink? Oh, that starts at Shannon Airport in Dublin. In 1952, Jack Koeppler (owner of the Buena Vista) was told about the coffee by a travel writer who frequented his bar. Jack wanted to duplicate the recipe, and they both tried many times but failed. So Jack flew to Ireland on the wings of intention to get the real recipe for Irish Coffee. He succeeded, and the rest is history. The recipe on this page is the one used at the Buena Vista Café.

A St Patrick's Day would not be complete without a green drink, so the Sweet Clover fits the bill. The recipe leans more toward what an Irish beauty's taste buds might welcome, so if you need to tweak it to be more of a manly Irish laddie

Irish Coffee

Ingredients

45 ml Irish whiskey
3 sugar cubes
150 ml freshly brewed strong black coffee
Whipped cream or double cream garnish

1. Preheat an Irish coffee glass.
2. Pour in the ingredients. Stir.
3. Garnish with whipped cream, or double cream poured over a spoon. Do not stir.

drink, then pour all the ingredients into a tall glass of ice and add an extra measure of whiskey.

ZOOM

The iconic American Lucky Charms cereal, with a leprechaun as a mascot, was created in 1963. The first lucky marshmallows were pink hearts, yellow moons, orange stars and green clovers. Others include purple horseshoes (1984), rainbows (1992), pots of gold (1994) and leprechaun hats (1996). British and Irish fans can buy Lucky Charms online from specialist importers of American products.

Even the colour matches the festive spirit.

Sweet Clover

Ingredients

Ice
45 ml Irish whiskey
30 ml melon liqueur
30 ml lemon juice
15 ml simple syrup
Washed and rinsed clover leaves for garnish

1. Chill a cocktail glass with ice.
2. Shake the ingredients with ice.
3. Strain into the glass. Add garnish

Lucky Charms-tini

Ingredients

Ice
45 ml blueberry vodka
60 ml strawberry milk
Handful of Lucky Charms cereal garnish

1. Chill a coupe-style glass with ice.
2. Shake the ingredients with ice.
3. Strain into the glass. Add garnish.

SUMMER PARTY DRINKS

Keep your cool by making some refreshing drinks for celebrating or just kicking back

To beat the heat, summer drinks should be mouth watering, light, refreshing, bubbly and, above all else, cold. The bounty of the season allows a wide assortment of fruits to be used, so you can let your imagination run wild, especially when you have so many fruity flavoured spirits to choose from as well. Let's take the Watermelon Kiwi Cooler. In cocktail terminology a cooler is wine with lemon-lime soda such as Sprite or 7-Up. So, this opens up other possibilities. You can use different wines, but make sure you stick with dry ones because you need to balance the sweetness of the soda you're adding. And if you need help finding what is available as a replacement for the lemon-lime soda, then just take a walk down

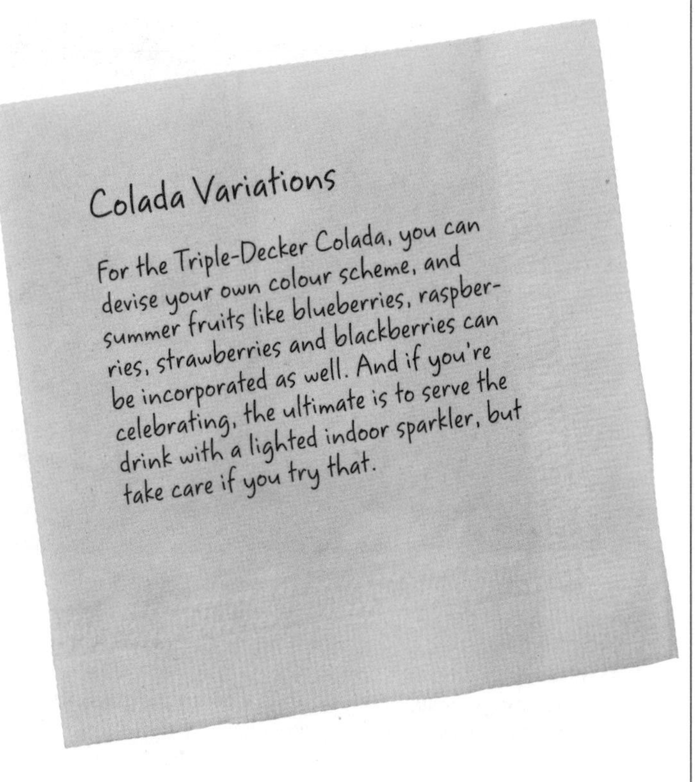

Triple-Decker Colada

Ingredients

15 ml grenadine
Ice
45 ml light rum
120 ml Piña Colada mix
15 ml blue Curaçao

1. Pour the grenadine into the bottom of a tropical glass.
2. Blend the rum and Piña Colada mix with a cup of ice.
3. Pour into the glass.
4. Float the blue Curaçao on top.

the soft drinks aisle in the supermarket. You can also choose sugar-free varieties. And you can add liqueurs and flavoured spirits. But keep the measures on the low side because you already have 120 ml of wine in the cooler to begin with. Other garnishes you can try are grapes, cantaloupe balls, nectarines, berries, cherries, cubes of pear, mango or pineapple, star fruit, star anise, edible flowers or citrus. It's really all up to you.

Provide cocktail sticks to make it easier to eat the garnish.

Watermelon Kiwi Cooler

Ingredients

Ice
120 ml dry white wine
30 ml lemon juice
120 ml lemon-lime soda
Watermelon balls and kiwi slices garnish

1. Half-fill a wine glass with ice.
2. Add all the ingredients and stir. Add garnish.

Strawberry Pom Lemonade

Ingredients

Ice
45 ml strawberry vodka
30 ml pomegranate juice
15 ml homemade lemonade
Lemon and strawberry garnish

1. Fill a tall glass with ice.
2. Shake all the ingredients with ice.
3. Strain into the glass. Add garnish.

HALLOWEEN DRINKS

Scare up some haunting and spooky drinks to get everyone in the spirit

Blavod black vodka is without a doubt the best Halloween spirit on the planet. It's the only black vodka in the world and has a multitude of uses in creating cocktail fun. The black-as-a-witch's-hat colour comes from catechu, which is extracted from the bark of sacred acacia trees found in India and elsewhere in southern Asia. Through the centuries, catechu has been used in medicine to cure colds, coughs, diarrhoea and fevers; boiled in water it has been added to baths to ease pain. It can be used as an astringent, breath freshener and body disinfectant. Commercially it's used for tanning, dyeing, preserving and printing. And in modern times it's best used for spooky-licious Halloween drinks. It doesn't affect the flavour:

Devil's Blood

Ingredients

Red sugar to rim
Ice
120 ml cranberry juice
45 ml black vodka

1. Rim a highball glass with red sugar, then fill with ice.
2. Pour in the cranberry juice.
3. Carefully layer the vodka over a spoon on top of the juice.

Rotten Pumpkin

Ingredients

Ice
120 ml orange juice
45 ml black vodka
Black sugar-dipped orange garnish

1. Fill a highball glass with ice.
2. Pour in the orange juice.
3. Carefully layer the vodka over a spoon on top of the juice.

Blavod black vodka tastes exactly like regular vodka, so there's no need to be afraid of the dark!

Also, don't be afraid to treat yourself and your friends to some tricks! You can give the black vodka extra interest by infusing it with a favourite flavour. This will open up a casket of possibilities. Also, why not drop in some lighted ice cubes? Glow sticks would be awesome in the Ghost Aura or any of these Halloween drinks. Wrapping them around the outside of the glass is a great option, too.

MAKE IT EASY

Liquid black food colouring became common on shelves a few years ago, and you should be able to find it in any cake decorating shop. If you can't find black vodka, then make your own! Simply put three drops of black colouring into a 750-ml bottle of vodka (or any other spirit, for that matter).

Ghost Aura

Ingredients

Ice
Grated coconut to rim glass
45 ml coconut rum
15 ml melon liqueur
150 ml lemon-lime soda

1. Rim a tall glass with grated coconut, then fill with ice.
2. Pour the first two ingredients into the glass. Stir.
3. Top up with lemon-lime soda.

Berry Scary-tini

Ingredients

Black sugar to rim glass
Ice
20 ml black vodka
20 ml blueberry vodka
30 ml raspberry liqueur
60 ml lemon juice
Raspberry garnish

1. Rim a cocktail glass with black sugar.
2. Shake all the ingredients with ice.
3. Strain into the glass. Add garnish.

WARMING WINTER DRINKS

These seasonal treats are just what you need on a dark, chilly night

The Honey Baked Turkey is a cold-weather variation on the ordinary, any-night cocktail nicknamed the Cosmo. Instead of vodka, this uses the award-winning Wild Turkey Honey Liqueur, which is made with honey, citrus, vanilla and, of course, bourbon. It's also 71 proof.

Hot Apple Pie is simple to make once the cider is warmed. The Tuaca makes all the difference. This Italian liqueur is sweet with vanilla, citrus and spices and makes a perfect combination with the warm cider. This drink is wonderful as a hot toddy, but if some family member has cranked the heat up, or in warm weather you crave something chilly and light slipping down your throat, then shake it up with ice, apple juice and lemon juice. It's equally yummy that way.

When family and friends are getting together, Blackberry Plum Wine is a warm and welcoming choice to offer guests as they arrive. It's perfect to make ahead of time and an easy

Honey Baked Turkey

Ingredients

Ice
60 ml Wild Turkey Honey Liqueur
30 ml lemon juice
30 ml cranberry juice

1. Chill a cocktail glass with ice.
2. Shake all the ingredients with ice.
3. Strain into the glass.

Hot Apple Pie

Ingredients

45 ml Tuaca
150 ml hot apple cider
Whipped cream garnish

1. Preheat a mug with hot water or set it in the microwave for 30 seconds.
2. Pour in the ingredients. Add garnish.

recipe to multiply to suit your guest list. The best thing is that you can make it with a less expensive red wine when you're catering for large numbers.

GREEN LIGHT

If you or your guests don't like plums and blackberries, then you can try many other autumn and winter fruit combinations with red wine. Possible variations include red apple fig wine, ginger pear wine and rhubarb orange zest wine. You can also replace the nutmeg with cinnamon, and there's nothing stopping you from using a pink or white wine.

Blackberry Plum Wine

Ingredients

Serves 4

1 750-ml bottle red wine
3 plums, sliced
175 g blackberries
1 teaspoon nutmeg
90 g sugar

1. Put the first three ingredients in a pan and bring to a simmer. Stir gently.
2. Stir in the nutmeg and sugar and simmer for 5 minutes, stirring gently.
3. Remove from heat and leave to infuse for at least 20 minutes before serving.

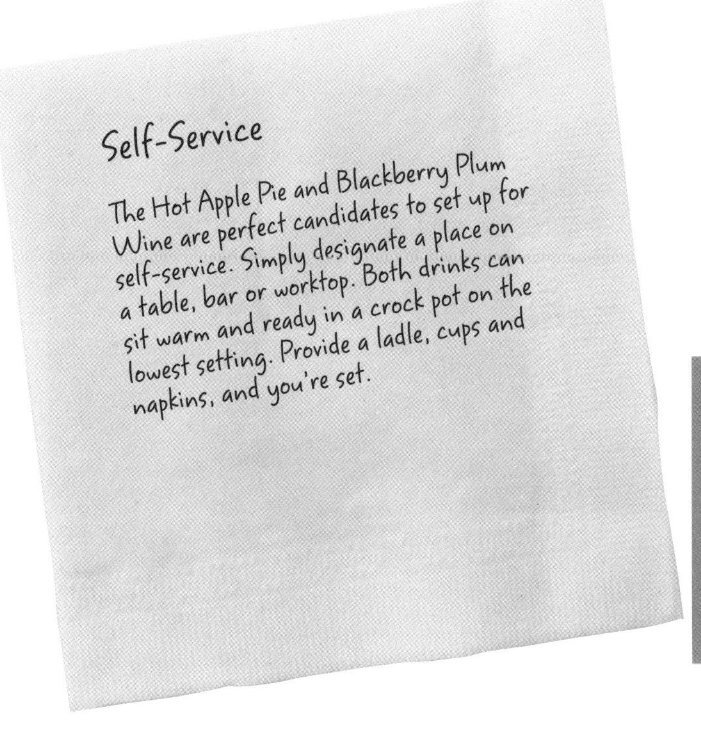

CHRISTMAS DRINKS

Get into the spirit of the season with some festive mixtures

Christmas is the exception to other festivities during the year because these days virtually the whole month of December is dedicated to celebration. So you need choices of drinks that vary in flavour and colour.

If you like coconut, chocolate and vanilla, then the ice blue Winter Wonderland is the perfect Christmas choice for you. To make the coconut-vanilla snowballs ahead of time, you'll need two baking trays, some vanilla ice cream and some grated coconut. Place one baking tray in the freezer, then spread the coconut on to the other tray. In assembly-line fashion, take a small scoop of ice cream, form it into a ball, then roll in the coconut. Place on the tray in the freezer and keep working like a North Pole elf until you've made the number of snowballs you need.

Dark rum is made with molasses, and when mixed with eggnog it creates a taste much deeper and richer than that

Winter Wonderland

Ingredients

Ice
60 ml coconut rum
30 ml white crème de cacao
Dash blue Curaçao
Coconut vanilla ice cream ball garnish

1. Chill a cocktail glass with ice.
2. Shake all the ingredients with ice.
3. Strain into the glass. Add garnish.

Molasses Eggnog

Ingredients

Ice
45 ml chilled dark rum
150 ml chilled eggnog
Nutmeg garnish

1. Chill a mug with ice.
2. Pour in the chilled ingredients. Add garnish.

of plain light rum or brandy. Aged and amber rums will work well with eggnog, and some people love spiced rum with it. It also tastes better if both the rum and eggnog start cold, so keep both in the fridge until you're ready to serve.

MAKE IT EASY

If you don't feel like crushing candy canes in your grinder or banging at it in a plastic bag, then make it easy on yourself and just drop a stripy sweet into the Candy Cane cocktail, or use a candy cane as a garnish. Browse around a Christmas sweet counter and you'll come up with lots of ideas.

Candy Cane

Ingredients

Crushed candy cane to rim glass
Ice
60 ml vanilla vodka
30 ml peppermint schnapps or white crème de menthe

1. Rim a cocktail glass with crushed peppermint candy.
2. Shake all the ingredients with ice.
3. Strain into the glass.

Mr Grinch Juice

Ingredients

Red sugar to rim glass
Ice
30 ml sour apple vodka
30 ml sour apple schnapps
60 ml lime juice

1. Rim a cocktail glass with red sugar.
2. Shake all the ingredients with ice.
3. Strain into the glass.

TRADITIONAL SANGRIA

Learn to create some traditional sangrias to help you grasp the basics

Sangria in its basic form is just wine, fruit, juices and spirit mixed together and topped with something bubbly. It's a kind of punch, often served by the jugful in bars, and although no one knows when the first sangria was made, it's believed to have a long history as a social drink in Spain and Portugal. A Spanish housewife probably needed to make some drinks for a convivial evening with friends, then looked to see what she had in her pantry and sangria was born.

The ideal way to prepare sangria is to allow most of the fruits to steep in the mixture overnight in the fridge to soak up the alcohol and flavour, but you can cheat and make it a few hours ahead as well. Fruits used mostly as decoration, such as

Spanish Sangria

Ingredients

Serves 8
1 750-ml bottle rioja
120 ml Spanish brandy
250 ml orange juice
120 ml lemon juice
50 g sugar
Orange slices
2 oranges, 2 lemons for garnish
Ice
750 ml soda water

1. Pour the first five ingredients into a jug and stir.
2. Add orange slices and leave in the fridge for 3–12 hours.
3. To serve, pour 180 ml sangria into fruit-garnished wine glasses half filled with ice.
4. Top up each glass with 90 ml soda water.

Italian Sangria

Ingredients

Serves 8
1 750-ml bottle Italian red wine
120 ml grappa
250 ml orange juice
120 ml lemon juice
50 g sugar
Orange and peach slices
2 oranges, 2 lemons for garnish
Ice
750 ml soda water

1. Pour first five ingredients into a jug. Stir.
2. Add orange and peach slices; leave in fridge for 3–12 hours.
3. To serve, pour 180 ml sangria into fruit-garnished wine glasses half filled with ice.
4. Top up each glass with 90 ml soda water.

star fruit, for example, can be added just before serving.

The red wine traditionally used in Spain for sangria is rioja. The sangria recipes below include ingredients that pertain to their countries of origin. Feel free to use other appropriate regional ingredients as well.

The overall taste of sangria should be slightly sweet. Different wines have different sweetness levels, but don't fret. If the sangria is too sour, then add more sweetener, and if it's too sweet, then add a sour note with more citrus juice.

MAKE IT EASY

One of the keys to sangria is the way you present the fruit. So think about the various ways you can cut fruit for the prettiest presentation. You can make balls, triangles, squares or circles from various fruits. If you have some interesting cookie cutters, you could press them into flat slices of large fruits such as pineapple and melons.

French Sangria

Ingredients

Serves 8
1 750-ml bottle French red wine
120 ml Grand Marnier
250 ml orange juice
120 ml lemon juice
50 g sugar
Orange slices
2 oranges, 2 lemons, and
175 g raspberries
Ice
750 ml soda water

1. Pour first five ingredients into jug. Stir. Add fruit slices and leave in fridge 3–12 hours.
2. To serve, pour 180 ml sangria into fruit-garnished wine glasses half filled with ice.
3. Top up each glass with 90 ml soda water.

Sangria Tips

- Less expensive wine works fine.
- Choose fruit in season.
- Serve over ice in garnished wine glasses.
- Try alternatives for soda water, such as lemonade.
- Try serving with bamboo skewers so that the fruit can be speared and eaten by your guests.

RED SANGRIA

Experiment with new flavours for your next gathering of friends

Now that you know the basics of sangria, you can branch out of the traditional and think up ideas of your own. First, determine what you have in your own fridge and storecupboard, then make a list of what you need.

Practically any liqueur, juice, spice, fruit or fizz is possible. As for spirits, you can use brandy, vodka, rum, gin, tequila and whiskey, in any flavours available. Liqueur choices abound, and juices can also be replaced with nectars and purées.

More flavour combinations to try include kiwi and strawberry, mango and vanilla, spiced pear, pineapple and ginger, raspberry and lychee, tangerine and clove, apple and amaretto, and chilli and lime.

To add a zing for your guests, you can also get creative by freezing fun edibles in ice cubes. For the recipes given here, you could make ice cubes with cherries, berries, pomegranate seeds or chopped apples, and lemons. Simply drop your

Chocolate Cherry Sangria

Ingredients

Serves 8

1 750-ml bottle red wine
120 ml cherry brandy
120 ml white crème de cacao
120 ml lemon juice
175 g maraschino or fresh cherries, stoned
Ice
750 ml black cherry soda

1. Pour the first four ingredients into a jug. Stir.
2. Add cherries and juice.
3. To serve, pour about 180 ml of sangria into fruit-garnished wine glasses half filled with ice.
4. Top up each glass with 90 ml black cherry soda.

Blackberry Apple Maple Sangria

Ingredients

Serves 8

1 750-ml bottle red wine
120 ml blackberry brandy
120 ml apple juice or cider
120 ml lemon juice
60 ml maple syrup
300 g blackberries, 2 red apples, and 2 lemons
Ice
750 ml lemon-lime soda

1. Pour the first five ingredients into a jug. Stir.
2. Add blackberries and apples.
3. To serve, pour 180 ml sangria into fruit-garnished wine glasses half filled with ice.
4. Top up each glass with 90 ml lemon-lime soda.

choice into the cavities of the ice trays, then fill with water and freeze. Continue the process over a number of days until you collect a nice big bowl of ice cubes in the freezer. That is, unless you have a large freezer and many trays that you can freeze at the same time.

ZOOM

At the 1964 World's Fair in New York, Spain spent US $7 million on building a romantic Spanish courtyard filled with Spanish art, music, flowers and fine dining. The air was filled with flamenco music as visitors strolled through the winding courtyard holding glasses of sangria. That just happened to be when the US was introduced to Spain's red wine punch.

For all sangrias, add the fruit after the initial ingredients & then leave in the fridge for 3-12 hours before serving.

Raspberry Pom Peach Sangria

Ingredients

Serves 8

1 750-ml bottle red wine
120 ml peach schnapps
120 ml pomegranate juice
120 ml lemon juice
2 peaches, 2 lemons, and 175 g raspberries
Ice
750 ml raspberry soda

1. Pour the first four ingredients into a jug. Stir.
2. Add peaches.
3. To serve, pour 180 ml sangria into fruit-garnished wine glasses half filled with ice.
4. Top up each glass with 90 ml raspberry-flavoured soda.

Red Chai Sangria

Ingredients

Serves 8

1 750-ml bottle red wine
120 ml Tuaca
120 ml apple juice or cider
120 ml lemon juice
1 teaspoon ground cinnamon
2 red apples, chopped
Ice
750 ml cream soda
Cinnamon candy garnish

1. Pour the first four ingredients into a jug. Stir.
2. Add apples and cinnamon.
3. To serve, pour 180 ml sangria into wine glasses half filled with ice.
4. Top up each glass with 90 ml cream soda and garnish with candy.

THEMED RED SANGRIA

Have vino-licious fun by stirring up some sangria on a theme for your friends

Without a doubt, sangria is a concoction meant to be shared with friends and family. There's no reason why you can't create a big jug or bowl to match a theme.

For a fiesta theme, go crazy with lots of colourful fruit, as if you were stuffing a piñata. The spirit used for Fiesta Sangria is tequila. You can replace it with flavoured tequila if you prefer.

Fiesta Sangria

Ingredients

Serves 8

1 750-ml bottle red wine
120 ml tequila
120 ml pineapple juice
120 ml orange juice
120 ml lime juice
60 ml agave syrup
Assorted colourful fruits
Ice
750 ml lemon-lime soda

1. Pour first six ingredients into a jug. Stir.
2. Add an assortment of fruit.
3. When ready pour 180 ml sangria into fruit-garnished wine glasses half filled with ice.
4. Top up each glass with 90 ml lemon-lime soda.

Agave syrup is also called 'agave nectar' and is made from the agave plant (which is the plant that tequila is made from). You can find it in wholefood stores.

The Midnight at the Oasis Sangria would be wonderful to serve at a party with an Arabian or desert theme. You could even whip some up for a midnight pool party! The name

Passionate Summer Holiday Sangria

Ingredients

Serves 8

1 750-ml bottle red wine
120 ml Alizé Red Passion liqueur
120 ml pineapple juice
120 ml lemon juice
60 ml honey syrup
300 g strawberries and 175 g seedless grapes
Ice
750 ml pink Champagne

1. Pour first five ingredients into a jug. Stir.
2. Add some of the fruit.
3. When ready pour 180 ml sangria into fruit-garnished wine glasses half filled with ice.
4. Top up each glass with 90 ml pink Champagne.

comes from the romantic song of the same title, and the song is filled with camels, cactus, belly dancers, harems, sultans, palm trees, a half moon and, of course, an oasis. Star fruit can represent the stars in the midnight sky, half orange slices look like half moons, raw sugar represents sand, and pineapple fronds stand in for palm trees. This romantic sangria also works for a romantic party of two.

YELLOW LIGHT

You'll notice ready-mixed sangria on the bottom shelf in the wine aisle. You don't want to buy these mixtures. They are for people who know nothing about sangria. Besides, they contain too much sugar and preservatives. Making your own is always better! However, the Lambrusco wine sitting next to these ready-made sangrias is worth using in sangria.

Midnight at the Oasis Sangria

Ingredients

Serves 8

1 750-ml bottle red wine
120 ml pineapple vodka
120 ml tangerine juice
120 ml lemon juice
50 g raw sugar
2 oranges, 175 g pineapple
Pineapple fronds and star fruit garnish
Ice
750 ml lemon-lime soda

1. Pour first five ingredients into a jug. Stir.
2. Add oranges and pineapple.
3. To serve, pour 180 ml sangria into fruit-garnished wine glasses half filled with ice.
4. Top up each glass with 90 ml lemon-lime soda.

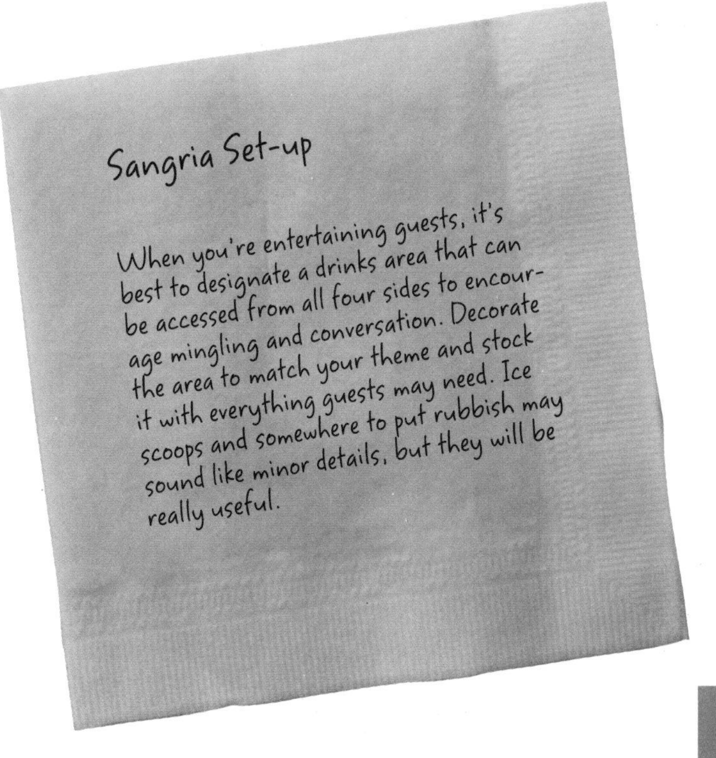

WHITE SANGRIA

Reach for a golden bottle of wine to make a lighter, yet still refreshing sangria

If you like traditional red sangria, you will love the white version! Some people prefer it, because it has a translucency that allows the beautiful fruit to shine through. White sangria is also known as Sangria Blanco, and the best wine to use for this is a dry wine like Sauvignon Blanc. This way the dryness of the wine will balance with the sweetness added to it. If you use a sweeter white wine like a Riesling or Chardonnay, you should balance the sweetness by adding more lemon or lime juice and omitting the sugar.

The pear brandy in the White Pear-adise Sangria can be replaced with pear schnapps or pear vodka. And if you don't care for honey, just substitute a sweetener of your choice.

Translucent Mixers

The classic white sangria is made with apple juice because for a long time light apple juice was the only translucent sweet juice available. Today you can also choose white grape or white cranberry juice. Lemon and lime juices are still great for the sour note needed to balance the sweetness in a white sangria, and clear spirit and liqueur choices are plentiful.

Classic White Sangria

Ingredients

Serves 8

250 ml apple juice
120 ml lemon juice
250 ml water
50 g sugar
2 cinnamon sticks
1 750-ml bottle cava
2 oranges, 2 red apples, 2 lemons, sliced
Ice
750 ml soda water

1. Gently heat the juices, water, sugar and spice for 15 minutes.
2. Stir in the wine and fruit and chill for 3–12 hours.
3. To serve, pour 180 ml sangria into fruit-garnished wine glasses half filled with ice; top up with 90 ml soda water.

Other flavours that would work well in this sangria include ginger liqueur, ginger ale, elderflower liqueur, peach and violet. Keep in mind that a violet liqueur or syrup would change the colour of the sangria to a light purple. This may or may not be something that appeals to you.

The White Granny Smith Mint Sangria can use sour apple schnapps in place of the sugar for a more intense green apple taste. The colour, of course, will change as well.

GREEN LIGHT

Remember that the wine you use can also be organic or alcohol free. Alcohol-free choices are great for children, pregnant women, designated drivers and other people who can't have or don't want to drink alcohol. You could always make one jug of non-alcoholic sangria and label it as such. Don't forget to leave out the spirit or liqueur as well.

White Pear-adise Sangria

Ingredients

Serves 8

1 750-ml bottle dry white wine
120 ml pear brandy
120 ml white grape juice
120 ml lemon juice
60 ml honey
2 pears, sliced
2 lemons, 300 g strawberries garnish
Ice
750 ml lemon-lime soda

1. Pour first five ingredients into a jug. Stir and add pears.
2. To serve, pour 180 ml sangria into fruit-garnished wine glasses half filled with ice.
3. Top up with 90 ml lemon-lime soda.

White Granny Smith Mint Sangria

Ingredients

Serves 8

1 750-ml bottle dry white wine
120 ml sour apple vodka
250 ml white cranberry juice
120 ml lemon juice
50 g sugar
Handful mint sprigs
2 Granny Smith apples and 2 lemons, sliced
Ice
750 ml soda water

1. Pour first five ingredients into a jug. Stir in fruit and mint.
2. To serve, pour 180 ml sangria into wine glasses half filled with ice. Top up each glass with 90 ml soda water and garnish with fresh mint sprigs.

THEMED WHITE SANGRIA

Learn how blondes have more fun when stirred up with festive creativity

The Tropical Luau Sangria can have so many flavourful substitutions and additions. Your favourite fruity flavoured sprits, such as mango, pineapple and mandarin, can be used; grated fresh coconut and cherries are options; and sweeteners such as coconut cream and sugar in place of the falernum would work. Taylor's Velvet Falernum, by the way, is a tropical syrup made in Barbados and used in many exotic drinks. It has a combination of flavours, including vanilla, lime, almond, ginger and cloves.

The goal of the Patriotic Sangria is to match the colours of the country of your choice; for red, white and blue you can use blueberries, strawberries, and stars. You could introduce

Tropical Luau Sangria

Ingredients

Serves 8

1 750-ml bottle dry white wine
120 ml coconut rum
120 ml white grape juice
120 ml pineapple juice
120 ml lemon juice
60 ml Velvet Falernum
Tropical fruits and flowers
Ice
750 ml lemon-lime soda

1. Pour the first six ingredients into a jug. Stir.
2. Add the fruit.
3. To serve, pour 180 ml sangria into garnished wine glasses half filled with ice.
4. Top up with 90 ml lemon-lime soda.

Patriotic Sangria

Ingredients

Serves 8

1 750-ml bottle dry white wine
120 ml strawberry vodka
250 ml white grape juice
120 ml lemon juice
50 g sugar
Strawberries, blueberries and star fruit
Ice
750 ml lemon-lime soda

1. Pour first five ingredients into a jug. Stir.
2. Pour 180 ml sangria into fruit-garnished wine glasses half filled with ice.
3. Top up each glass with 90 ml lemon-lime soda.

different colours by infusing star fruit slices in water with food colouring added in the fridge overnight.

Pool Party Sangria incorporates blue Curaçao so that it looks like a cool swimming pool. Make citrus rings to look like floats and throw in some grapes for beach balls. If you don't have blue Curaçao, replace it with triple sec and add a little blue food colouring. Also, you can easily change the name to 'Under the Sea Sangria' or 'Beach Party Sangria.'

Have fun and come up with your own themed sangria! Here are a few more ideas to spark your imagination. You could try the Colour Purple Sangria, made with violet syrup with plums and grapes, Billy Joel Sangria, made with a bottle of white and a bottle of red, or Kitchen Sink Sangria, made with whatever you have in your kitchen.

Pool Party Sangria

Ingredients

Serves 8

1 750-ml bottle dry white wine
120 ml blue Curaçao
250 ml white grape juice
120 ml lemon juice
2 lemons, 2 oranges, 250 g blueberries and 250 g seedless grapes
Ice
750 ml lemon-lime soda

1. Pour first four ingredients into a jug. Stir.
2. Add fruit.
3. To serve, pour 180 ml sangria into garnished wine glasses half filled with ice.
4. Top up with 90 ml lemon-lime soda.

Down Under Sangria

Ingredients

Serves 8

1 750-ml bottle dry Australian white wine
120 ml mango vodka
250 ml white grape juice
120 ml lemon juice
50 g sugar
2 kiwi fruits, 2 papayas and 2 mangos, sliced
Ice
750 ml soda water

1. Pour first five ingredients into a jug. Stir.
2. Add fruit.
3. To serve pour 180 ml sangria into garnished wine glasses half filled with ice.
4. Top up each glass with 90 ml soda water.

PINK SANGRIA

Tickle yourself and your friends pink by experimenting with rosy-hued wine

These days you can find stores on the internet that sell virtually anything you want in the colour pink. So why not have a pink sangria?

Pink sangrias are perfect for a girls' night in, a baby shower or a hen night, or for any celebration for a person who just loves pink. You can use any rosé wine or pink Champagne.

The Pretty in Pink Sangria is very versatile and can handle fun flavour changes with ease. You can experiment with cherry vodka with cherries, raspberry vodka or rum with raspberries, grape vodka with grapes, orange vodka with oranges, pear vodka with pears, and so forth. The Rose Parade Sangria is a little different from the other sangrias in this chapter

Pretty in Pink Sangria

Ingredients

Serves 8
1 750-ml bottle rosé wine
120 ml limoncello
120 ml white cranberry juice
120 ml pink grapefruit juice
120 ml lemon juice
2 pink grapefruit, sliced
8 lemon spirals and 300 g raspberries or strawberries
Ice
750 ml lemon-lime soda

1. Pour first five ingredients into a jug. Stir.
2. Add pink grapefruit.
3. To serve, pour 180 ml sangria into fruit-garnished wine glasses half filled with ice; top up each glass with 90 ml lemon-lime soda.

Rose Parade Sangria

Ingredients

Serves 8
120 ml cherry vodka
175 ml white grape juice
120 ml lemon juice
60 ml rose simple syrup
125 g white seedless grapes, 125 g cherries and 2 lemons
Rose petals to garnish
Ice
2 750-ml bottles rosé brut Champagne

1. Pour first four ingredients into a jug and stir in fruit.
2. To serve, pour 60 ml of the mixture into rose petal- and fruit-garnished wine glasses half filled with ice.
3. Slowly pour about 120 ml pink Champagne on top.

because it combines the wine and fizz by using Champagne (or another sparkling wine). Feel free to combine it with any flavoured spirit or liqueur of your choice. You won't be able to soak the fruit in this sangria because you can't pop the bottle until you're ready to serve.

Of course, any shape can be cut from watermelon flesh, but the hearts in the Pink Heart Sangria give it a feeling that you made it with love. And love is always hip.

MAKE IT EASY

Cutting fruits into lots of different shapes takes extra preparation time, but the visual effect is worth it. If it's not the season for star fruit, for example, you can slice up citrus wheels, then make angled cuts until you have a star shape. Taking strips out of the rind with a canelle knife before you slice the fruit will give you an interesting shape like a cogwheel.

Pink Heart Sangria

Ingredients

Serves 8

1 750-ml bottle rosé wine
120 ml watermelon schnapps
250 ml white grape juice
120 ml lemon juice
1 cantaloupe melon, balled, and 8 watermelon hearts
Ice
750 ml soda water

1. Pour the first four ingredients into a jug or large container. Stir.
2. Add the canteloupe balls.
3. To serve, pour about 180 ml sangria into fruit-garnished wine glasses half filled with ice.
4. Top up with 90 ml soda water and garnish with a watermelon heart.

Watermelon Hearts

To make the watermelon hearts, start with a seedless watermelon. Use a long knife to cut 12-mm slices across the melon. If your knife is not long enough, simply cut the melon lengthwise first, then slice up half rounds. Use a heart-shaped cookie cutter to cut out the hearts, or cut them freehand using a paring knife.

TWISTED CLASSICS

Learn how to twist and shake up well-known cocktails into something new

Party drinks should be fun. There should always be something unique about a party drink, whether it's the colour, garnish, flavour or name. Link it to the theme of your party if you can. Your goal when presenting party drinks to your guests is to see a look of excitement on their faces. When you see that look, you know you've succeeded.

Party drinks are perfect for small gatherings of ten or fewer. For more guests, I would suggest setting up a self-service table or bar with instructions and all the preparation of ingredients already taken care of. The best solution for larger crowds is to hire a bartender so you're not spending all your time cleaning the table or bar or making drinks for your guests.

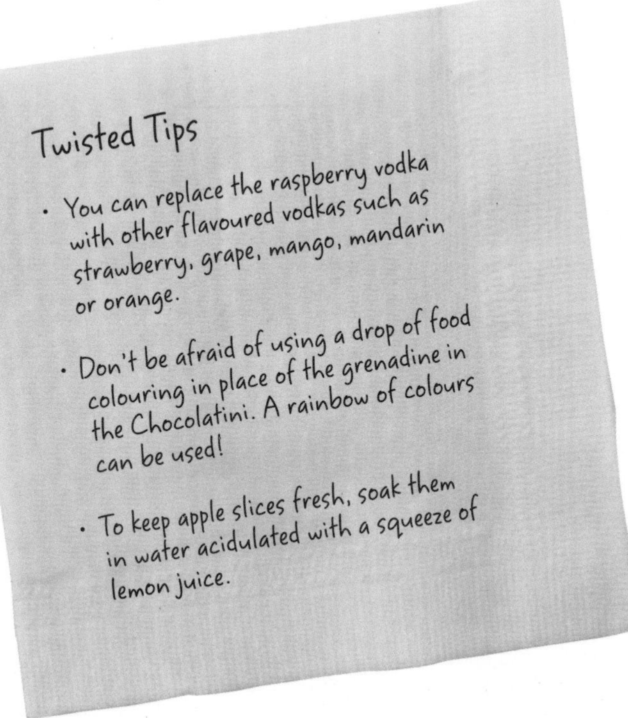

White Raspberry Cosmo

Ingredients

Ice
20 ml raspberry vodka
20 ml citrus vodka
20 ml Cointreau
15 ml fresh lime juice
60 ml white cranberry juice
Raspberry garnish

1. Chill a cocktail glass with ice.
2. Shake all the ingredients with ice.
3. Strain into the glass. Add garnish.

The best place to start with a party drink is a classic recipe for a well-known cocktail. Then twist it. Here we started with a Cosmopolitan, Chocolate Martini and an Appletini. The big twist on the Cosmo is using white cranberry juice in place of red cranberry juice. To bump up the flavour factor, we added raspberry vodka. 'Pink chocolate' sounds intriguing, so by adding a little grenadine you achieve a whole new presentation. And who can resist the playfulness of a gummy worm munching through an apple slice?

MAKE IT EASY

If you don't have a friend to tend your bar or a tame bartender you can ask, see if there's a bartending course run in your area, or try contacting your local catering college. Students are always looking for real world practice to hone their new skills.

Pink Chocolatini

Ingredients

Shaved chocolate to rim glass
60 ml vanilla vodka
45 ml white crème de cacao
7.5 ml grenadine

1. Rim a cocktail glass with shaved chocolate.
2. Shake all the ingredients with ice.
3. Strain into the glass.

Forbidden Appletini

Ingredients

Ice
60 ml citrus vodka
60 ml sour apple schnapps
Green apple slice and gummy worm garnish

1. Chill a cocktail glass with ice.
2. Shake all the ingredients with ice.
3. Strain into the glass. Add garnish.

FUN RIMMED PARTY DRINKS

Learn a whole range of ways you can rim a glass to grab immediate attention

Rimmed drinks scream fun, and fun is the main component needed for a great party drink. So far you've seen some great drinks in this book whose rims are crowned with assorted edibles. Now it's time to learn about other possibilities.

The first thing to consider is balancing the contents of the drink with the chosen rim ingredient. Both will be providing flavour and need to complement each other. For example, any cocktail with a sugar-based rim needs to have an element of sourness for balance.

The most basic drink rims consist of coarse salt or sugar. Salt can be coloured or mixed with a variety of flavours, such as chilli powder and other ground peppers, cracked espresso

Ultraviolet

Ingredients

Purple sugar and edible purple glitter to rim glass
60 ml Van Gogh açaí-blueberry vodka
7.5 ml Chambord raspberry liqueur
30 ml lemon juice

1. Rim a cocktail glass with the purple sugar mixture.
2. Shake all the ingredients with ice.
3. Strain into the glass.

Pop Star

Ingredients

Strawberry popping candy to rim glass
Ice
60 ml green apple vodka
60 ml sour strawberry schnapps
30 ml lemon juice
Star fruit slice garnish

1. Rim a cocktail glass with the strawberry popping candy.
2. Shake all the ingredients with ice.
3. Strain into the glass. Add garnish.

beans, citrus zest, ginger, rosemary, mint or sage. Sugar choices include using coarse crystals, granulated and castor sugar. These can be coloured or flavoured with spices such as cinnamon, but sugar rims give you much more scope because you can also use hundreds and thousands, hot chocolate powder or any hard candy sweets.

Other choices for special rims include crushed nuts, grated chocolate, frosted chopped cherries, shredded coconut, crushed biscuits and edible gold or silver flakes.

MAKE IT EASY

Crush ingredients for rims by putting them into a plastic bag and gently hitting with a heavy object. The ingredients you use will require different sticking power depending on their weight. For salt and sugar rims can be rubbed with lemon juice or dipped into liqueurs. Biscuit crumbs, coconut and chunky rims require something stickier, like golden or chocolate syrup or honey.

Insane Plantain

Ingredients

Lime zest and salt to rim glass
45 ml reposado tequila
30 ml banana liqueur
30 ml lime juice

1. Rim a cocktail glass with lime zest mixed with salt.
2. Shake all the ingredients with ice.
3. Strain into the glass.

Ring of Fire (Birthday Drink)

Ingredients

Ice
60 ml vanilla vodka
30 ml amaretto
30 ml Amarula cream liqueur
90 ml single cream
Assorted doughnuts and birthday candles for the special guest

1. Shake all the ingredients with ice.
2. Strain into the glass.
3. Set a doughnut on top of the drink.
4. Poke holes for the candles with a cocktail stick. Insert birthday candles.

FLOWER POWER PARTY DRINKS

Blooming ideas help you add an extra special taste to your cocktails

Flower power party drink ideas are plentiful! You can use flower-flavoured spirits, liqueurs, syrups, waters or garnishes to create flower-empowered drinks.

Flavoured spirit and liqueur choices on the market include elderflower liqueur, parfait amour, rose vodka and crème de violette. You can also make your own flower-flavoured spirits, syrups and waters by infusing fresh or dried flowers or using flower extracts.

Nontoxic flowers that can be used in cocktails include dandelion, rose, impatiens, violet, pansy, lilac, hibiscus, calendula, chamomile, marigold, cattail, gardenia, orchid, peony, chrysanthemum, carnation, gladiolus, jasmine, snapdragon, tulip and any flower from common culinary edibles such as citrus and herbs. However, you should always wash flowers gently before using unless you know they were grown organically or you've grown them yourself.

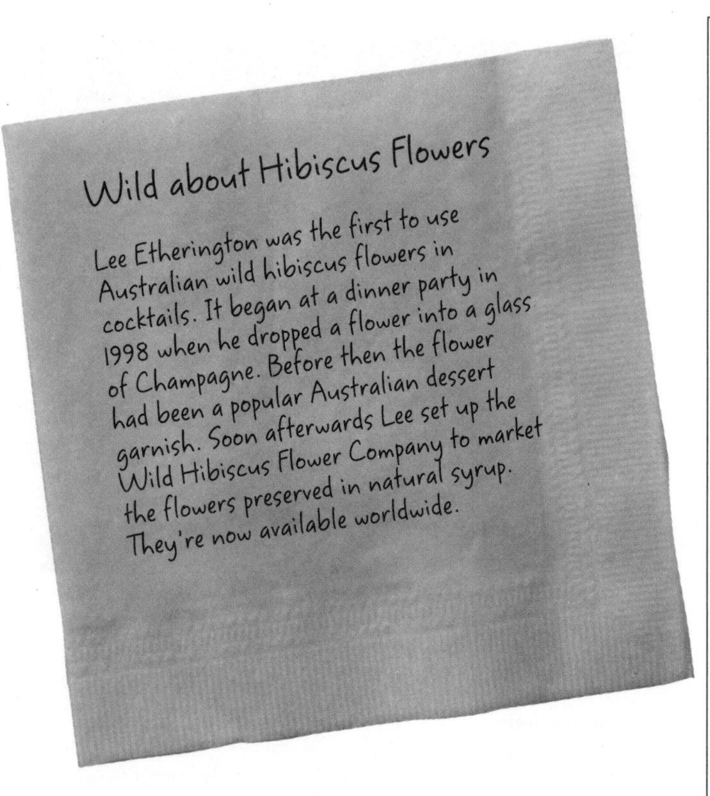

Tropical Hibiscus

Ingredients

Ice
30 ml mango rum
30 ml cranberry juice
30 ml pineapple juice
15 ml hibiscus syrup
90 ml dry sparkling wine or brut Champagne

Sugarcane stick and a wild hibiscus flower turned inside out for garnish

1. Fill a tall glass with ice.
2. Shake the first four ingredients with ice.
3. Strain into the glass, then top with sparkling wine. Add garnish.

Toxic flowers that you must never use include morning glory, lily of the valley, poinsettia, oleander, wisteria, sweet pea, azalea, daffodil, hyacinth, periwinkle, rhododendron, foxglove, bird of paradise, narcissus and nightshade.

The Tropical Hibiscus can be garnished with the wild hibiscus flower many ways. You can place it in the drink, float it on top of the drink, or skewer it. Perrier Jouet is the Champagne choice for Stop and Smell the Flowers because the bottle is painted with flowers, but you can substitute another Champagne if you prefer.

ZOOM

The flowering tea buds in Blooming Jasmine Toddy are imported from China. They are hand-sewn into rosettes but open quickly when hot liquid is added to them. Make sure you choose a large, pretty and thick glass that can be held when filled with the hot toddy. This is perfect for warming up a party in the dead of winter.

Stop and Smell the Flowers

Ingredients

Ice
15 ml rose vodka
15 ml elderflower liqueur
15 ml violet liqueur
15 ml lemon juice
120 ml Perrier Jouet Champagne
Spray of rose water
Rose petal garnish

1. Half-fill a wine glass with ice.
2. Add the first four ingredients.
3. Add Champagne, then spray the top of the drink with rose water.
4. Add garnish.

Blooming Jasmine Toddy

Ingredients

45 ml honey liqueur
15 ml lemon juice
Jasmine blooming tea flower
180 ml hot water

1. Pour the honey liqueur and lemon juice into a thick glass.
2. Place a jasmine blooming tea flower in the bottom of the glass.
3. Pour in the hot water.

ICE & LIGHT DRINKS

Hot ice drinks and glowing garnishes will light up your life

Nothing skyrockets a party mood faster than drinks that light up the night or the creative use of ice. Hopefully some of these ideas will help you spark ideas of your own.

Fortune Teller has an ice crystal ball that will be a great conversation starter for your guests. Ice balls can be purchased from internet companies or made from moulds found in novelty stores, or at a pinch you can freeze water-filled balloons. Keep the balloon shape as round as possible.

Ice cones frozen around straws have been around in tiki bars since the 1950s. Make your own by packing a paper cup with crushed ice, adding water (or juice), then sticking a pencil or chopstick in the middle to create a hole for the straw.

Tap water freezes cloudy because of chemicals and air bubbles. To make your ice creations as clear as possible, use filtered water. For crystal-clear ice, boil filtered water, then allow it to cool. Boil it again, and then it's ready to use.

Fortune Teller

Ingredients

Ice and ice ball
60 ml Hpnotiq
30 ml VooDoo spiced rum

1. Chill a cocktail glass with ice.
2. Place an ice ball in the cocktail glass.
3. Shake all the ingredients with ice.
4. Strain into the glass. Read your fortune.

Tiki Traffic Cone

Ingredients

Orange juice straw cone
Ice
45 ml dark rum
15 ml orgeat syrup (or amaretto)
30 ml red passion fruit syrup
30 ml pineapple juice
30 ml lime juice

1. Place the straw cone in a highball glass wide enough to fit the cone.
2. Shake all the ingredients with ice.
3. Strain into the glass.

Other fun ice you can try is dry ice. Put a large chunk into the bottom of a thick glass, then add ice on top of the chunk. Never store dry ice in an airtight container or touch it with your bare hands, especially if they are wet. Follow these simple precautions, and all will be fine. You can also freeze edibles in ice cube trays for extra fun. Try berries, coffee beans, herbs, fruits and so forth.

Starry Starry Night will appeal to artists everywhere. It was inspired by one of Van Gogh's most famous paintings, which was painted while he was in an asylum in 1889. To make 'black' black cherry vodka, simply add three drops of black food colouring to a bottle of black cherry vodka.

Starry Starry Night

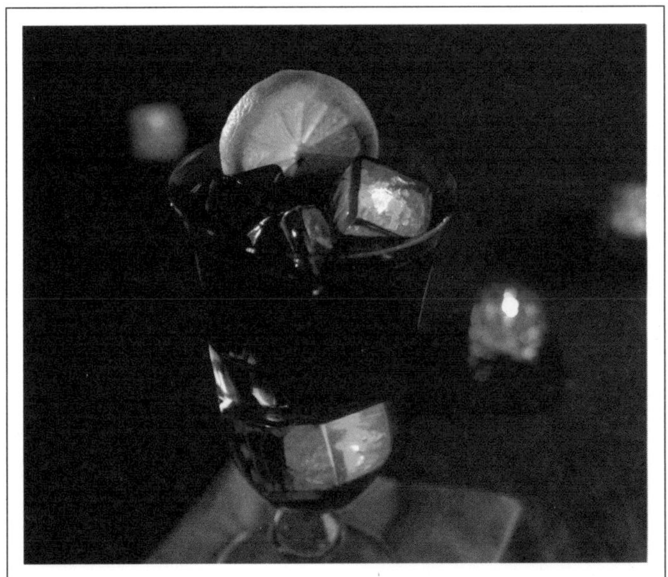

Ingredients

Blue ice cube lights
Ice
15 ml blue Curaçao
15 ml lemon juice
120 ml lemon-lime soda
45 ml black black cherry vodka
Lemon wheel

1. Place a blue light cube into the bottom of a tall glass, then fill with ice.
2. Pour in the blue Curaçao, lemon juice, and soda water.
3. Slowly layer the black black cherry vodka on top.
4. Add another blue light cube and a wheel of lemon.

Mexican Glow Worm

Ingredients

Glow necklace
Ice
45 ml blanco tequila
30 ml melon liqueur
30 ml lime juice
15 ml agave syrup
120 ml soda water

1. Slowly spiral a glow necklace into a balloon glass as you add ice.
2. Shake the next four ingredients with ice.
3. Strain into the glass, then top up with soda water.

FUN GARNISH PARTY DRINKS

Keep the party lighthearted by taking a little time to make some fun garnishes

Garnishes are the crowning touch to a drink, and guests always love to see something out of the ordinary sitting on top of or in their cocktail.

Everyone loves fortune cookies because they add a sense of whimsical magic. Why not dip some in chocolate? You could even add sprinkles and other decorations to them. Sloe Boat to China is the perfect tall, cool drink to have a dipped fortune cookie set on its rim.

The Black Leather String Bikini is a simple drink that smells like suntan lotion. If you prefer a Red Leather String Bikini, simply use red shoestring liquorice in place of the black.

You'll need to make a simple card template to make the

Sloe Boat to China

Ingredients

Ice
30 ml sloe gin
30 ml white crème de cacao
120 ml soda water
Chocolate-dipped fortune cookie

1. Fill a tall glass with ice.
2. Shake the next two ingredients with ice.
3. Strain into the glass, then top with soda water. Add garnish.

Black Leather String Bikini

Ingredients

Black bootlace liquorice
Ice
60 ml coconut rum
150 ml white cranberry juice

1. Slowly spiral black shoestring liquorice into a tall glass as you add ice.
2. Shake ingredients with ice.
3. Strain into the glass.

garnish for the Yin Yang-tini. Just turn the glass you will be using upside down on the cardboard and trace around the edge. Now draw the yin-yang design to fit the circle and cut it out. The chocolate buttons can be found in cake supply stores or sweet shops, or you can make your own by melting chocolate, spreading it out on silicone paper, and allowing it to cool. When it's set, find something around the kitchen like a bottle cap to use as a cutter to make small chocolate discs.

MAKE IT EASY

Other fun garnish ideas include stencils that fit the theme of the party, melon balls, chocolate-covered strawberries or a maple leaf for a drink that contains maple syrup. You can use shaped hole punches to cut shapes from citrus rinds, and cookie cutters to make shapes with sliced fruit. You'll also find lots of ideas in sweet shops.

Yin Yang-tini

Ingredients

Ice
60 ml vanilla vodka
60 ml dark crème de cacao
30 ml hazelnut liqueur
30 ml single cream
Grated white chocolate and chocolate buttons

1. Blend all the ingredients with half a cup of ice.
2. Pour into the glass.
3. Place a cardboard yin-yang template (see above) over one side of the top of the drink and sprinkle on grated white chocolate. Place the chocolate buttons on top of the drink.

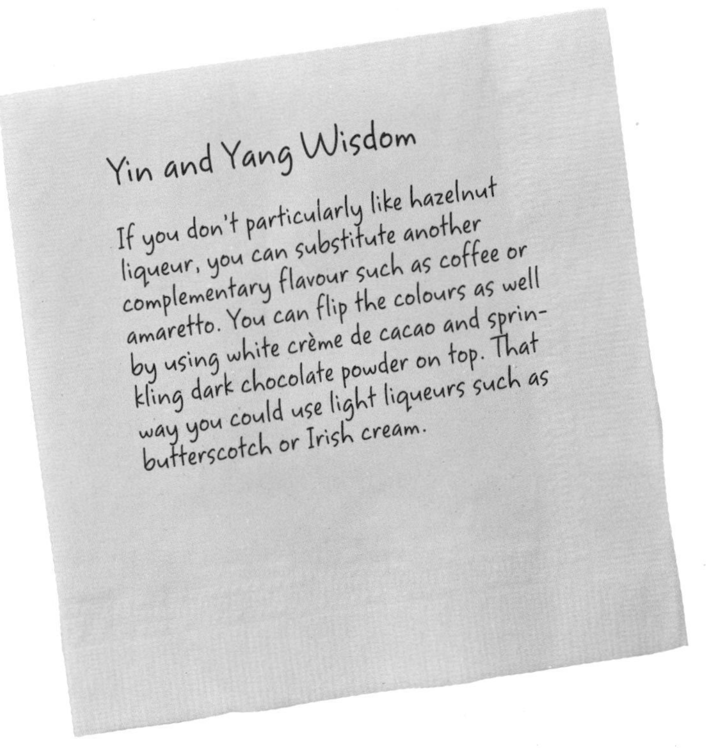

Yin and Yang Wisdom

If you don't particularly like hazelnut liqueur, you can substitute another complementary flavour such as coffee or amaretto. You can flip the colours as well by using white crème de cacao and sprinkling dark chocolate powder on top. That way you could use light liqueurs such as butterscotch or Irish cream.

SPECIAL-TOUCH PARTY DRINKS

Make some party drinks that require your extra personal touch

Sometimes party drinks require an extra touch. We've all seen the drink markers, rings and tags that keep everyone's drinks organized, so why not try some other ideas? One is to stick some of those translucent, rubbery window clings on to glasses. They come in a variety of designs and can be found in craft stores. They can even be cut down to size.

The cocktail Kiss My Glass is a clever idea to try. Simply slather on some lipstick and kiss the glass where your lips can fit. Be sure to leave enough of the surface unkissed for someone to hold the glass without lipstick all over their hand. This drink would be great for Valentine's Day, an anniversary, a romantic evening or just to flirt with the cutie across the room.

The Lucky Ladybird looks just like a ladybird. It could also be called the 'Watermelon', because it tastes like watermelon, and the chocolate dots look like watermelon seeds. You can experiment with lots of polka-dotted things! How about

Kiss My Glass

Ingredients

Dark pink, red, or white lipstick
Ice
60 ml X-Rated vodka
60 ml X-Rated fusion liqueur

1. Kiss the outside of a glass with lipstick.
2. Half fill with ice.
3. Shake the ingredients with ice.
4. Strain into the glass.

Lucky Ladybird

Ingredients

Dark chocolate
Ice
60 ml Southern Comfort
30 ml crème de noyeaux
60 ml orange juice

1. Melt the chocolate in a microwave.
2. Dip a finger in the chocolate and make dots inside a cocktail glass. Double coat if necessary.
3. Put glass in freezer to set.
4. Shake ingredients with ice and strain into the glass.

making a yellow drink and calling it the 'Itsy Bitsy Teenie Weenie Polka Dotted Bikini'? You could use white chocolate, too. And white chocolate can be made into any colour, so that leaves you free to experiment.

MAKE IT EASY

You'll need to make the Message Martini clear or white to be able to read the message. You can also experiment with other coloured thick syrups on the market. The little tubes of cake 'writing icing' work well, too. Just make sure that you strain the drink into the glass very slowly so as not to disturb your message.

Message Martini

Ingredients

Chocolate syrup
Ice
60 ml chocolate vodka
60 ml white chocolate liqueur
30 ml single cream

1. Write message inside a cocktail glass with chilled chocolate syrup.
2. Shake the ingredients with ice.
3. Slowly strain into the glass.

Chocolate Design Tips

- Transfer chocolate syrup to a condiment bottle for better control.
- Chilled chocolate syrup writes better and lasts longer.
- For more control, paint with chocolate using a small paintbrush.
- Place glasses in freezer to set.
- Use letters or numbers to write a message that fits the occasion. Remember that you'll have to write backwards.

TRADITIONAL PUNCH

Stir up some vintage bowls using centuries-old recipes handed down by our ancestors

The idea of mixing drinks with fruit juice and other flavourings is a very old one, and 'punch' is a general name for this kind of mixture. The word is said to come from the Hindu word *panch*, meaning a drink with five ingredients, which was brought to England from India in the 17th century. The earliest recipes were based on brandy, but when the English took control of Jamaica in 1655, Jamaican rum became the most popular base for punch.

Punch is mentioned in George Washington's diary, and Fish House Punch got its start among the founding fathers and their friends in Philadelphia in the 18th century. These influential men founded their own club and called it 'State in

Fish House Punch

Ingredients

Serves 20–25
1 litre fresh lime juice
500 ml fresh lemon juice
250 ml water
1 kg brown sugar
1 750-ml bottle dark Jamaica rum, chilled
1 750-ml bottle light rum, chilled
1 750-ml bottle peach brandy, chilled
Block of ice

1. Mix the freshly squeezed juices, brown sugar, and water together until all the sugar has dissolved.
2. Add the alcohol, then stir.
3. Serve in a bowl with a block of ice.

Wassail

Ingredients

Serves 20–25
2.5 litres unfiltered apple cider or juice
500 ml cranberry juice
115 g brown sugar
12 whole cloves
12 allspice berries
6 cinnamon sticks
3 large apples, chopped
1 large orange, chopped
1 750-ml bottle sherry
2 bottles brown ale

1. Put the first 9 ingredients into a large pan. Simmer gently for 1 hour.
3. Add sherry and brown ale. Stir gently.
4. Transfer to a crock pot and keep warm while serving.

Schuylkill Fishing Corporation'. They built a clubhouse near the Schuylkill River, created a special punch, and established the motto 'Fish, drink, and eat!' The club is still around today and is the oldest gentlemen's club in continuous existence in the world.

'Wassail' is a medieval word that basically means 'Your health!' Wassailing was also a popular tradition in which people walked from door to door with a big wooden bowl while singing, then yelled out 'Wassail!' as neighbours filled their bowl with ingredients to make punch.

MAKE IT EASY

Keep in mind that all punch recipes can be modified to fit your guest list. Simply guesstimate how many drinks your guests may drink, then adjust the recipe by doubling or halving the ingredients in the recipe. Punch servings are normally around 180 ml.

Whiskey Milk Punch

Ingredients

Serves 20

2 750-ml bottles blended whisky, chilled
3.5 litres whole milk
400 g sugar
3 tablespoons grated nutmeg
Extra nutmeg for garnish

1. Mix everything together in a large jug.
2. Place in fridge until ready to serve.
3. Pour cold into glass cups.
4. Grate a little nutmeg on top.

Pegleg Sullivan

It is believed that on 8 October 1871, Daniel 'Pegleg' Sullivan started the Great Chicago Fire, which killed hundreds of people, destroyed 10 sq km of the city and burned for three days. He was reported to have been stealing milk from a cow to make Whiskey Milk Punch when the cow kicked a lighted lantern into the hay.

ICE CREAM PUNCH

Have fun making some creamy sub-zero punches for your next party

Everything on the serving table for these ice-cold punches must be cold. For the root beer float punch, first clear out a space in the freezer to line up your glasses or mugs. Pour the vodka and schnapps into a jug, then place it and the root beer in the fridge. Fifteen minutes before your guests arrive you will need to arrange three large containers or bowls of ice on the punch table: they will hold the glasses or mugs, the ice cream and the root beer. Set the jug on the table and have plenty of straws, long-handled spoons (spoon straws would be a nice touch), and napkins.

Another presentation idea for the vodka and schnapps would be to freeze a block of ice around the bottles then funnel the mixture back into them. All you need is an empty rinsed 2-litre juice or milk carton. Just cut the top off, then set the bottle inside, fill with water, and freeze (the mixture won't freeze solid). When you're ready, simply peel off the carton,

Root Beer Float Punch

Ingredients

Serves 20–25
1 750-ml bottle vanilla vodka
1 750-ml bottle root beer schnapps
1 litre vanilla ice cream
4 litres cold root beer

1. Pour the vodka and schnapps into a jug and chill.
2. To serve, pour 60 ml of the cold mixture in the jug into frozen glasses or mugs.
3. Add 1 scoop of ice cream to each glass or mug.
4. Top up with chilled root beer.

Tropical Iced Punch

Ingredients

Serves 20–25
1 750-ml bottle coconut rum, chilled
2 litres pineapple juice, chilled
500 ml tropical fruit sorbet
2 litres chilled ginger ale
Pineapple flags garnish

1. Pour the first two ingredients into a jug and chill.
2. To serve, pour chilled mixture into a punch bowl.
3. Set the sorbet in the middle of the punch, then pour in the chilled ginger ale. Add garnish.

and you'll have a block of ice around a bottle. Pop a pourer on top, and you're ready to set it on a deep dish on the table. Your guests will love the extra-effort presentation.

GREEN LIGHT

Feel free to add tropical elements to the Tropical Iced Punch table: maybe you could arrange everything on straw mats or banana leaves. And add lots of multi-coloured straws and little paper umbrellas.

Fried Coffee Punch

Ingredients

Serves 20–25

1 750-ml bottle coffee liqueur
1 750-ml bottle Irish cream
2 litres cold coffee
500 ml vanilla and 500 ml chocolate ice cream, pressed together and frozen
60 ml 151 rum
1 teaspoon ground cinnamon

1. Pour first three ingredients into a large container and chill.
2. When ready to serve, pour the chilled mixture into a glass punch bowl.
3. Set the ice cream in the middle of the punch.
4. Pour 151 rum on top of ice cream, light, then sprinkle with cinnamon.

Fried Coffee Punch Tips

- Dim the lights after igniting the ice cream because the cinnamon sprinkle will create a mini fireworks display for your guests.
- Always be very careful when working with fire. Make sure there is nothing flammable around the punch bowl. Do not serve until the fire has died away.
- Rubber gloves help when working with the ice cream.

GLOBAL PUNCH

Try using ingredients that represent countries from around the planet to make themed drinks

Punch doesn't have to be served in a big bowl. Jugs can work just as well, and you can always have backup jugs in the fridge ready to pull out as one empties. For parties on the go or outdoors, large water coolers with taps work very well. Of course, these types of containers can be a little unattractive for a party, so feel free to cover or decorate them. Indoors you can also use large plastic containers with spigots, of the kind used for home brewing or wine making.

Keeping punch cold is a main concern. Back in the day, our founding fathers chipped blocks from frozen lakes to throw into the bowl. Today, thanks to modern conveniences, there are many creative ways to keep the punch cold. One of the

American Punch

Ingredients

Serves 10
500 ml Southern Comfort
500 ml Jack Daniel's
500 ml orange juice
500 ml pineapple juice
250 ml lemon juice
120 ml grenadine
Ice
Cherries garnish

1. Pour all the ingredients into a jug and stir.
2. Chill punch in the fridge until ready.
3. To serve, fill tall glasses with ice.
4. Pour in the punch. Add garnish.

German Punch

Ingredients

Serves 10
500 ml Jägermeister
500 ml peach schnapps
500 ml cranberry juice
500 ml pineapple juice
250 ml lemon juice
Ice
Peach garnish

1. Pour all the ingredients into a jug and stir.
2. Chill punch in the fridge until ready.
3. To serve, fill tall glasses with ice.
4. Pour in the punch. Add garnish.

most popular is to freeze water in a ring mould to float in the punch bowl. But you don't have to freeze only water. Why not freeze some of the mixer being used in the punch? You can also throw in some of the garnishes. More ideas include freezing garnishes in ice cube trays, freezing mixers in ice cube trays, using freezable plastic ice cubes, and using a bowl made of ice (see next page).

MAKE IT EASY

You can buy canned lychees in syrup in any supermarket, but fresh lychees are often available too. Their red skins against the white flesh look very pretty used as a garnish for the Asian punch: half peel the fruits to make the most of their appearance.

French Punch

Ingredients

Serves 20
1 750-ml bottle strawberry vodka
1 750-ml bottle Chambord
250 ml Grand Marnier
250 ml cranberry juice
250 ml lemon juice
1 bottle Champagne, chilled
Ice
Strawberry garnish

1. Pour all the ingredients except the Champagne into a jug and stir.
2. Chill in the fridge until ready.
3. To serve, pour into wine glasses three-quarters filled with ice.
4. Top with chilled Champagne. Add garnish.

Asian Punch

Ingredients

Serves 40–50
1 750-ml bottle sake
1 750-ml bottle lychee liqueur
1 750-ml bottle Hangar One Citron Buddha's Hand vodka
4 litres white cranberry juice
Ice
2 litres ginger ale, chilled
Lychee or fortune cookie garnish

1. Pour first four ingredients into a large container and stir.
2. Chill in the fridge until ready.
3. To serve, pour into wine glasses three-quarters filled with ice.
4. Top with chilled ginger ale. Add garnish.

ICE BOWL PUNCH

Chill out and impress your guests with your ice-sculpting skills

One of the main challenges with punch served in bowls is keeping the punch cold. You can make ice moulds by filling just about anything with water or mixer or even throw in a block of ice as our founding fathers did. But why not make the bowl itself out of ice? How cool is that? You can also freeze all kinds of items in the bowl to suit a party theme.

The only real issue with an ice bowl is what to set it on to absorb or drain the water when it is on the punch table. The best solution I've found is disposable nappies. The chemical inside them is sodium polyacrylate, which is extremely absorbent. Simply open a few nappies out flat over and around a plate, then lay an attractive cloth over the diapers and set the ice bowl on top. Decorate around the bowl.

Tap water was used for the Bowl of Cherries Punch and the Patriotic Punch. To achieve the crystal-clear ice seen in the Garden Party Punch, you will have to prepare the water. All

Ice Bowl Mould

- You need a large plastic bowl and a smaller plastic bowl to nest inside it.
- Half-fill the large bowl with water. More can be added later.
- Add weights to the smaller bowl until its rim is on a level with the larger bowl.
- Tape to secure and freeze. When ready to use, thaw for 15 minutes and the bowls will pop off.

Bowl of Cherries Punch

Ingredients

Serves 20–25
1 750-ml bottle cherry vodka
2 litres pink lemonade
2 litres grapefruit soda

1. Mix the vodka and lemonade in a jug. Chill in the fridge.
2. To serve, three-quarters fill the ice bowl with the vodka and lemonade.
3. Top up with cold grapefruit soda.
4. Replenish as needed.

you do is boil a large pot of water, then allow it to cool. Bring it to a boil again, and then it's ready.

MAKE IT EASY

The flowers were placed in the garden party bowl with the water before freezing, because they float. The bowl of cherries was frozen first, then microwaved for 15 minutes. The cherries were added, then the bowl was refrozen. The strawberries on the Patriotic Punch bowl will stay in place only if cocktail sticks are frozen into the rim of the bowl to set them on.

The ice in this bowl is crystal clear.

Garden Party Punch

Ingredients

Serves 20–25
1 750-ml bottle St-Germain elderflower liqueur
1 750-ml bottle pear vodka
4 bottles brut Champagne

1. Mix the liqueur and vodka together in a jug. Chill in the fridge.
2. To serve, divide the jug mixture into four equal parts.
3. Pour one part into the ice bowl and top with a chilled bottle of Champagne.
4. Replenish as needed using the same ratio.

Patriotic Punch

Ingredients

Serves 20–25
1 750-ml bottle strawberry vodka
500 ml blue Curaçao
2 litres lemonade
2 litres lemon-lime soda, chilled

1. Mix the vodka, blue Curaçao and lemonade in a jug. Chill in the fridge.
2. To serve, three-quarters fill the ice bowl with the mixture in the jug.
3. Top up with chilled lemon-lime soda.
4. Replenish as needed.

WARM PUNCH

Heat up your party by mixing batches of punch on those cold, wintry days

When it's cold outside, nothing warms friends' hearts more than whipping up a batch of warm punch.

The Hot Buttered Rum recipe is made without adding the dark rum to the mixture before serving. Some guests may not want alcohol for various reasons, and others may want to add as little or as much as they please. You'll also notice that there are three ways to use the mixture. If you want to store it in a container in the fridge, it should keep for one month.

For the Spicy Fruit Punch, you can also add fruits such as chopped apples, oranges and pineapples. And the cranberry and apple juice blend can be replaced with equal parts of cranberry juice and apple juice.

Hot Buttered Rum Mix Ideas

The mix can be added to 4 litres of hot water and poured into a crock pot. It can also be placed into ice cube trays, then frozen: simply pop out the cubes and store in a freezer bag until ready to use. When you want to make the punch, drop one cube into a cup, add the amount of rum you like, then fill with hot water.

Hot Buttered Rum

Ingredients

Serves 20–25
675 g brown sugar
225 g unsalted butter, softened
30 ml honey
1 tablespoon ground cinnamon
1 tablespoon ground cloves
1 tablespoon ground nutmeg
1 litre vanilla ice cream
1 750-ml bottle dark rum

1. Pour all the ingredients except the dark rum into a large bowl. Mix together. Keep mixture in the fridge until ready to serve.
2. Scoop 2 tablespoons of the mixture into a coffee mug.
3. Add 30 ml dark rum, then fill with hot water. Stir.

Gingerbread cookies can be served alongside the Gingerbread House Punch if desired. You can also use a variety of candy sticks as stir stick garnishes.

Always keep in mind that hot punches can be kept warm in an electric crock pot on a low setting. Simply supply your guests with a ladle, cups, garnishes, if any, and napkins.

MAKE IT EASY

Why not invite friends over for a gingerbread gathering? Serve the Gingerbread House Punch while making gingerbread man cookies. Or you can make gingerbread houses – hold a contest for the best house. Provide bowls of assorted sweets for decorations, icing, tools, tubes of icing and gingerbread squares.

Spicy Fruit Punch

Ingredients

Serves 20–25

225 g brown sugar
20 whole cloves
4 sticks cinnamon
1.5 litres cranberry and apple juice
500 ml pineapple juice
500 ml water
1 750-ml bottle Tuaca
500 ml Grand Marnier
Star anise garnish

1. Pour all the ingredients except the Tuaca and Grand Marnier into a large pan.
2. Simmer gently for 1 hour, then strain out spices.
3. Stir in the Tuaca and Grand Marnier.
4. Ladle into cups. Add garnish.

Gingerbread House Punch

Ingredients

Serves 20

2 litres chai tea
750 ml eggnog
1 750-ml bottle ginger liqueur
Cinnamon sticks or candy cane garnish

1. Mix the chai tea with the eggnog and heat gently.
2. Stir in the ginger liqueur.
4. Ladle into cups. Add garnish.

THEMED FOUNTAIN PUNCH

Create a centrepiece of flowing liquid goodness for all to enjoy

What better way to get the party started than to create a towering punch waterfall? Not only is it pleasing to the eyes, but also its trickling sound is soothing to the ears.

These fountain punch examples are themed to help give you some ideas for your party. Other occasions when a fountain would be appropriate are a graduation of any kind, hen party or bridal shower, reunion, anniversary, homecoming, retirement party, or any event that attracts a roomful of people. Try to set the fountain on a table away from the wall so that it can be approached from all sides. This setting commands attention and encourages conversation.

You should know a few things about fountains. First, you need to decide whether to buy or rent one. There are lots of party suppliers that will hire out small to extra-large, grandiose fountains that will keep up to 10 litres of punch cold because they contain a chiller. Until recently this was the only

Wedding Punch

Ingredients

Serves 50–60
3 750-ml bottles amaretto
1 750-ml bottle vanilla rum or vodka
11 litres whole milk
2 litres single cream
3 tablespoons ground nutmeg
Frozen milk cubes and clear light cubes

Option 1. Mix all ingredients together, then funnel into large jugs. Refrigerate.
Option 2. Fill fountain bowl with punch. Add more as needed.

Birthday Punch

Ingredients

Serves 40–50
2 750-ml bottles dark rum
2 750-ml bottles spiced rum
3.75 litres pineapple juice
3.75 litres pulp-free orange juice
3.75 litres lemonade
500 ml grenadine
Frozen ice balloons

Option 1. Mix all ingredients together, then funnel into large jugs. Refrigerate.
Option 2. Fill fountain bowl with punch. Add more as needed.

way to experience a fountain, and you normally saw them only at weddings. Now there are several small to medium-sized clear acrylic fountains on the market. They work very well but don't contain a chiller.

The Wedding Punch (which tastes like wedding cake) is kept cold with frozen milk cubes. The Birthday Punch is kept chilly with frozen water-filled balloons. Hint: let the balloons thaw a little so that the rubber thickens before placing them in the fountain. For the Baby Shower Punch, the rubber ducks were filled with water and frozen. Always think about creative ways to keep punch chilled without too much dilution and always keep backup punch in the fridge for refilling. For mixed drinking crowds you can put the cold mixer in the bowl and leave the alcohol next to it, allowing guests to choose to add or not to add alcohol.

Baby Shower Punch

Ingredients

Serves 40–50
2 750-ml bottles raspberry vodka
2 750-ml bottles citrus vodka
11 litres white cranberry juice
3–6 drops blue food colouring
Ice-filled rubber ducks

Option 1. Mix all ingredients together, then funnel into large jugs. Refrigerate.
Option 2. Fill fountain bowl with cold white cranberry juice. Either add cold vodka to the bowl or set beside the bowl.

Fountain Punch Tips

- Never pour into the fountain anything containing pulp, seeds, gelatine or ice cream, or anything small and chunky. Doing so will ruin the motor.
- Never let the fountain run dry because doing so will burn out the motor.
- The fountains shown here need 8–10 litres of liquid to start.

MODERN VODKA COCKTAILS

Discover possibilities using ingredients made from herbs and flowers

The first golden age of cocktails occurred during the first two decades of the 20th century. Bartenders took the art-form of crafting classic cocktails and new creations very seriously. But in America all this ended in January 1920 because of Prohibition. Eighty years later, around the millennium, the cocktail entered its second golden age. Bartenders and enthusiasts worldwide united to help preserve the craft of the cocktail. A museum was even established to celebrate the cocktail as an American icon. You can visit online at museumoftheamericancocktail.org.

Cocktails of today began simply from the desire to use the freshest ingredients possible. Soon after that there was a

Oz

Ingredients

Ice
45 ml rose petal and blue poppy seed-infused premium orange vodka
30 ml green Chartreuse
30 ml fresh Meyer lemon juice
Rose water

1. Chill a 120–180-ml cocktail glass with ice.
2. Shake all ingredients except the rose water with ice.
3. Strain into a cocktail glass.
4. Spray a mist of rose water across the top of the drink.

Dusk

Ingredients

Ice
15 ml pear vodka
30 ml St-Germain elderflower liqueur
30 ml crème de violette
30 ml fresh Meyer lemon juice

1. Chill a 120–180-ml cocktail glass with ice.
2. Stir all ingredients with ice.
3. Strain into a cocktail glass.

marriage of the kitchen and the bar, resulting in new buzz-words like 'bar chef' and 'mixologist'. This led to researching and mastering classic cocktails of the early 20th century.

Imaginative avant-garde mixologists today experiment with pink peppercorns, lemongrass, truffles, squid ink and bacon. They also incorporate historic ingredients such as bitters, falernum, absinthe and a variety of vermouths. Popular techniques include puréeing, muddling, misting, foaming, infusing, double straining and suspending. Other ingredients you may find in a modern cocktail include herbs such as sage, rosemary and coriander, flowers such as hibiscus, rose, elderflower and lavender, and fruits such as lychee, jackfruit and calamansi.

The Oz gets its name from the poppy seeds and flower petals used to infuse the orange vodka as well as the green Chartreuse, whose colour is reminiscent of the Emerald City.

When the sun sinks below the horizon, it produces dreamy colours across the evening sky. This time of day is called 'dusk'. The Dusk cocktail looks like one of those colours. Crème de violette was extinct for many years but has now been resurrected thanks to the demands of modern bartenders.

Tainted Virtue

Ingredients

Ice
45 ml Madagascar vanilla bean-infused vodka
15 ml Drambuie
15 ml raw simple syrup
30 ml cold espresso
60 ml fresh cream garnish

1. Chill a 12–180-ml cocktail glass with ice.
2. Shake all ingredients except cream with ice.
3. Strain into the cocktail glass.
4. Layer the cream on top.

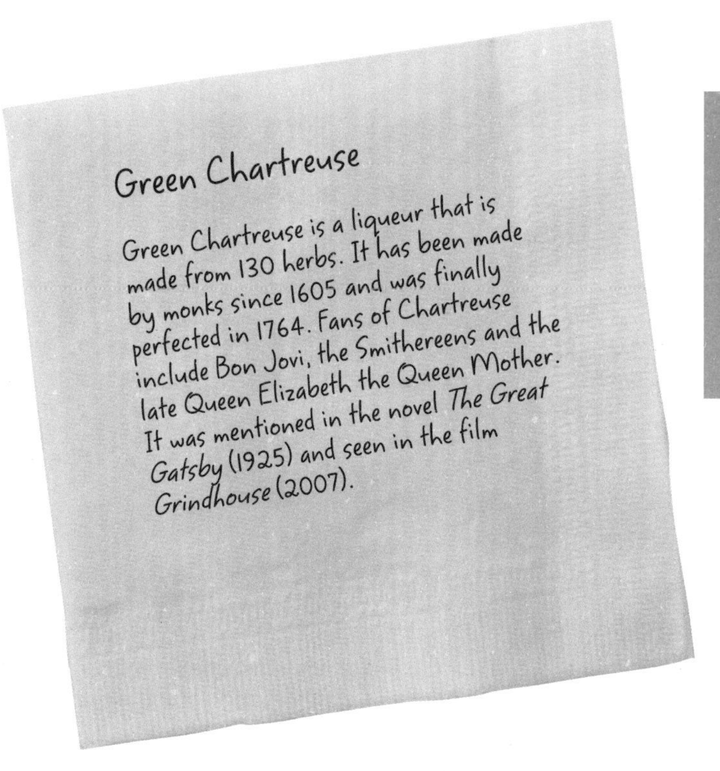

Green Chartreuse

Green Chartreuse is a liqueur that is made from 130 herbs. It has been made by monks since 1605 and was finally perfected in 1764. Fans of Chartreuse include Bon Jovi, the Smithereens and the late Queen Elizabeth the Queen Mother. It was mentioned in the novel *The Great Gatsby* (1925) and seen in the film *Grindhouse* (2007).

MODERN GIN COCKTAILS

Shake and strain the old and the new to create some delectable concoctions

Gin is one of the spirits that modern mixologists love to experiment with, because it embodies many herbs and botanicals; it has been featured in cocktail recipe books since 1862.

Modern bartenders love marrying fresh ideas with historic ingredients, and the Gypsy Bloodless Mary is a great example. The original Bloody Mary was made with gin, and this modern cocktail is a little twist on this tomato-based creation . . . without the tomato. Noilly Prat French dry vermouth has been handcrafted in the South of France, in the small village of Marseillan on the Mediterranean coast, since 1813. Celery bitters can be found in historic cocktail books but have not been available (commercially at least) since the mid-1900s.

Gypsy Bloodless Mary

Ingredients

Ice
Celery salt to rim glass
60 ml cucumber-infused gin
15 ml Noilly Prat dry
2 dashes The Bitter Truth Celery Bitters
Cucumber or celery garnish

1. Chill a 120–180-ml cocktail glass with ice, then rim with celery salt.
2. Stir all ingredients with ice.
3. Strain into the cocktail glass. Add garnish.

Pineapple Butterscotch Collins

Ingredients

Ice
30 ml pineapple-infused gin
30 ml butterscotch schnapps
30 ml pineapple purée
30 ml fresh Meyer lemon juice
120 ml fresh soda water
Pineapple garnish

1. Shake the first four ingredients with ice.
2. Strain into a tall glass or Collins glass of ice.
3. Top up with fresh soda water. Add garnish.

The Bitter Truth Celery Bitters is a recent introduction (2006), invented by Stephan Berg and Alexander Hauck in Munich. An online search will lead you to sites where you can obtain it in the UK. To make the lengthwise cucumber slice garnish, you will definitely need a slicer.

If you want to make fresh soda water for the Pineapple Butterscotch Collins, you'll need to invest in a soda siphon. The first soda siphon was patented in 1829 and it was used for many cocktails until the 1940s. This is why you see it so often in films from the 1930s–40s. The commercial production of bottled soda water caused the decline of the siphon, but modern bartenders love resurrecting vintage barware, so the modern soda siphon can be found in all cocktail bars dedicated to the craft. You simply fill it with filtered water and attach the charger, and it's ready to go.

Loose honeysuckle tea can be found at local tea merchants or online. To avoid bitterness, don't infuse the gin for the Suckle with the tea for more than four hours.

Suckle

Ingredients

Ice
60 ml honeysuckle tea-infused gin
30 ml Rhum Clément Créole Shrubb
30 ml fresh lemon juice
2 dashes Angostura bitters

1. Chill a cocktail glass with ice.
2. Shake all the ingredients with ice.
3. Strain into the chilled cocktail glass.

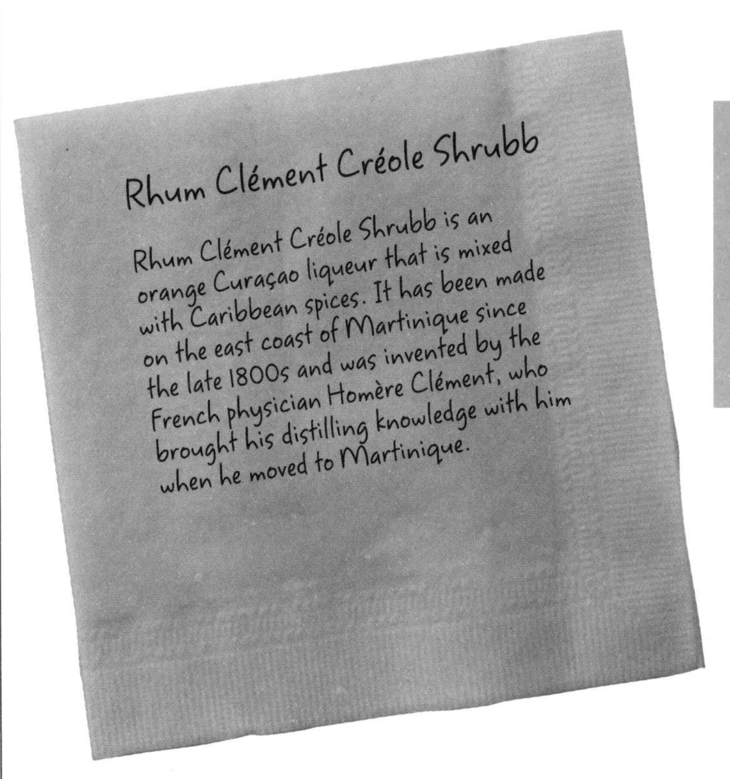

MODERN RUM COCKTAILS

Create extraordinary rum cocktails using out-of-the-ordinary ingredients

The cocktail name 'Kong' is a play on the banana rum and the strong flavour of the coffee. You can use any type of espresso beans you wish, but experts agree that Arabica beans have a balanced flavour. The cacao nibs are the beans that chocolate is made from. If you don't have the time to wait for all these beans to infuse your banana rum, just add 15 ml chocolate liqueur to the recipe to give the chocolate flavour. The pure vanilla whipped cream is achieved by adding a teaspoon of pure vanilla extract as you are whipping the cream. Look out for Mexican chocolate in specialist shops. This chocolate is unlike any chocolate you've ever tasted. It's mixed with spices and coarse-grained sugar.

Strong Kong

Ingredients

30 ml Arabica espresso bean and roasted cacao nib-infused banana rum
30 ml coffee liqueur
150 ml fresh hot coffee
1 teaspoon brown sugar
Pure vanilla extract, whipped cream, and Mexican chocolate chunk garnish

1. Pour all the ingredients into a coffee glass.
2. Stir. Add garnish.

Rhuby Slipper

Ingredients

Ice
45 ml rhubarb and strawberry-infused gold rum
30 ml fresh lime juice
30 ml falernum
120 ml dry white wine
60 ml fresh filtered soda water
Fanned strawberry garnish

1. Half-fill a medium wine glass with ice.
2. Add all the ingredients except for the fresh soda water. Stir.
3. Top up with fresh soda water. Add garnish.

When infusing the gold rum with rhubarb and strawberries to make the Rhuby Slipper, make sure you don't put the rhubarb leaves into the infusion because they are toxic. The stalk is the only part that is edible. Gardeners know to grow rhubarb on the outskirts of their garden for this reason. Falernum is the sweetening agent in this cocktail. It can be found in gourmet shops or online. You can also make the Rhuby Slipper by substituting the infused vodka with 30 ml strawberry vodka and 30 ml rhubarb liqueur, then use only 15 ml of the falernum.

When infusing the mango rum for the Heatwave, crack the peppercorns a little by placing them in a plastic bag and giving them a couple of good hits with something heavy. A variety of peppercorn types can be found in gourmet stores, including mixtures of white, black, pink and green peppercorns.

Heatwave

Ingredients

Fresh-ground cinnamon and organic sugar to rim glass
Ice
60 ml rainbow peppercorn-infused mango rum
30 ml tropical fruit purée
30 ml fresh Meyer lemon juice
2 dashes Angostura bitters
Mini-mango chequerboard-cut arched garnish

1. Rim a chilled cocktail glass with the cinnamon sugar.
2. Shake all the ingredients with ice.
3. Strain into the glass. Add mini-mango garnish.

Wild Hibiscus Mojito

Ingredients

3 wild hibiscus flowers in syrup and 3 peppermint sprigs
30 ml peppermint leaf and lime zest-infused light rum
30 ml fresh lime juice
30 ml wild hibiscus syrup
Ice
120 ml fresh filtered soda water
30 ml gold rum
Peppermint stem, inside-out wild hibiscus flower garnish

1. Muddle flowers and peppermint in a tall glass.
2. Add infused rum, lime juice, and syrup. Fill with ice and fresh filtered soda water.
3. Float gold rum. Add garnish.

MODERN TEQUILA COCKTAILS

Shake up some new cocktails Mexico would be proud of

The Blanco y Negro cocktail calls for Patrón XO Café, a tequila-based coffee liqueur that was introduced around 2004. Most coffee liqueurs are low proof and sweet. This one is 70 proof and not so sweet, so the addition of a little ginger-infused maple simple syrup (see page 215) is a good marriage.

Anyone who has ever driven around Florida has heard about the Indian River, because of the Indian River fruit stands seen everywhere. The river is 225 km long and runs along the Atlantic coast, and the fruit grown in the area is so luscious and juicy that the stands even offer to ship gift boxes. The Indian River Sage cocktail includes pineapple, a fruit introduced to Florida in 1860, and sage, which can be a little peppery, so the sweetness and spiciness of the two create a nice balance.

For the Tea-juana, you'll notice that there are two types of oranges listed. This is because thin-skinned Valencia oranges

Blanco y Negro

Ingredients

60 ml Patrón XO Café
15 ml ginger-infused maple simple syrup
Ice
30 ml fresh cream
White and dark chocolate stick garnish

1. Chill a 120–150-ml glass.
2. Shake the Patrón XO Café and ginger-infused maple simple syrup with ice.
3. Strain into the glass.
4. Gently float fresh cream. Add garnish.

Indian River Sage

Ingredients

Ice
60 ml 100 per cent agave blanco tequila infused with sage and pineapple
30 ml pineapple purée
15 ml Patrón Citrónge orange liqueur
2 fresh sage leaves torn in half
60 ml fresh lime juice
Sage sprig garnish, bruised to release aroma and oils

1. Chill a cocktail glass with ice.
2. Shake ingredients with ice.
3. Strain into the glass. Add garnish.

are best for juicing, and the thick-skinned navel oranges are best for making zests. Ginger beer originated as an alcoholic drink in England in the 1700s. Most commercial ginger beer no longer contains any alcohol, but the spiciness of the ginger means it does have a kick.

ZOOM

The most popular drinks made with ginger beer are the Moscow Mule and the Dark 'n' Stormy. The Moscow Mule was the very first vodka drink to be introduced to the USA in the 1940s. The inventor visited thousands of bars nationwide trying to spread the word about Smirnoff vodka. The Dark 'n' Stormy was invented in Bermuda.

Tea-juana

Ingredients

Ice
60 ml 100 per cent agave reposado tequila infused with carrot cake tea
30 ml fresh Meyer lemon juice
30 ml fresh Valencia orange juice
30 ml date purée
90 ml ginger beer
Navel orange zest garnish

1. Chill a cocktail glass with ice.
2. Shake the tequila, juices and purée with ice.
3. Strain into the glass.
4. Add ginger beer. Add garnish.

Carrot Cake Tea

Carrot cake tea is a popular herbal tea blend in America, made with carrot, rooibos (redbush tea), cinnamon and walnuts. To make carrot cake tea-infused tequila, pour a bottle of tequila into a sterile, wide-mouthed jar and add 250 ml loose tea. Let it infuse for not more than 3–4 hours. Agitate, then strain and funnel into a sterile bottle. If you can't get hold of any carrot cake tea, you could try making your own mix of its ingredients for the infusion.

MODERN WHISKEY COCKTAILS

Pour some whiskey cocktails using ingredients you've never thought possible

Try the first three modern whiskey cocktails on an autumn or winter day and the fourth in the spring or summer.

To make the walnut-infused Woodford bourbon for Knock on Wood, you'll need to toast 115 g unshelled walnuts at 200°C for 20 minutes, then leave them to cool. Pour a bottle of bourbon into a wide-mouthed jar and add the walnuts. Leave it to infuse for a week, shaking the jar daily. When it's finished, simply strain the bourbon and funnel it into a sterilized bottle.

If it's not the right season for clementines, which are available around Christmas, you can substitute mandarin oranges; if you can't find those, then use tangerines.

Knock on Wood

Ingredients

Ice
60 ml black walnut-infused Woodford Reserve Small Batch bourbon
30 ml dark maple simple syrup infused with clementine zest
2 dashes Peychaud's bitters
Orange twist garnish

1. Fill a rocks glass with ice.
2. Stir the ingredients with ice.
3. Strain into the glass. Add garnish.

Barrel of Cracker Jacks

Ingredients

Ice
60 ml real buttered popcorn and roasted peanut-infused Jack Daniel's Single Barrel whiskey
30 ml caramel liqueur
60 ml fresh cream
Caramel popcorn garnish

1. Chill a 120–150-ml cocktail glass with ice.
2. Shake the infused whiskey and caramel liqueur with ice.
3. Strain into the glass.
4. Top with fresh cream. Add garnish.

Your curiosity may be piqued when you read about the real buttered popcorn and peanut-infused Jack Daniel's in the Barrel of Cracker Jacks. Yes, modern bartenders have found a way to infuse spirits with fats such as butter and bacon fat. There are three steps to making the infusion, but it's well worth it. First roast 50 g peanuts and infuse in a bottle of Jack Daniel's like the walnuts for Knock on Wood. Strain, then place 100 g popcorn wrapped in cheesecloth in the Jack Daniel's for 24 hours. Remove the popcorn, then melt 115 g butter, stir it into the whiskey and leave for 4 hours. Place the container in the fridge so that the fat rises to the top and solidifies. Scoop off the fat, and it's ready. When you add caramel liqueur to the recipe, it will taste like a grownup version of the caramel popcorn and peanut confection Americans have known for over a century as Cracker Jacks.

Kreteks are Indonesian cigarettes flavoured with cloves. Clove comes from the infused Grand Marnier, and the smoke comes from the Islay region Scotch whisky (the smokiest of the malts). To flame orange oil, put it in a mister, then spray at a flame. It will caramelize over the cocktail.

Kretek

Ingredients

Ice
60 ml Islay region Scotch whisky
3 ml clove-infused Grand Marnier
15 ml fresh Meyer lemon juice
15 ml fresh Valencia orange juice
Dash of Fee Brothers Whiskey Barrel Aged Bitters
Spray of flamed essential orange oil

1. Chill a 120–150-ml cocktail glass with ice.
2. Shake all ingredients with ice; strain into glass.
3. Hold a flame over drink, then spray mist of essential orange oil at the flame.

Sweet Rye Reverie

Ingredients

Ice
3 fresh sweet basil leaves (one for garnish)
30 ml fresh lime juice
60 ml Sazerac rye whiskey
7.5 ml Carpano Antica Italian vermouth
30 ml pear purée

1. Chill a 150–200-ml cocktail glass with ice.
2. Muddle two sweet basil leaves and lime juice in a mixing glass.
3. Add ice, rye, Carpano Antica and pear purée.
4. Add garnish, then shake with ice and double-strain into the glass. Garnish with basil.

MODERN BRANDY COCKTAILS

Mix brandy and fruits to craft cocktails that taste like the nectar of the gods

Eden is the first place mentioned in any version of the Bible, with apples being the first fruit mentioned in the first chapter. And as you learned in Chapter 4, Laird's Applejack was the first commercial distillery in the USA, and to continue with this string of firsts there is documented proof that the first president of the United States, George Washington, wrote to the Laird family requesting the recipe for applejack. Velvet Falernum is a paradise-like sweetener that originated in Barbados in 1890. With all that information, the Eden cocktail should taste like heaven.

The Pisco Sour has been a popular South American brandy cocktail since the late 1800s. The twisted one here uses Key

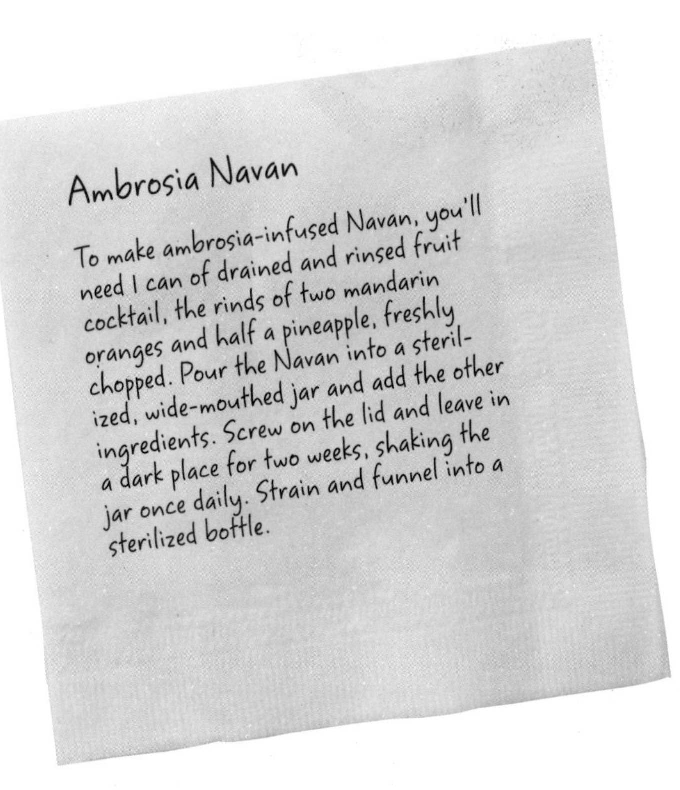

Eden

Ingredients

Organic raw sugar and freshly ground cinnamon to rim glass
Ice
60 ml Laird's Applejack
30 ml Velvet Falernum
30 ml fresh Meyer lemon juice

1. Rim a 120–150-ml chilled cocktail glass with raw sugar and cinnamon.
2. Shake the ingredients with ice.
3. Strain into the glass.

lime juice and gomme syrup. You can purchase the syrup or make your own from sugar, water and gum arabic. Simply mix 25 g gum arabic powder with 60 ml water and leave for 3 hours. Heat 400 g sugar with 250 ml water, stirring to dissolve the sugar. Bring to the boil, then add the gum arabic and bring to the boil again. Remove from the heat and skim off the scum that rises to the top with a large spoon. Leave to cool, then strain into a sterile bottle. Gomme syrup makes a silky sweetener for your cocktails.

MAKE IT EASY

Make marshmallow orange blossom honey foam by mixing 60 ml orange blossom honey, 60 ml Marshmallow Fluff, 30 ml fresh lemon juice, 3 egg whites and 475 ml filtered water. Transfer to a whipped cream dispenser. Charge the canister with a nitrous oxide cartridge and chill in the fridge for at least 1 hour before using.

Key Lime Pisco Sour

Ingredients

Ice
60 ml pisco
30 ml fresh Key lime juice
15 ml gomme syrup
½ organic egg white
1 dash Angostura bitters

1. Chill a 200–275-ml glass of choice.
2. Shake the ingredients hard with ice.
3. Strain into the glass.
4. Dash bitters on top.

Ambrosia

Ingredients

60 ml ambrosia-infused Navan
15 ml Disaronno Originale amaretto
90 ml brut Champagne
Marshmallow orange blossom honey foam garnish
Toasted coconut sprinkle garnish (optional)

1. Shake the infused Navan and amaretto with ice.
2. Strain into the glass.
3. Add Champagne.
4. Add foam.
5. Add coconut garnish (optional).

SIMPLE SYRUP

Learn how simple it is to make one of the key cocktail ingredients

Simple syrup is simply sugar and water mixed together to make a liquid sugar. Sugar in syrup form is the ideal way to add sweetness to a cocktail – crystalline sugar doesn't dissolve as well.

For the simple syrup recipe, a ratio of 1:1 works fine, but some people prefer it a little thicker and will use twice as much sugar as is called for in this recipe. You'll discover your preference after you begin to experiment. For the water, try to use the highest quality available, and for sugar you can choose from raw, organic, brown and more.

To make infused simple syrups, just add clean herbs, fruits, vegetables, spices and so forth to the water. Bring to the boil, add the sugar, and stir until the sugar has dissolved. Remove from the heat, cover and leave to cool and steep. After about 30 minutes you can strain the syrup and funnel it into a jar or bottle. It will keep in the fridge for a month.

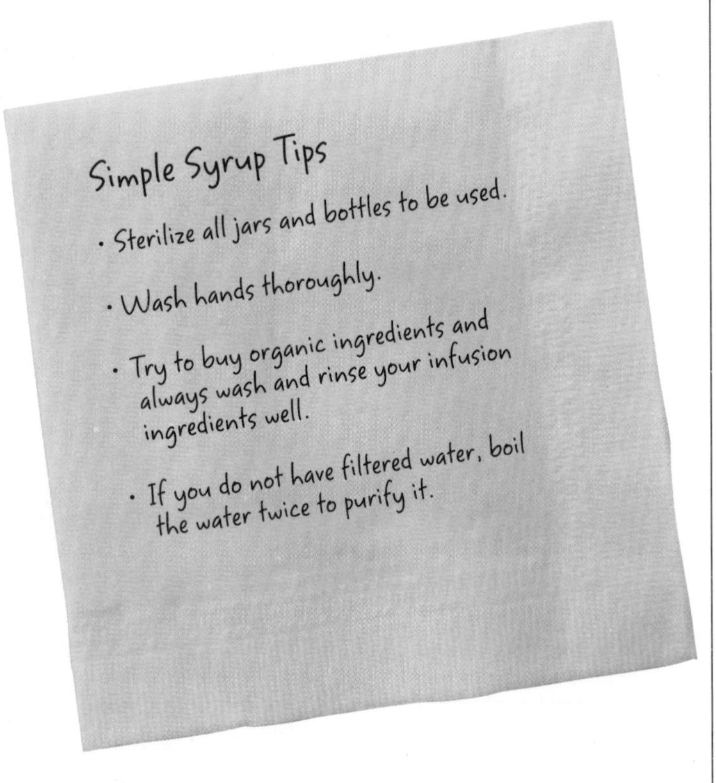

Simple Syrup

Ingredients

475 ml water
400 g sugar

1. Bring the water to the boil.
2. Pour in the sugar. Stir until dissolved.
3. Remove from heat and leave to cool.
4. Funnel into a jar or bottle.

For a no-heat sugar-free simple syrup, use filtered room-temperature water and shake it hard with Splenda in a jar or bottle. You'll notice that the Splenda dissolves very quickly. Simply refrigerate.

GREEN LIGHT

There's really no limit to what you can infuse in simple syrup. Popular infusions include vanilla, mint, ginger, citrus (use the zested rind), rose petals, lavender and tea bags. Other ideas you can try are roasted coffee beans, peppercorns and pumpkin. And don't forget that you can combine flavours such as vanilla with ginger, or cacao bean and chilli.

Tri-citrus Infused Simple Syrup

Ingredients

475 ml water
Zest from 1 lime, 1 lemon and 1 orange
400 g sugar

1. Bring the water and the citrus zest to the boil.
2. Pour in the sugar. Stir until dissolved.
3. Remove from heat and leave to cool and steep for 30 minutes.
4. Strain and funnel into a jar or bottle.

No-heat Simple Syrup

Ingredients

400 g sugar
475 ml lukewarm water

1. Funnel the sugar and water into a bottle.
2. Seal and shake hard for 10 seconds.
3. Leave to stand for 1 minute, then shake hard again. Repeat until sugar has dissolved. Cloudiness will clear.

HONEY & MAPLE SYRUP

Learn more about the birds and the bees and the flowers and the trees

Honey and maple syrup are two other sweeteners that can be used to sweeten drinks, or made into simple syrups or infused simple syrups to add sweetness to cocktails. As you know, bees make honey from the nectar of flowers, and the flowers they visit affect the flavour of the honey. The most popular honey is made from clover, but others that are easily found include heather, acacia, limeflower, orange blossom, eucalyptus and chestnut. It all just depends on where the bees buzz. Flavours that mix well with honey are citrus, mint, ginger, hot peppers, vanilla, cinnamon, clove, thyme, rose, lavender and almond. Alcohols that mix well with honey are vodka, rum, tequila, whisky and Champagne.

Simple Honey Syrup

Ingredients

475 ml water
475 ml honey

1. Bring the water to the boil.
2. Pour in the honey. Stir until dissolved.
3. Remove from the heat and leave to cool.
4. Funnel into a jar or bottle.

Jalapeño-infused Honey Syrup

Ingredients

475 ml water
200 g fresh jalapeño peppers, sliced
475 ml honey

1. Bring the water and jalapeño peppers to the boil.
2. Pour in the honey. Stir until dissolved.
3. Remove from heat and leave to cool and steep for 30 minutes.
4. Strain and funnel into a jar or bottle.

Maple syrup is made from the sap of maple trees. Canada is the world's largest producer of maple syrup, but it can be made with sap from any maple tree that grows in a cold climate anywhere. The sap is collected in the spring; light syrup is made in the early season, and dark syrup in the late season. Flavours that mix well with the flavour of maple syrup include apple, apricot, cranberry, allspice, ginger, cardamom, vanilla, whisky, mint and lavender. Alcohols that mix well with maple syrup are whisky, applejack and rum.

MAKE IT EASY

Whenever you use dried herbs or spices for infusions, remember to use only half the amount you would use if the herbs or spices were fresh. Growing your own is an option as well. Herbs are probably the simplest plants to learn to grow. Some growing herbs can be bought in supermarkets, but you'll have a far wider choice if you grow your own herbs from seed.

Ginger-infused Maple Syrup

Ingredients

475 ml water
200 g fresh ginger, sliced
475 ml dark maple syrup

1. Bring the water and ginger to the boil.
2. Pour in the syrup. Stir until dissolved.
3. Remove from heat and leave to cool and steep for 30 minutes.
4. Strain and funnel into a jar or bottle.

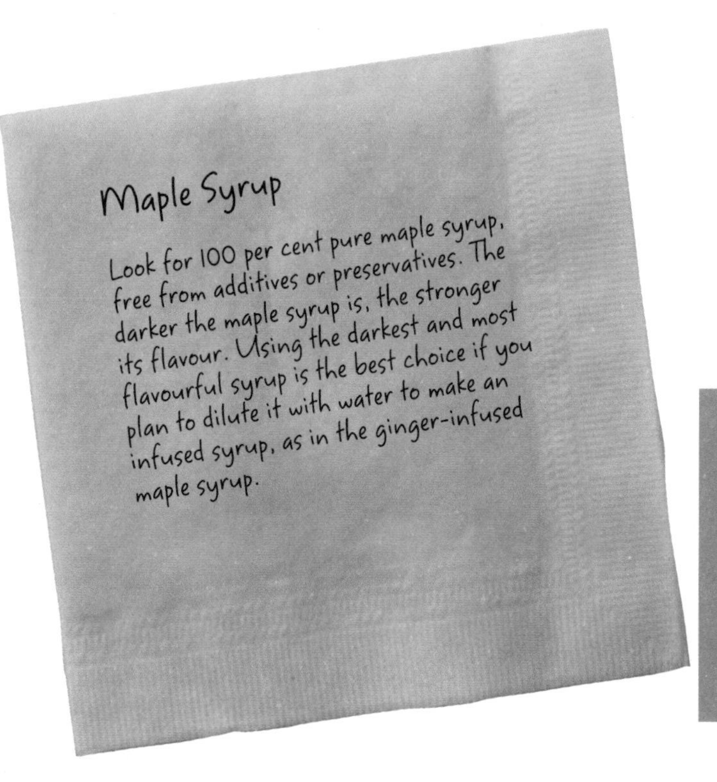

INFUSED SPIRITS

Make your own flavoured spirits, for your own use or as a great gift

If you believe that good things take time, then infusing spirits is right up your alley. To infuse spirits, all you need are alcohol, your chosen infusion ingredients, a wide-mouthed jar, and time. Simply pour the spirit into a sterilized wide-mouthed jar, add the washed and rinsed flavouring ingredients of your choice, and seal the jar. Leave it in a dark place such as a cool cupboard and every day turn it upside down once and back. After a few days, you can open the jar and taste-test it.

Some ingredients require a longer infusion but nothing takes longer than two weeks. Stronger flavours will take only three to four days: they include vanilla, basil, mint, garlic, dill, oregano, rosemary, citrus rinds, lavender and thyme. Most fruits take up to a week, including stoned cherries, figs, dates, cucumber, apples, raspberries, rose petals, watermelon, peaches, lychees, strawberries, blueberries, blackberries, mangos and papaya. Fibrous edibles such as peppers,

Infused Vodka and Rum

Ingredients

1 750-ml bottle premium vodka or rum
3 vanilla pods, cut and scraped

1. Pour the vodka or rum into a sterile, wide-mouthed jar.
2. Add vanilla pods. Seal jar.
3. Leave in a dark cool place and agitate once daily for four days.
4. Strain and funnel into a sterile jar or bottle.

Cucumber-infused Gin

Ingredients

1 750-ml bottle premium gin
1 cucumber, chopped or sliced

1. Pour the gin into a sterile, wide-mouthed jar.
2. Add cucumber. Seal jar.
3. Leave in a cool dark place and agitate once daily for one week.
4. Strain and funnel into a sterile jar or bottle.

lemongrass, ginger, pineapple, cinnamon sticks, whole cloves, beans and chillies take up to two weeks. Bear this in mind if you combine flavours, as you may need to add the ingredients at different times.

A new technique known as fat washing allows you to make creative infusions using ingredients such as buttered popcorn (see page 209) and bacon. It involves melting fat and stirring it into a spirit; once the flavour has infused, the mixture is chilled and the fat, which rises to the surface, sets in a solid block that can be lifted off. If you're using butter for this method you can give it a deeper, nutty flavour by browning it in the pan rather than just melting it.

To make bacon-infused bourbon, fry some bacon and pour 60 ml of the fat into 750 ml bourbon in a jar. Leave to infuse for 4 hours, then chill and remove the fat.

Coffee and Cacao Bean-infused Tequila

Ingredients

1 750-ml bottle premium tequila
75 g roasted coffee beans
75 g cacao nibs

1. Pour tequila into a sterile, wide-mouthed jar.
2. Add coffee beans and cacao nibs. Seal jar.
3. Leave in a cool dark place and agitate once daily for two weeks.
4. Strain and funnel into a sterile jar or bottle.

Cherry-infused Whisky

Ingredients

1 750-ml bottle premium whisky
300 g pitted cherries (not Maraschinos)

1. Pour whisky into a sterile, wide-mouthed jar.
2. Add cherries. Seal jar.
3. Leave in a cool dark place and agitate once daily for one week.
4. Strain and funnel into a sterile jar or bottle.

INFUSED WATER

Learn centuries-old ways of aromatizing and flavouring water

Infused water in cocktails adds flavour when you don't want to add extra sweetness or alcohol as well. One popular way by which infused waters are used is misting: simply funnel the flavoured and scented water into a mister, then mist on top of a cocktail.

When mixed with a sparkling water or wine, infused waters provide a light, aromatic quality, with just a subtle hint of flavour that is perfect for light refreshment.

One of the most important considerations when making infused waters is the quality of the water. Never use water taken out of your tap and put straight into the pot. You may have a filter on your tap, but it's still best to boil the water at least once for extra purification. Or you can buy distilled or de-ionized water for infusions.

The most popular flavoured waters are infused with non-toxic flower petals. Rose, lavender, hibiscus and lilac are the

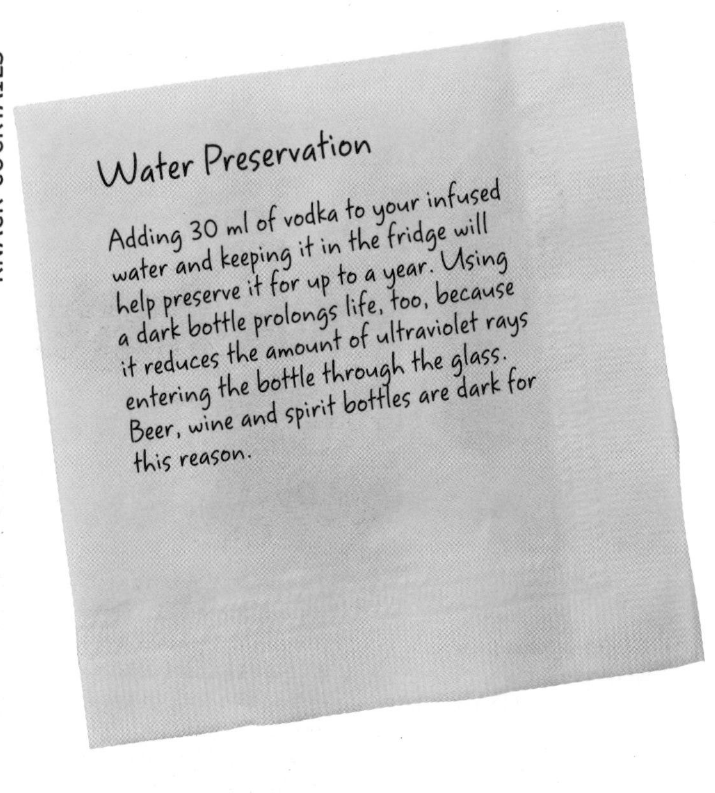

Rosewater

Ingredients

750 ml purified water
500 ml clean rose petals
30 ml vodka

1. Pour purified water into a pan and add rose petals.
2. Bring to the boil, then simmer for 30 minutes with a lid on the pan.
3. Leave to cool.
4. Strain and funnel into a sterile jar or bottle. Add vodka.

most common. For extra refreshment, you can even spray yourself or your sheets with the water!

The preferred way to make infused waters requires a large pan with a lid, a 500 ml Pyrex measuring jug, a clean brick and some ice. Place the brick in the bottom of the pan, then set the measuring jug on top of the brick. Fill the pan with your chosen ingredients to the top of the brick, then add distilled water up to the level of the brick. Place the lid on the pan upside down, then bring the water to the boil. Fill the inverted lid with ice, then lower the temperature to a simmer. As the steam rises, the cold pan lid will cause it to condense and drip into the Pyrex jug. Every 15 minutes empty the jug. This is basic distillation.

These infused waters add flavour without sweetness

Cinnamon Apple Water

Ingredients

750 ml purified water
2 apples, chopped
3 cinnamon sticks, broken
30 ml vodka

1. Pour purified water into a pan and add apples and cinnamon.
2. Bring to the boil, then simmer for 30 minutes with a lid on the pan.
3. Leave to cool.
4. Strain and funnel into a sterile jar or bottle. Add vodka.

Turkish Delight Water

Ingredients

750 ml purified water
250 ml clean rose petals
handful fresh mint leaves
75 g natural unshelled pistachio nuts
1 cinnamon stick, broken
30 ml vodka

1. Put all the ingredients except the vodka into a pan.
2. Bring to the boil, then simmer for 30 minutes with a lid on the pan.
3. Leave to cool.
4. Strain and funnel into a sterile jar or bottle. Add vodka.

PUREES

Use your food processor to mash up full-bodied flavours for your cocktails

Fruit purées add bursting, concentrated flavour to a cocktail. You can find a range of puréed fruit in the baby food aisle of your local supermarket, but nothing compares with making your own purées.

Making purées is pretty simple. Basically, you peel and chop your chosen fruit or vegetable, then heat it and mash it. Heating options include baking, boiling and steaming. The preferred method is steaming, because it keeps a lot of the flavour and vitamins intact. Baking is fine, but it takes a long time and uses a lot of energy.

Once your ingredients are cooked, simply use a food processor to mash them up. At this point, you can mix in more

Peach Purée

Ingredients

4 peaches, skinned, stoned and chopped
30 ml simple syrup if desired

1. Steam peaches until soft.
2. Process in the food processor for 1 minute.
3. Taste, then add simple syrup if desired.
4. Spoon into sterile jars or containers. Refrigerate.

Tropical Purée

Ingredients

1 mango, peeled, stoned, and chopped
½ fresh pineapple, peeled and chopped
1 ripe banana
30 ml simple syrup or falernum if desired

1. Steam mango and pineapple until soft.
2. Place in the food processor with the banana and process for 1 minute.
3. Taste, then add simple syrup or falernum if desired.
4. Spoon into sterile jars or containers. Refrigerate.

ingredients or other purées if you wish. When the mixture is smooth you can spoon it straight into small sterile jars or plastic containers. Some people prefer to push the purée through a sieve first to make it extra smooth.

You can keep purées in the fridge ready for use, or freeze them in ice trays. When they're frozen, pop out the purée cubes and store in a freezer bag for future use. You can put them straight in the blender if you're making a frozen drink, or allow them to thaw.

ZOOM

The Tropical Purée can contain any of your favourite tropical fruits, such as papaya, mandarin oranges, lychees, kiwi and tangerines. Cornucopia Purée can be made with any autumn or winter ingredients, such as pears, squash, ground nuts, cranberries, persimmons, oranges and ground allspice. You could even make a spa purée using cucumber, mint and lemons.

Cornucopia Purée

Ingredients

2 red apples, skinned, cored and chopped
200 g chopped pumpkin
1 teaspoon ground cinnamon
30 ml simple syrup or honey syrup if desired

1. Steam apple and pumpkin until soft.
2. Place in the food processor with the cinnamon and process for 1 minute.
3. Taste, then add simple syrup or honey syrup if desired.
4. Spoon into sterile jars or containers. Refrigerate.

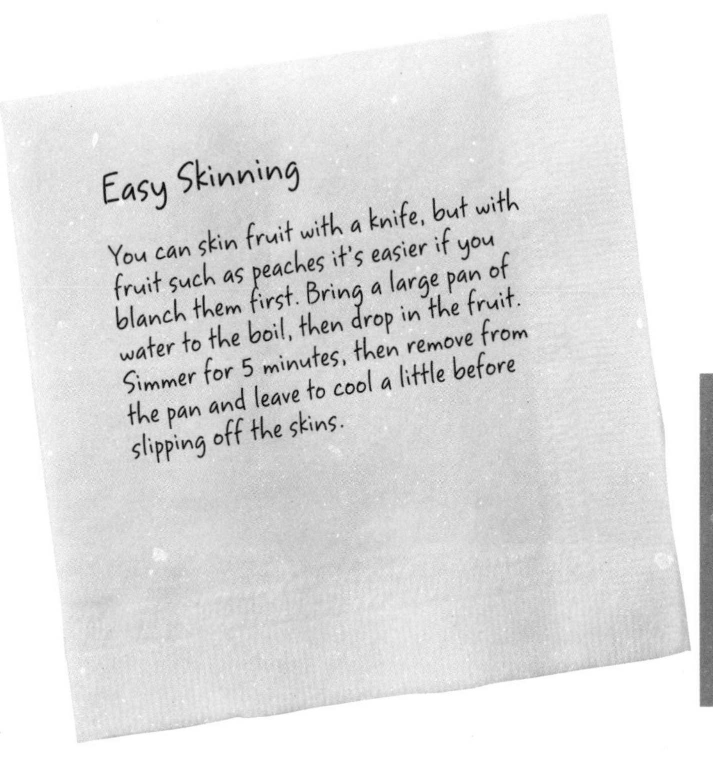

HOMEMADE CLASSIC DRINK MIXES

Try your hand at making essential bar mixers in your own kitchen

Two of the most confusing mixers to the layperson are Margarita mix and sweet-and-sour mix. That's no surprise, because you can buy a wide assortment . . . full of fake colourings and words you can't pronounce to ensure shelf life.

The first thing you need to know is that Margarita mix has a lime base and sour mix has a lemon base. You wouldn't make a whiskey sour with Margarita mix, and you shouldn't make a Margarita with sour mix. The next thing to know is that each mix should contain only three ingredients: water, sugar and citrus juice. That's it. Now stop for a minute and flip back through some recipes in this book, and you'll see that many of them call for 30 ml lemon juice and 30 ml simple syrup. That's sour mix (a little bit of sweet and a little bit of sour)! Look at the Margaritas in the Margarita chapter, and you'll see 30 ml lime juice and 30 ml simple syrup. That's Margarita mix! And in some recipes you'll see that simple syrup can be

Margarita Mix

Ingredients

475 ml fresh lime juice
475 ml simple syrup

1. Mix the juice and simple syrup together.
2. Pour into a sterile bottle. Refrigerate.

Sweet-and-sour Mix

Ingredients

475 ml fresh lemon juice
475 ml simple syrup

1. Mix the juice and simple syrup together.
2. Pour into a sterile bottle. Refrigerate.

replaced by other sweeteners such as grenadine, honey or agave syrup.

Some people like to make an all-purpose sour mix that uses half lemon and half lime juice, and that's fine for lots of tropical drinks, but it limits you with other drinks.

When mixing the simple syrup and juice together, your goal is to reach a balance of sweet and sour. Feel free to adjust the sweetness or sourness, depending on your taste preferences. Also, don't forget that you can make a sugar-free mix by using Splenda simple syrup.

Grenadine

Ingredients

475 ml pomegranate juice
175 g granulated sugar
30 ml vodka

1. Put the pomegranate juice in a pan and bring to a simmer.
2. Stir in the sugar until dissolved.
3. Funnel into a sterile bottle. Add vodka. Refrigerate.

Just so you know, grenadine was originally made from pomegranates, as it is in the recipe given here. However, commercially available grenadine often contains cheaper and sometimes artificial ingredients.

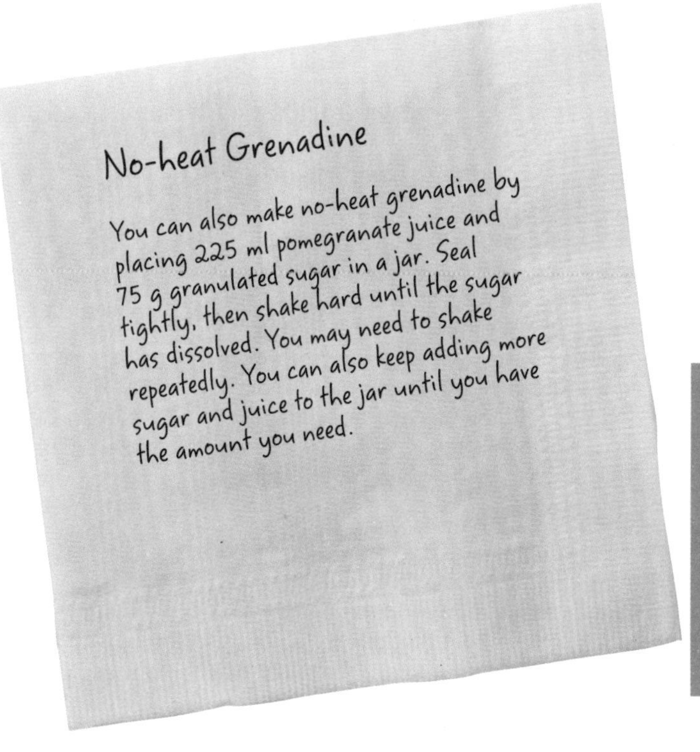

RESOURCES

Cocktail connoisseurs, modern mixologists & liquid chefs

Angus Winchester

barmetrix.com

- Angus is a veteran bartender of 20 years. He is an ambassador for the modern professional bartender, travelling the world hosting training sessions and tastings. Angus also owns and maintainsalconomics.com and therumclub.com.

Anistatia Miller and Jared Brown

martiniplace.com, euvs.org, mixellany.com

- Anistatia Miller and Jared Brown are credited with establishing the first bar and cocktail website (martiniplace.com) on the internet in 1995. Today they are the directors/curators of Exposition Universelle des Vins et Spiritueux on Ile de Bendor, France. They are also publishers of *Mixologist: The Journal of the American Cocktail,* the scholarly journal on cocktails and spirits of the Museum of the American Cocktail, of which they are co-founders.

Ardent Spirits

ardentspirits.com

- Gary Regan is a spirit and cocktail expert and author of many books, including *The Joy of Mixology*. He also maintains a worldwide bartender newsletter that keeps up with all the latest drink trends and happenings.

CocktailDB

cocktaildb.com

- Ted 'Dr Cocktail' Haigh is a cocktail historian, speaker, consultant, and author of *Vintage Spirits and Forgotten Cocktails*. He is also the curator for the Museum of the American Cocktail and co-founder of cocktaildb.com. He lives in Los Angeles.

Darcy O'Neil

theartofdrink.com

- Darcy O'Neil is a bartender and chemist in London, Ontario. He publishes *The Art of Drink* and writes cocktail-related articles for many publications.

DrinkBoy

drinkboy.com

- Seattle-based Robert Hess's site is dedicated to providing clear and concise information about the art of the cocktail.

Jamie Boudreau

spiritsandcocktails.com

- Jamie's thirst for cocktail minutiae is infamous. He has a love for the classics but at the same time is always looking for new, exciting ingredients with which to try out new recipes. He is known for his molecular mixology.

Jeff Berry

beachbumberry.com

- Jeff 'Beachbum' Berry is the author of *Beachbum Berry's Grog Log,* which the *New York Times* hailed as the world's first serious tiki cocktail book. Jeff is the world authority on all tiki cocktails, and his creations have been featured in many publications and served in famous bars around the world. Je[ff] serves on the advisory board of the Museu[m] of the American Cocktail.

Jeffery Morgenthaler

jeffreymorgenthaler.com

- Jeffrey Morgenthaler is a master mixologist who writes about bartending and mixology from Eugene, Oregon.

King Cocktail

kingcocktail.com

- Dale 'King Cocktail' Degroff is credited with pioneering the revival of the classic cocktail He's the world's foremost mixologist and is the president and founder of the Museum o[f] the American Cocktail and the author of *Th[e] Craft of the Cocktail*.

Natalie Bovis-Nelsen

theliquidmuse.com

- Los Angeles-based author, cocktail blogger, mixologist, spirits columnist, and online cocktail show host Natalie Bovis-Nelsen has a passion for cocktail culture that defines he[r] career. She keeps a close eye on drink trend[s,] the people who set them, and bars around the world where connoisseurs can share a quality tipple.

Paul Clarke

cocktailchronicles.com

- A Seattle-based cocktail enthusiast, Paul Clarke's site is an ongoing exploration of fine spirits, creative cocktails and classic mixology.

Simon Difford

diffordsguide.com

- Simon Difford is best known for his yearly colour recipe book, *Difford's Guide to Cocktails*. Simon constantly travels the world in search of the best bars and their best cocktails.

Stanislav Vadrna

stanislavvadrna.com

- Stan is from Bratislava, Slovakia. He first made cocktail history when he won a world cocktail menu contest for the bar he worked at called 'Paparazzi'. Since then he has founded Stanislav Vadrna's School of Bartending and Mixology and a joint project with the Redmonkeygroup.

Stephen Beaumont

worldofbeer.com

- Stephen Beaumont has been documenting the world of beer, spirits, food and travel for almost 20 years. He writes for many related blogs, including thatsthe spirit.com and onthehouse.typepad.com.

Organizations

Museum of the American Cocktail

museumoftheamericancocktail.org

- This non-profit organization celebrates the American cocktail and welcomes a global network of the most passionate and talented bartenders, collectors, historians and writers on the subject.

UK Bartenders Guild

ukbg.co.uk

- A national trade association founded in 1933 to train bartenders, promote their professional skills and maintain standards in the industry, It fosters the development of new recipes through the sponsorship of competitions.

US Bartenders Guild

usbg.org

- The guild works to improve customer-bartender relations, increase the prestige of bartenders, and perform public relations for the alcoholic beverage industry.

Best cocktail consultants to learn from

Bar Magic

barmagic.com

- Bar Magic is a Las Vegas-based drink design business owned by Tobin Ellis. Tobin provides worldwide services for development, operations, and marketing services for hospitality, foodservice and nightlife operations.

BarMedia

barmedia.com

- Robert Plotkin is BarMedia. His mission is to serve the needs of aspiring professionals and enlighten the social host on the nuances of creative mixology.

Cuff & Buttons

cuffandbuttons.com

- Cuff & Buttons is a partnership between three bartenders from New York City's cocktail vanguard. It brings together the talents of Sasha Petraske, Christy Pope and Chad Solomon.

Liquid Architecture

liquid-architecture.com

- Liquid Architecture is a beverage consultancy owned by Kim Haasarud, who creates signature liquid cuisine and turns bar concepts into beverage masterpieces.

Liquid Relations

liquidrelations.com

- Ryan Magarian heads Liquid Relations, a beverage development company based in Seattle. He has a unique, cheflike approach to the craft of mixology and develops innovative bar programmes.

Liquid Solutions

liquidsolutions.org

- Philip Duff heads Liquid Solutions. He is a renowned bar and beverage consultant and award-winning mixologist who travels the world to advise and train major drinks companies, hotels, bars, restaurants and nightclubs in the fields of brands, bartending and cocktails.

INDEX

WHITE STAR
CHAMPAGNE
Veuve Clicquot Ponsardin
BRUT
A REIMS-FRANCE
CHAMPAGNE
G.H.MUMM
Brut

H

M

N

O

P

R

S